IMAGES
of America

CLEVELAND'S VANISHING SACRED ARCHITECTURE

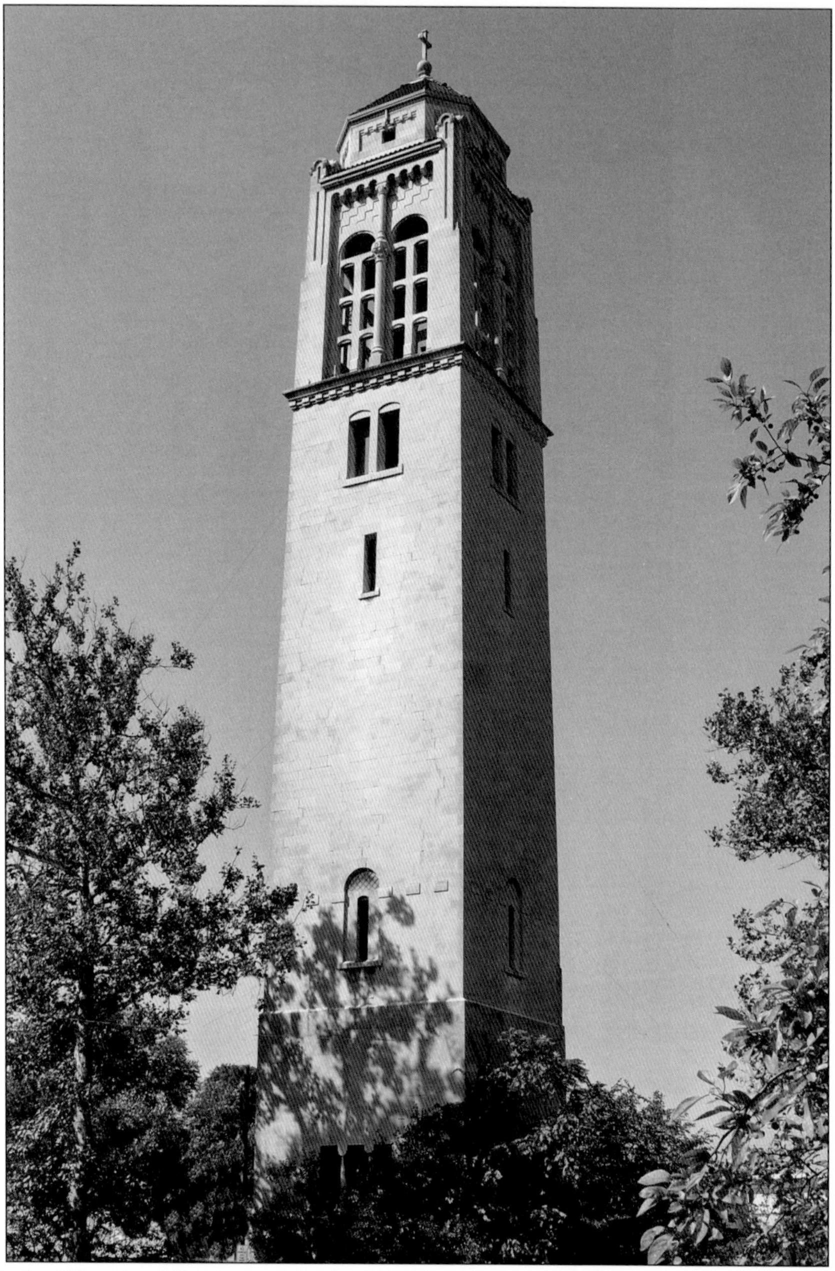

In 1916, the Church of St. Agnes was built at East Seventy-Ninth Street and Euclid Avenue. Through the years, it was considered "the Crown Jewel" of the Catholic churches of Cleveland, but during the last half of the century, St. Agnes was no longer the asset that it had been. It became a liability and, after much emotion, was closed and torn down in 1975. However, to satisfy protesters, the bell tower was left as a monument to this great church. Today tens of thousands of people pass by this intersection and have no idea what the tower is or what it represents; someday, it too will be gone. (Walter Grossman.)

ON THE COVER: This photograph shows a stunning panoramic view of the front of St. James Church in Lakewood, Ohio. (Walter Grossman.)

IMAGES
of America

Cleveland's Vanishing Sacred Architecture

Barry K. Herman and Walter Grossman
Introduction by Dennis Kucinich

ARCADIA
PUBLISHING

ISBN 978-0-7385-8442-3

Published by Arcadia Publishing
Charleston SC, Chicago IL, Portsmouth NH, San Francisco CA

Printed in the United States of America

Library of Congress Control Number: 2010920455

For all general information contact Arcadia Publishing at:
Telephone 843-853-2070
Fax 843-853-0044
E-mail sales@arcadiapublishing.com
For customer service and orders:
Toll-Free 1-888-313-2665

Visit us on the Internet at www.arcadiapublishing.com

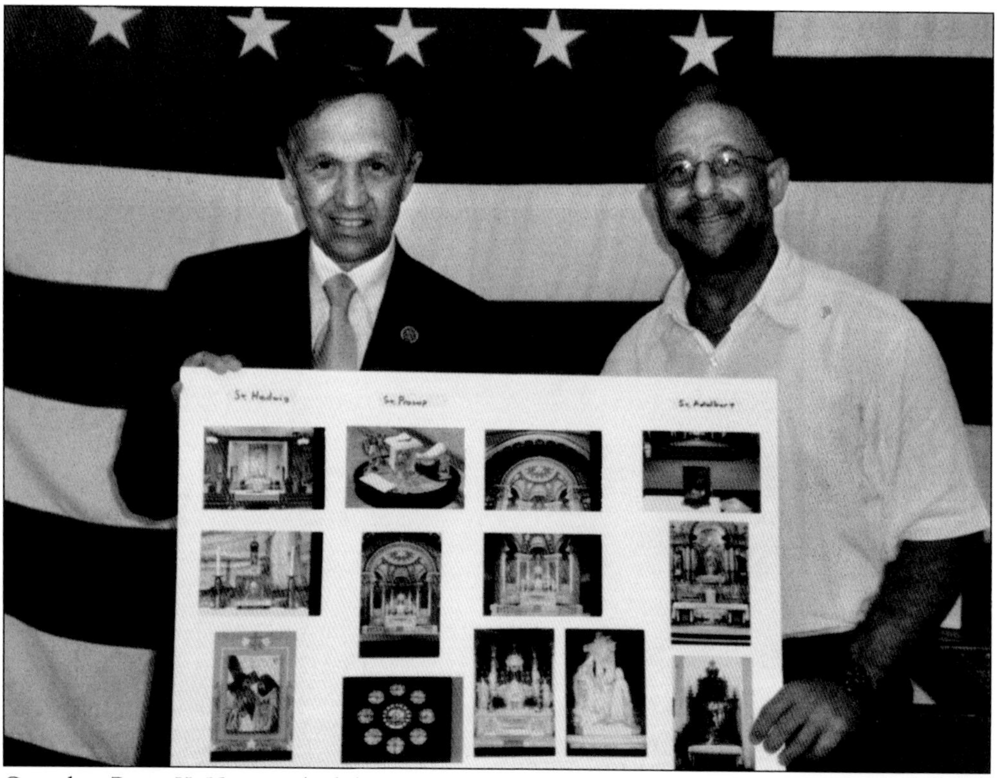

Coauthor Barry K. Herman (right) poses with Congressman Dennis Kucinich while holding a display of the photographs of Walter Grossman. (Sharon Herman photograph.)

Contents

ACKNOWLEDGMENTS

Although the book was a labor of love for us, many people were indispensable in making it a reality. We would like to thank the pastors of these churches for their commitment to both their flocks and our project. We dedicate this book to them. Many of these pastors have been at these churches for years, and the closings were as much of a shock to them as to their parishioners. We thank them for their friendship, assistance, and for teaching us the true meaning of spirituality.

Thanks to Walter's wife, Luda, and children, Alex and Stacy, who virtually lost the head of their family for the past six months; their support and understanding were much appreciated.

Thanks also to Barry's wife, Sharon, who was full of encouragement and support, and to his favorite kids, Jessica and her sister Sydney, who make him proud every day. Thanks also to Barry's mother and sister, who still admit they're related to him after all these years. Mostly, thanks to Barry's father, "Papa Will," to whom Barry says, "Dad, I love you, and you're with me every day. I hope you're one-tenth as proud of me today as I have been my whole life to be your son."

Thanks to Congressman Dennis Kucinich and his office for the support they have given for our project.

Lest we forget, we want to thank our publisher, editor, and production coordinator, John, Melissa, Rob, for caring as much as we do!

PREFACE

The surface of this planet, especially where people are involved, is constantly changing. Things come. Things go. People come. People go. Even neighborhoods have an ebb and flow. Houses of worship that spanned generations seem so stable and immovable, but even they are not. Here in Cleveland, as in many other American cities, churches are closing—and they are closing rapidly. Some of these houses of worship are magnificent; some are modest. But to their parishioners, they are all special, and to those who take the time to explore them, they are all beautiful.

In years past, some Roman Catholic churches in Cleveland became victims of vanishing neighborhoods and were closed down. Among these were the parishes of St. Agnes, St. Joseph, and St. Thomas Aquinas. It is my understanding that these churches were glorious, for I have never seen them. Good pictures of these churches may exist but are not easily found, especially within a single source. Unfortunately most younger generations today do not know these churches even existed.

As this book is being written, approximately 30 Catholic churches are closing in the Cleveland area. Much of the city of Cleveland was built around the neighborhoods that, in turn, were constructed around these churches. Many of these were ethnic in origin, thus making them even more significant in the development of the city. This is truly a historical event in the making. Chances could be that the next generation will never know what these churches were like or that they ever existed.

It is our opinion that we cannot allow this to happen again—not this time. With this publication, we are trying to make a fair presentation of these churches as they are today, using both original pictures and text. We are making an effort to capture the spirit of each church as best we can via their architecture, art, and artifacts; we hope to create a single source of reference for this historic information.

Initially we planned to incorporate all of the closing churches in one single book. This proved to be unrealistic, for it would have done none of them justice. We have selected 10 churches to present in this volume. It is our hope to present the others in future volumes. All photography, except where credits are given, was provided by Walter Grossman. Text and layout was done by Barry K. Herman. We hope you approve.

INTRODUCTION

It was not a difficult decision to write the introduction for *Cleveland's Vanishing Sacred Architecture*. When I was approached by Barry Herman and Walter Grossman regarding saving the memory of these churches, and to assist in any way my office could, it was a privilege.

I have an abiding interest in the preservation of the buildings that were constructed and supported by generations of Catholics and non-Catholics, including friends, neighbors, and the people of the cities in which the churches are located. The rich cultural, ethnic, and religious history belongs to the people of Cleveland. The churches are a monument to the heroic efforts of past generations who came from around the globe and built churches with their hands and hearts. Churches now slated for closure and possible demolition have been gathering places for immigrants seeking both religious and political freedom.

Many of these churches also serve as international centers. The nationality groups that founded many of the churches of Cleveland retain close ties with their countries of ethnic origin. Historically and currently, Cleveland is an important international city. The churches of Cleveland continue to serve as focal points for maintaining and renewing our relationship with our global neighbors in our city's ever-increasing need for trade and our nation's constant quest for peace.

These churches, as well as others in the Cleveland area, have served the people of northeast Ohio—some for more than a century. Although many people have moved out of the city, these houses of worship still serve as gathering places for social, cultural, and ethnic celebrations. If preserved, the churches will continue as neighborhood anchors to attract people interested in moving back into the city. Left to the elements, they will destabilize neighborhoods and require demolition. I am also well aware that the great works of these churches are not performed by the buildings but by the people who support the churches, Catholic and of every creed.

I am working closely with Mayor Frank Jackson under my authority as a member of Congress to encourage the use of federal funding and other incentives to support the effort of preserving some of these historical structures. I believe the good faith of this community that built these important institutions will show its presence again at this critical juncture. In the meantime, let us all enjoy these pictures, so lovingly taken by Walter Grossman, of the churches that are currently on the "block." I salute Barry Herman and Walter Grossman for their part in the preservation of the memory of these beautiful and sacred places.

—Congressman Dennis J. Kucinich

One

St. James the Greater

Located at 17514 Detroit Avenue, St. James majestically looms over the Lakewood community. On July 1, 1908, five years after the City of Lakewood became a village on the west side of Cleveland, St. James was founded. Bishop Ignatius Horstmann, Cleveland's third bishop, approved the naming of the Lakewood church after James the Greater, one of the 12 apostles. Not wanting another mono-ethnic church, he gave his blessing to the blending of the city's German-Catholic and Irish-Catholic founding families. The cornerstone was laid on October 12, 1912, and by the 1920s, with over 1,000 families and almost 5,000 members, the church had become a mainstream, English-speaking congregation.

Taking to heart the charge by the bishop at the founding of the new parish, Fr. Michael D. Leahy, the first pastor and creative influence behind the church, traveled to Europe in the company of architect Edward T. P. Graham in 1924. After making the grand tour, Leahy decided on the Sicilian Romanesque style of the 11th-century Cathedral Monreal in Palermo Sicily along with an exterior loosely based on the beautiful cathedral of Cafelu. The Great Depression virtually doubled the length of construction, and the bells were finally installed almost 20 years later. The church was dedicated on May 25, 1935, but the last brushstroke on the iconographic painting was not completed until 1944. The cost of the church was $569,000. Since its completion, there have been no significant changes to the church, inside or outside.

Both the interior and exterior show very apparent overtones of the Byzantine and Saracen/Arab influence. (Sicily was under Islamic rule in 1174 when Monreal was built.)

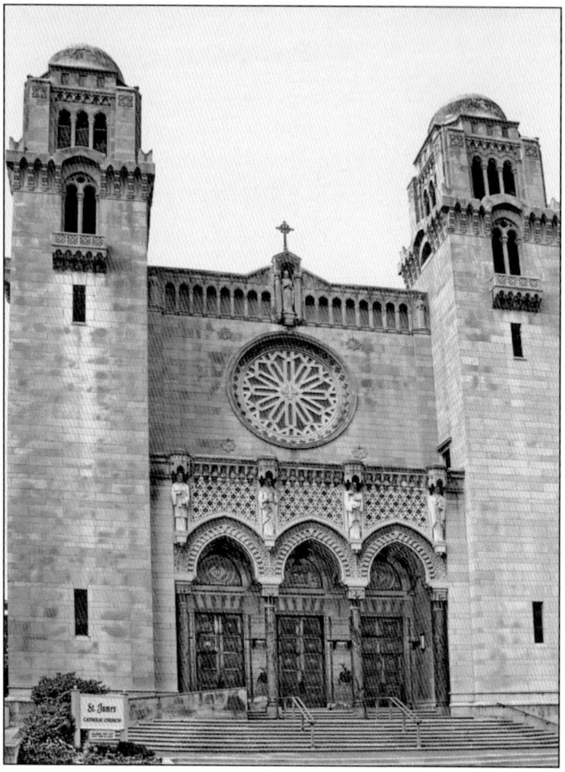

The lofty facade of St. James is representative of the Sicilian Romanesque style, with the twin towers reflecting a definite Norman influence. However, a very pronounced Middle Eastern influence is seen both on the exterior and in the interior. Above the doors are stone statues of the Four Evangelists, with their names carved below each. The outside walls are made of Indiana limestone, and the steps are carved out of Minnesota granite. The outside columns are of rainbow granite with sandstone caps quarried from Berea, Ohio.

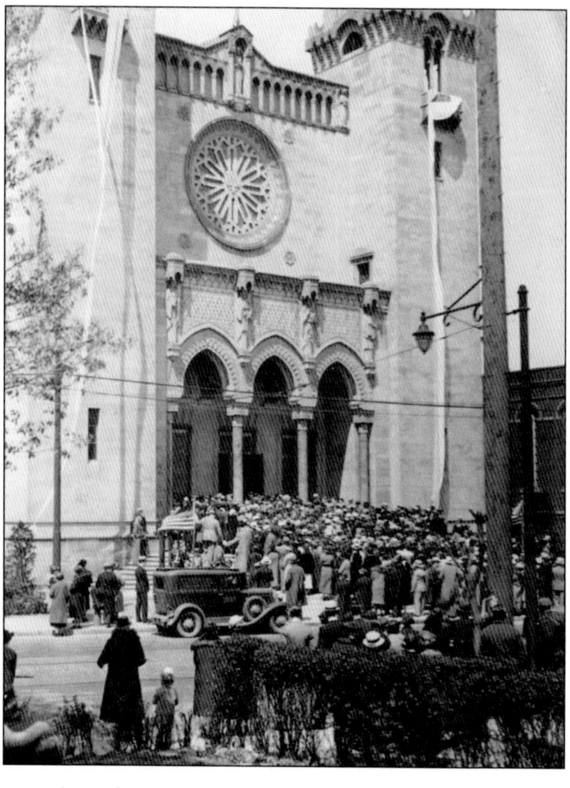

This May 25, 1935, photograph depicts an eventful day in the new city of Lakewood, the dedication of St. James Church. Overflowing crowds marked the day; here a vintage automobile drops off yet more people. (Cleveland State University, *Cleveland Press* photograph.)

The three arched porticos surround three sets of bronze double doors, which cost $6,450. The center doors bear the symbols of the Evangelists, SS. Matthew and Luke on the left and SS. Mark and John on the right. The two end doors have the St. James sword representing a cross.

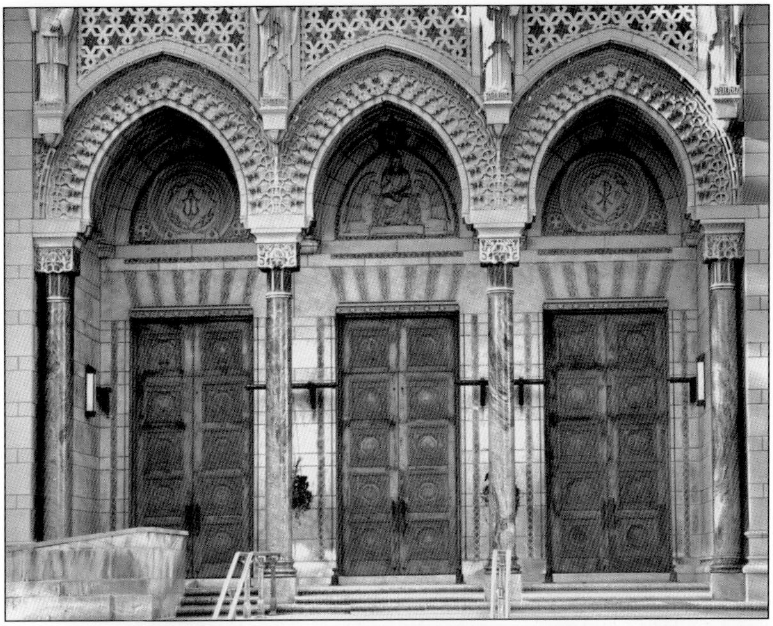

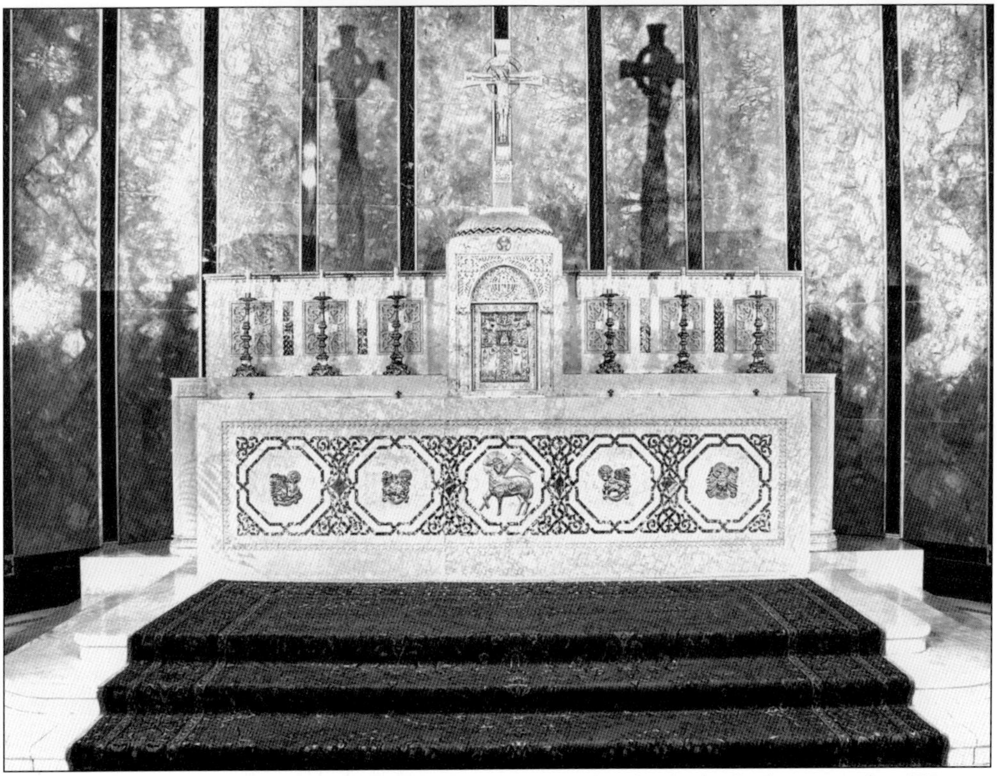

Inside St. James is a variety of stone unmatched in Cleveland. The high altar is made of Verona marble. The six candles represent the six days of creation. Centered on the altar is the Agnus Dei (Lamb of God), flanked by symbols of the Four Evangelists—all in polished bronze. The wall behind the altar and the walls of the floor level are composed of panels made of dark red Numidian marble from Africa. Between these panels are strips of black and gold Levanto marble.

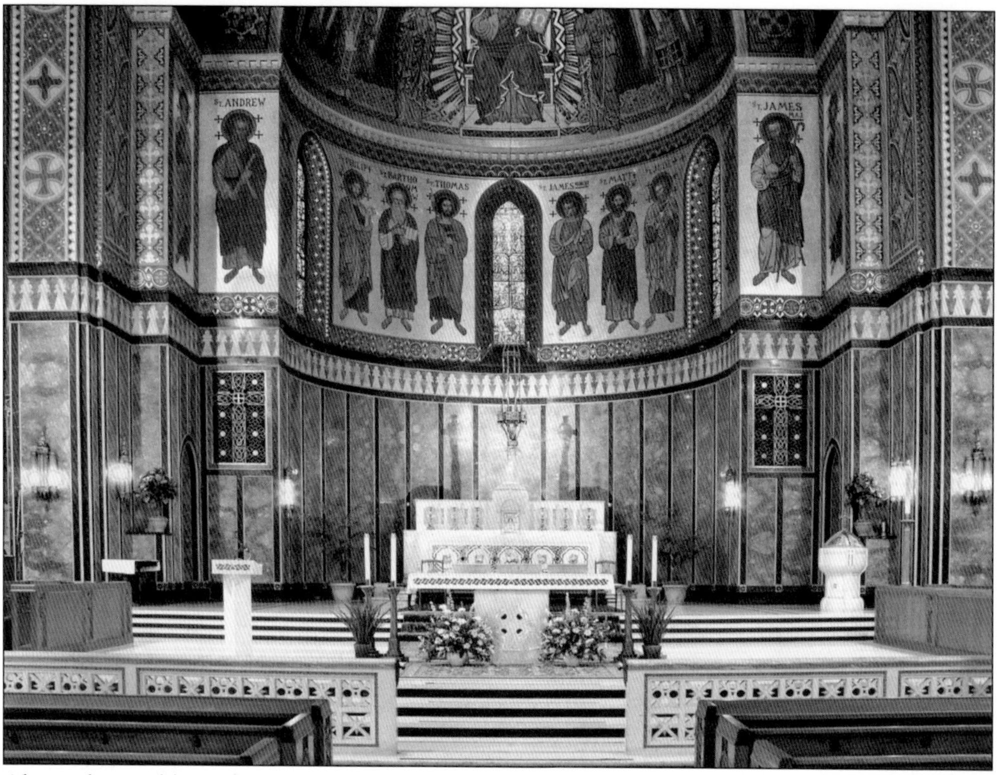

Above the marble surrounding the altar are iconic paintings of the 12 Apostles, all represented with their characteristic symbols. Even the ventilation grills beneath them are adorned with great detail.

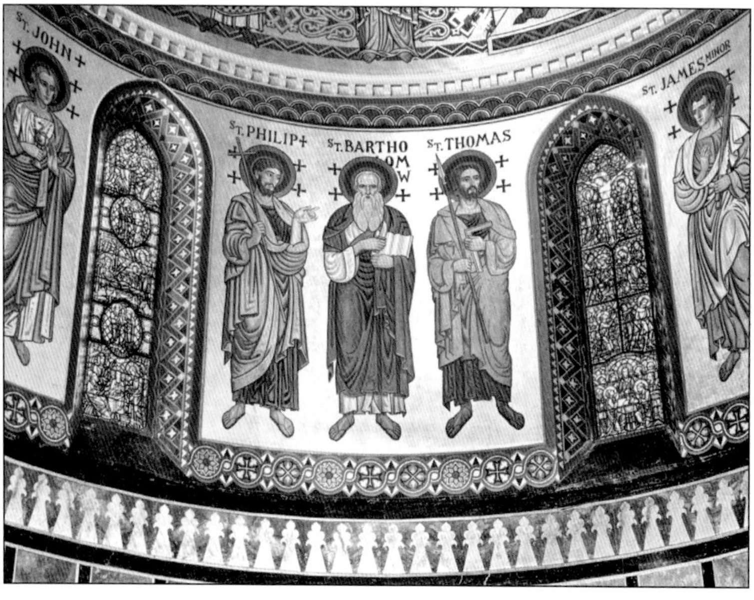

In each of the three arched windows at that level, one of the mysteries of the rosary is depicted. In the left window are the Joyful Mysteries, the center depicts the Sorrowful Mysteries, and the Glorious Mysteries appear in the right (not shown in this image). The George W. Sotter Studios of Pennsylvania made all the stained glass in St. James.

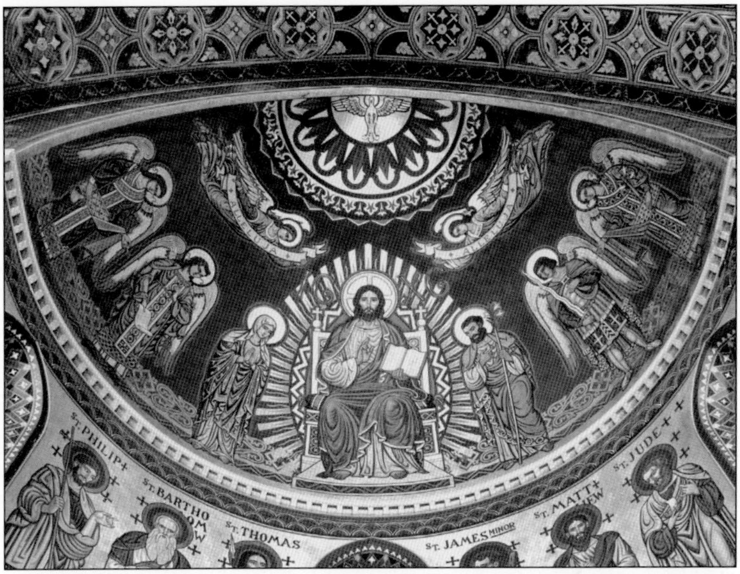

Above the paintings of the apostles, on the apse (or canopy), are the iconic figures of Christ (Agnus Dei) enthroned in Heaven, flanked by the Blessed Mother and St. Joseph. Local artist David Scott Brown did the painting, and it is very indicative of the Byzantine influence prevalent in 12th-century Sicily.

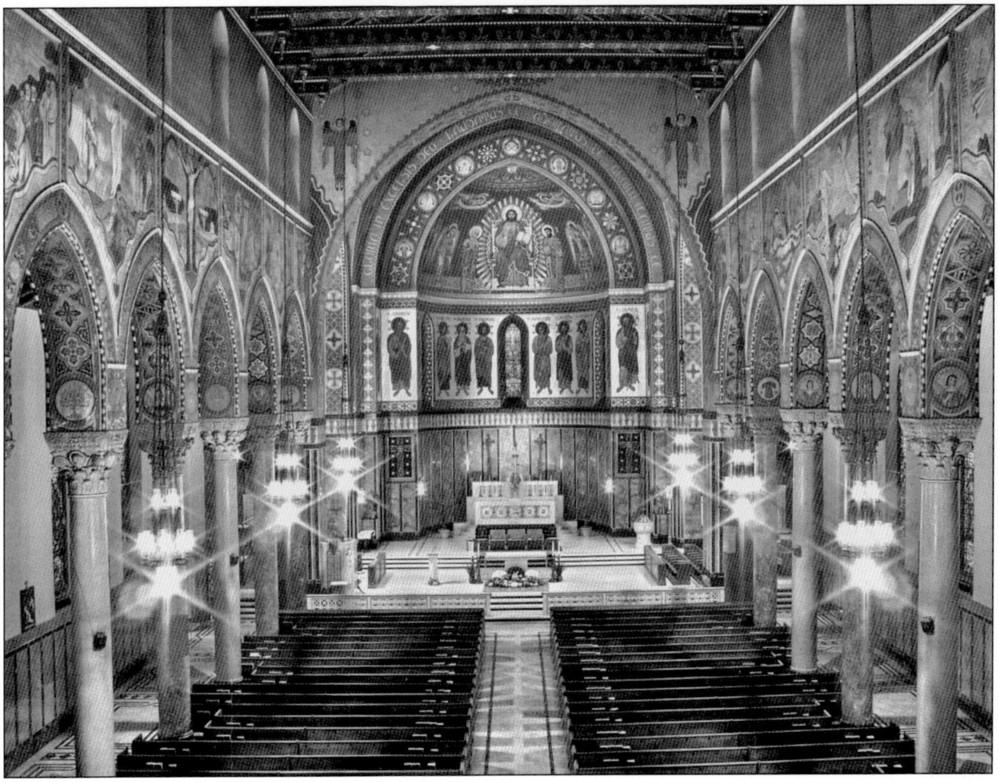

A panoramic view of the front of the church shows the elaborately decorated arches and the continuous story of the faith in the frescoes above the arches. There are 18 columns at the sides of the nave. These 17-foot-high columns are of four different stones: Porta Santa marble, Verona red marble, red Levanto marble, and Belgian black marble. Close inspection reveals the inclusion of fossils in some of the columns.

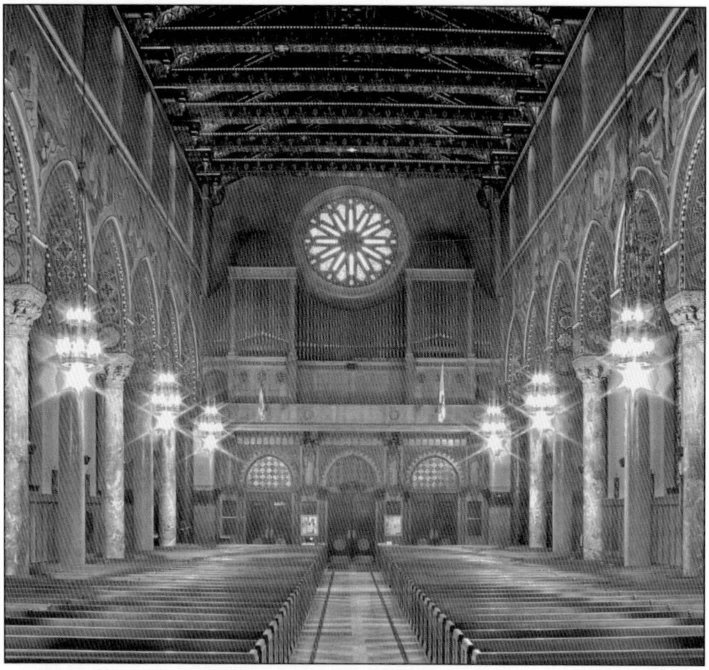

At the back on each side are Belgian black marble columns. The second, fourth, and sixth from the back are columns of Porta Santa marble. These columns were most likely recycled from a structure in antiquity, and there is convincing evidence that this marble was quarried from Chios in ancient Greece. Today this marble is present in only four churches in the world: the Holy Gate in St. Peter's Basilica in Rome, the Lateran in Rome, the Basilica of St. Mark in Venice, and St. James in Lakewood.

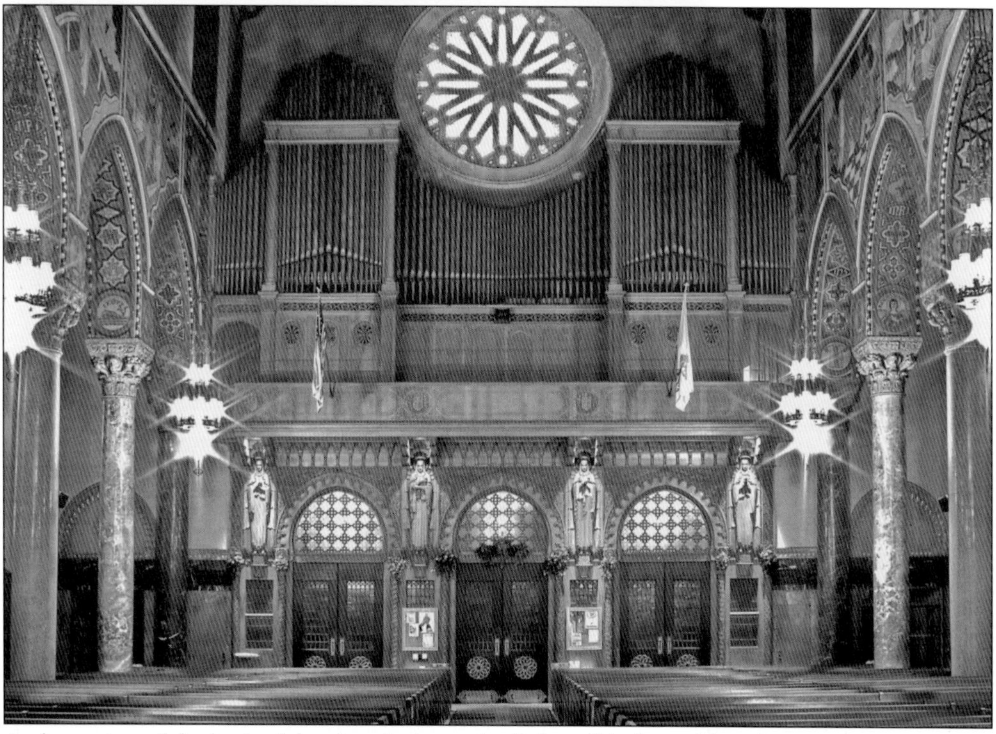

A closer view of the back of the church shows the Belgian black marble columns in contrast with the adjacent Porta Santa marble and the light Verona red in front of that. The doors at the back are padded leather and are surrounded by intricately carved wood that extends upward into the loft. The four carved wooden statues above the doors represent the four attitudes of prayer. From right to left, they are adoration, contrition, thanksgiving, and supplication.

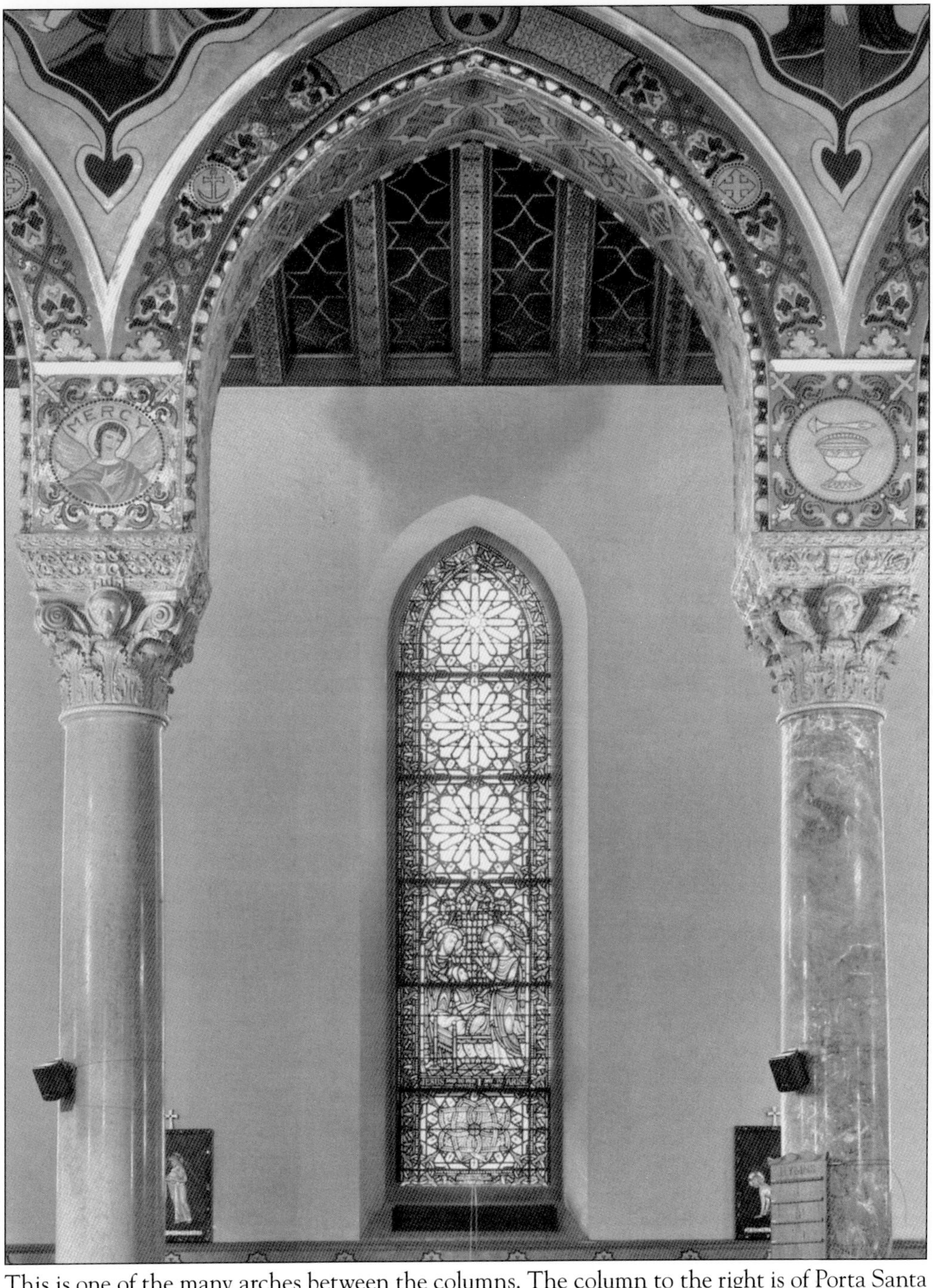

This is one of the many arches between the columns. The column to the right is of Porta Santa marble. Beyond it is one window in the lower row of stained-glass murals. This window depicts one of Jesus's miracles in which he says, "Damsel, I say to thee arise." Note also the differing capitals above the marble columns and the symbols above each cap representing one of the virtues. The caps themselves are of unpolished Rosato marble, and each is unique.

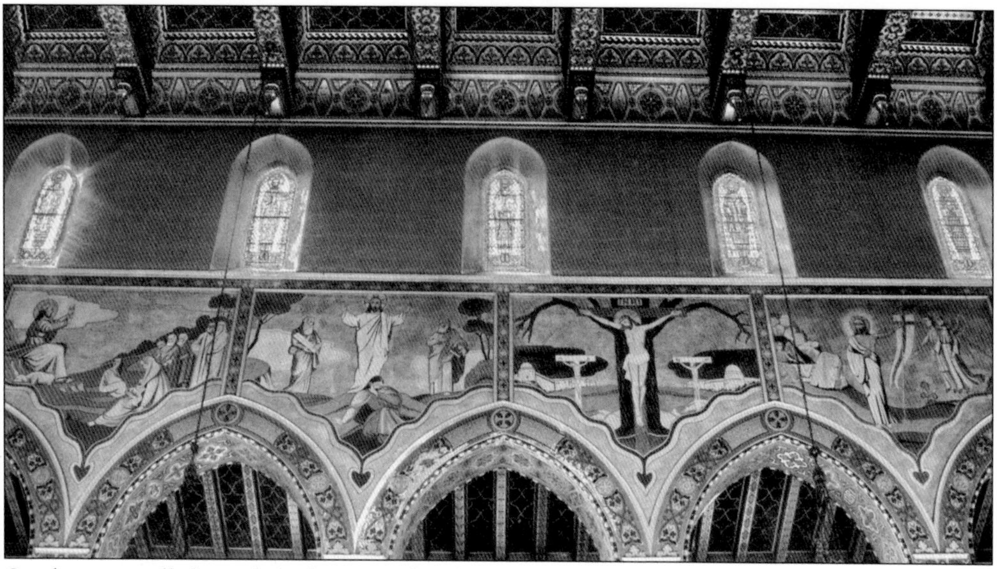

On the west wall above the columns and arches, large panels depict events from the life of Christ as told in the New Testament. Above these is the upper row of windows, where each features a Greek or Latin patriarch of the Church. In this picture, the summer sun is directly behind the left window, but the colored glass is so dense that the figure in the window is not obscured. This is testimony to the quality of glass used.

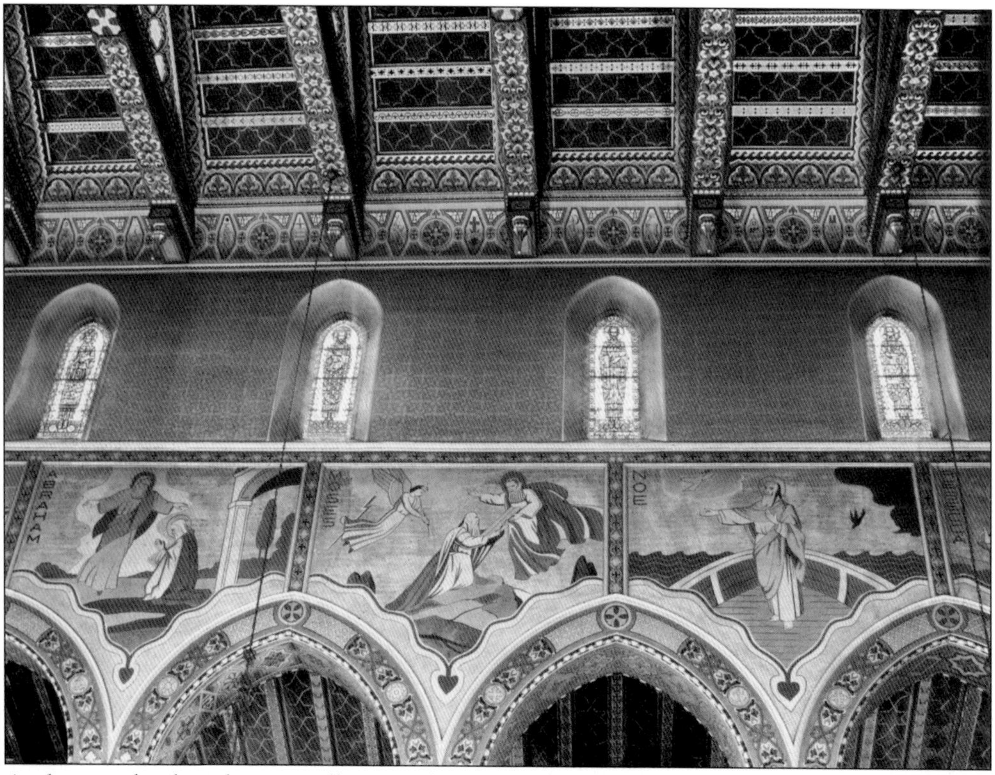

At the same level on the east wall are similar panels depicting characters and events from the Old Testament. Logically, the prophets of the Old Testament are featured in the windows above.

This telephoto view of the detail in one of the upper windows on the east wall depicts the prophet Daniel. These windows are so high that the only way to see them clearly from the floor is to move to the opposite wall of the church.

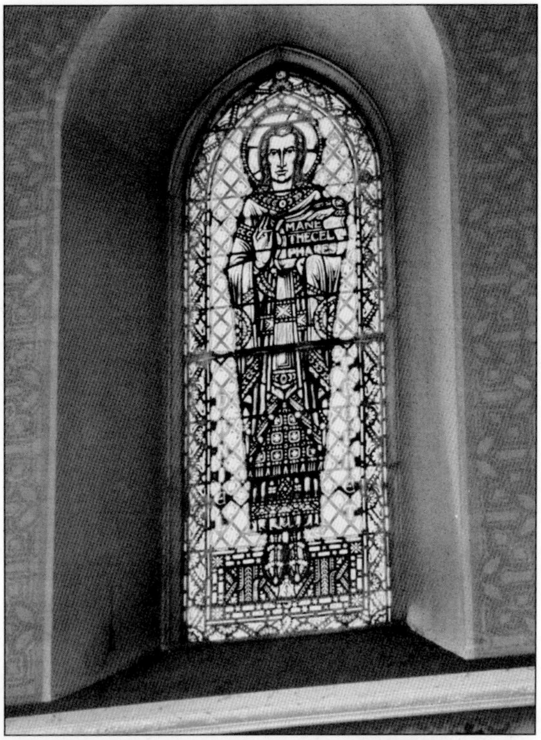

The city of Lakewood's significance is illustrated here as World War II hero Gen. Douglas MacArthur's motorcade passes St. James on its way from the airport to downtown Cleveland in 1951. The crowd of people lining the street speaks for itself. (Cleveland State University, *Cleveland Press* photograph.)

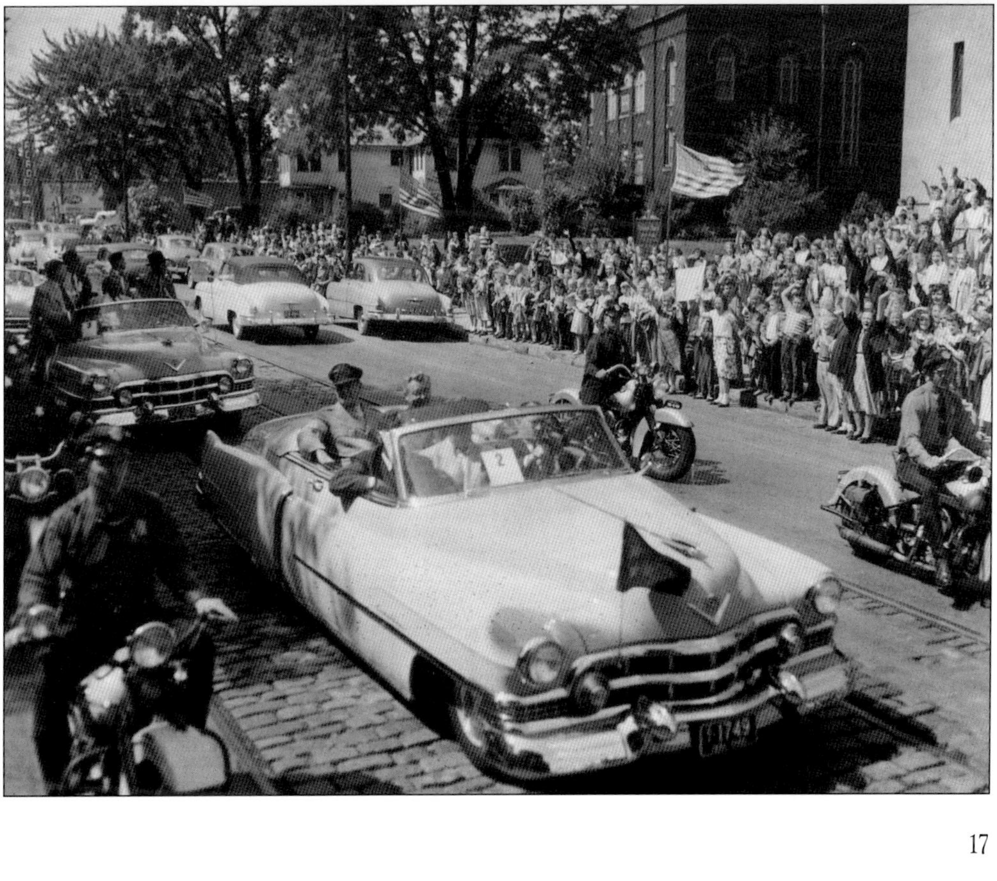

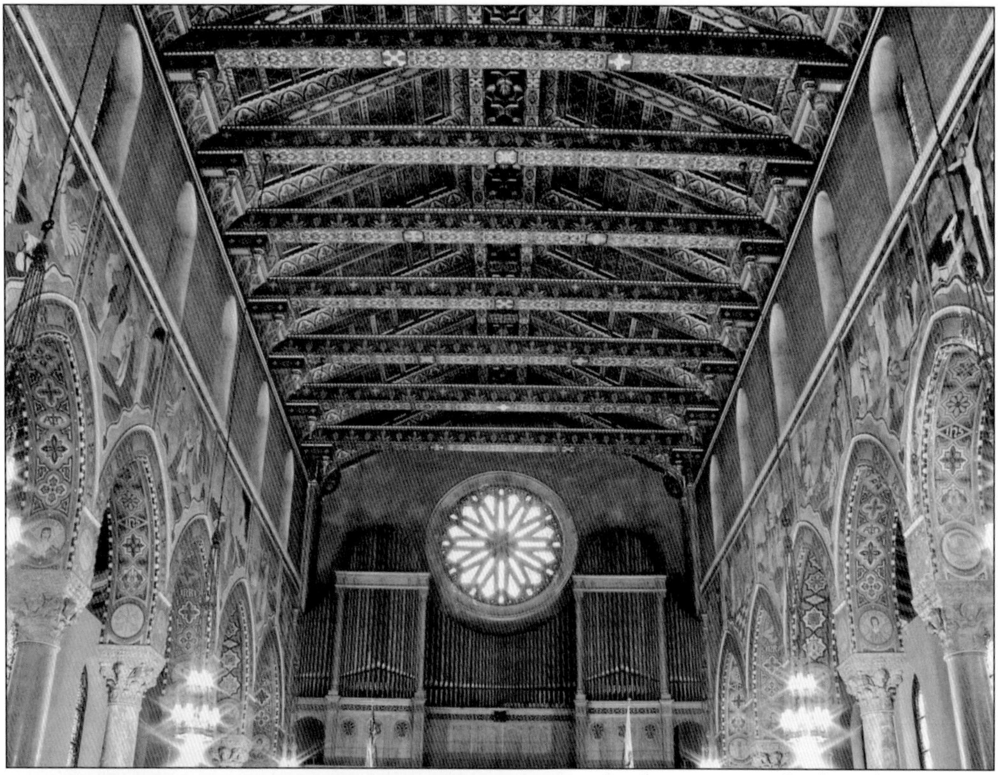

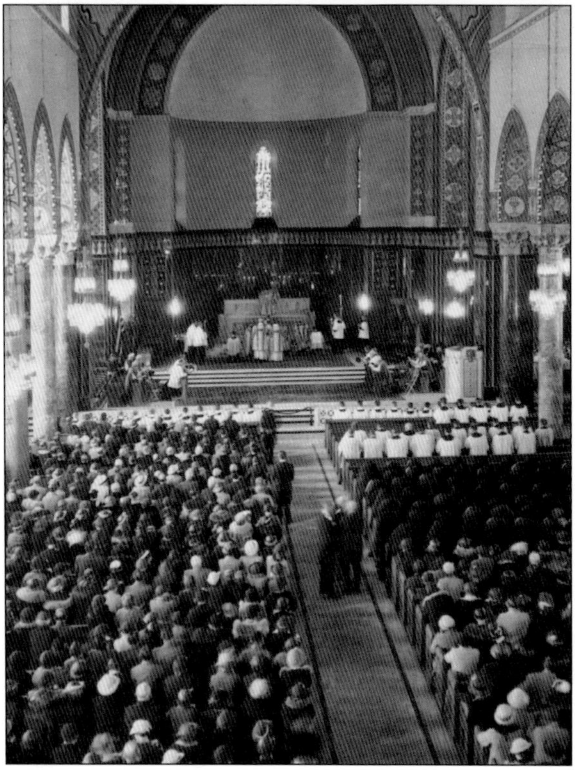

Looking up even higher, the spectacular ceiling of the church comes into view. Few ceilings in the world can match the intricately painted ceiling of St. James. Every square inch of the ceiling and horizontal beams are covered with perfectly created patterns, all done freehand with no shortcuts or stencils. Many believe this to be the finest example of ceiling art in modern times.

Priests and the congregation celebrate the church's dedication Mass on May 15, 1935. On St. James's first day, the beautiful church interior might have appeared finished to most parishioners, but over the next few years every available space would be adorned. The iconic frescoes have not yet been painted, and the pulpit is on the right side of the sanctuary rather than the left as it is today.

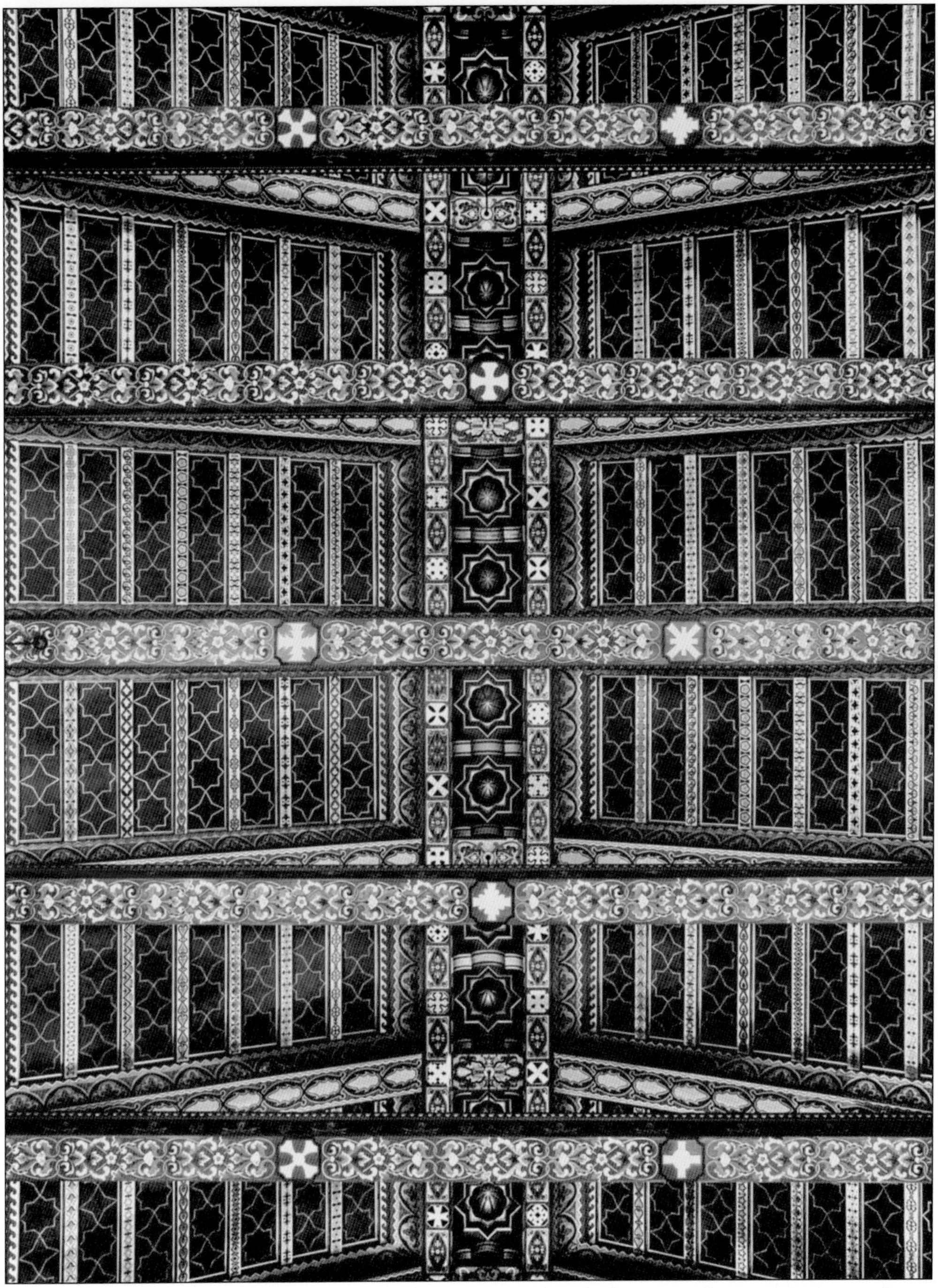

An extreme wide-angle photograph shows what one sees when looking straight up at this magnificent ceiling from the center aisle. Note especially the decorative strip that runs through the ceiling at its crest. On it are painted star-like figures. Within these stars are shapes that resemble rosebuds. Between the stars are striped ribbons.

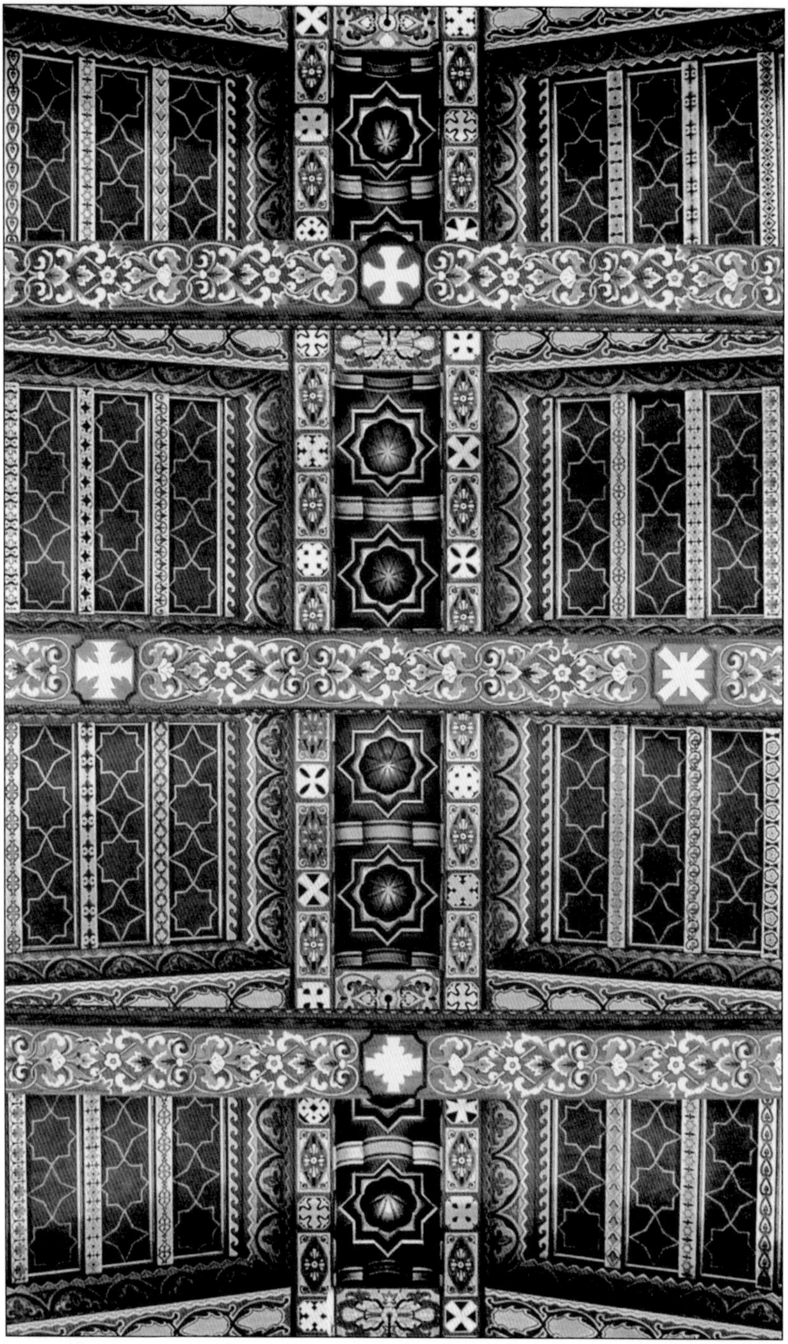

Zooming in on the previous plate, the ceiling becomes even more dazzling. Note again the rosebud figures within the stars. The center buds are pointing straight down. As one looks at the adjacent buds, they seem to be pointing at an angle toward the center. In this photograph, the buds closer to the top and bottom of the picture seem to be pointing at an even more severe angle toward the center (see the previous plate), but this is an illusion. As the viewer walks up and down the center aisle, while looking upward, the buds always seem to be pointed toward the viewer, moving as the viewer moves.

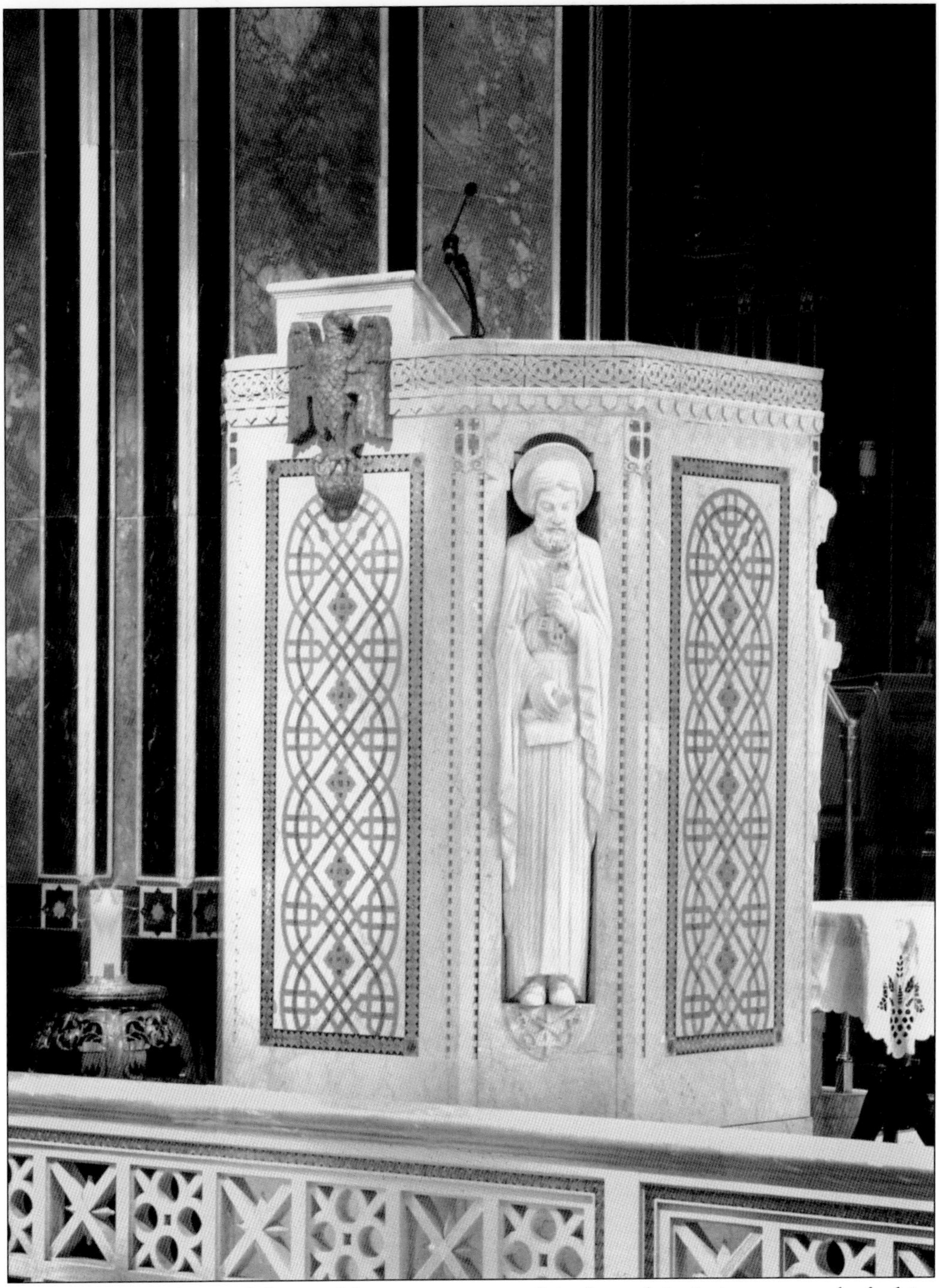

Immediately in front of the marble communion rail is the pulpit. It is composed of white Botticino marble with a golden eagle of Verona marble on the front. (The eagle is the symbol of John the Evangelist.) On the front corner is the image of St. Peter holding the keys to the Kingdom of God.

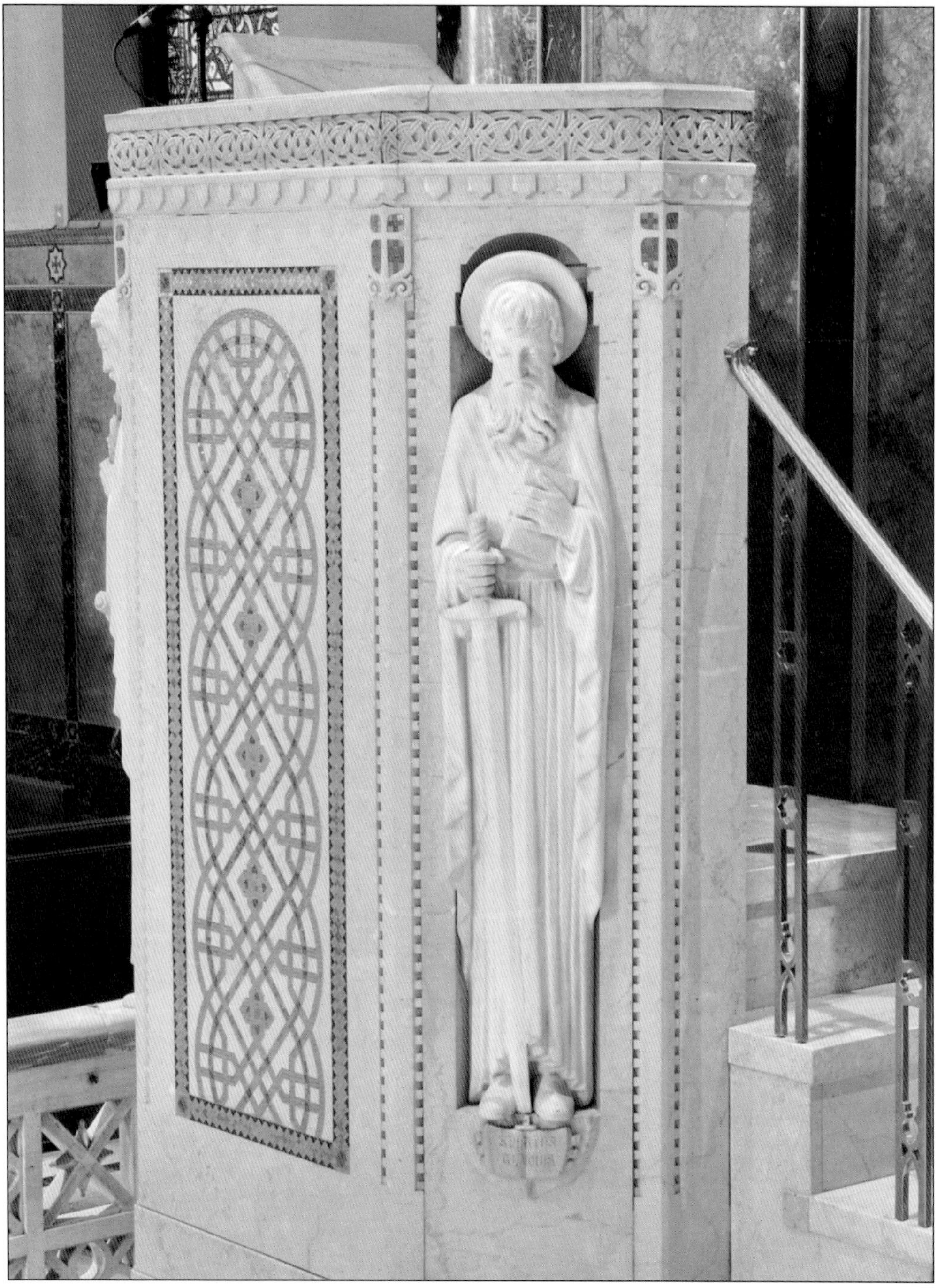

On the rear corner of the pulpit facing the altar is the image of St. James the Greater, the namesake of the church, with his sword. James was the brother of the Apostle John and son of Zebedee and Salome and older than the other apostle James the Less. He was martyred in Jerusalem by Herod Agrippa himself. James became known as a valiant knight who later miraculously appeared to fight against the Moors for the protection of Spain. Cervantes wrote that James had "been given by God to Spain for its patron and protection."

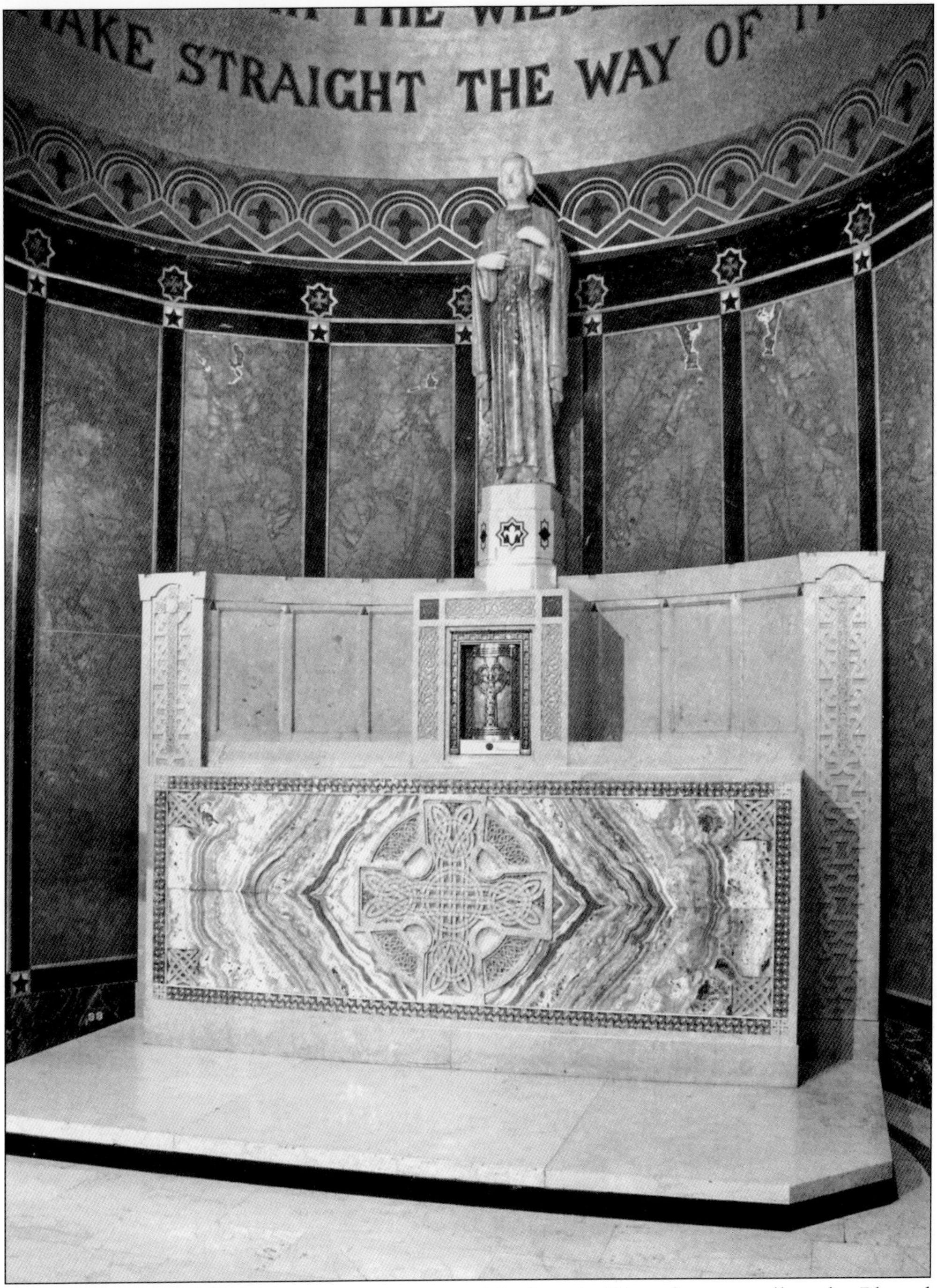

On the east side of the sanctuary is the altar of St. Joseph. This altar, as well as the Blessed Mother altar to the west, was built from Perla Campo marble inlaid with Algerian Onyx from Africa. The front panels bear the Greek cross and are laced with the type of complex geometric patterns often found on Norman Romanesque artifacts.

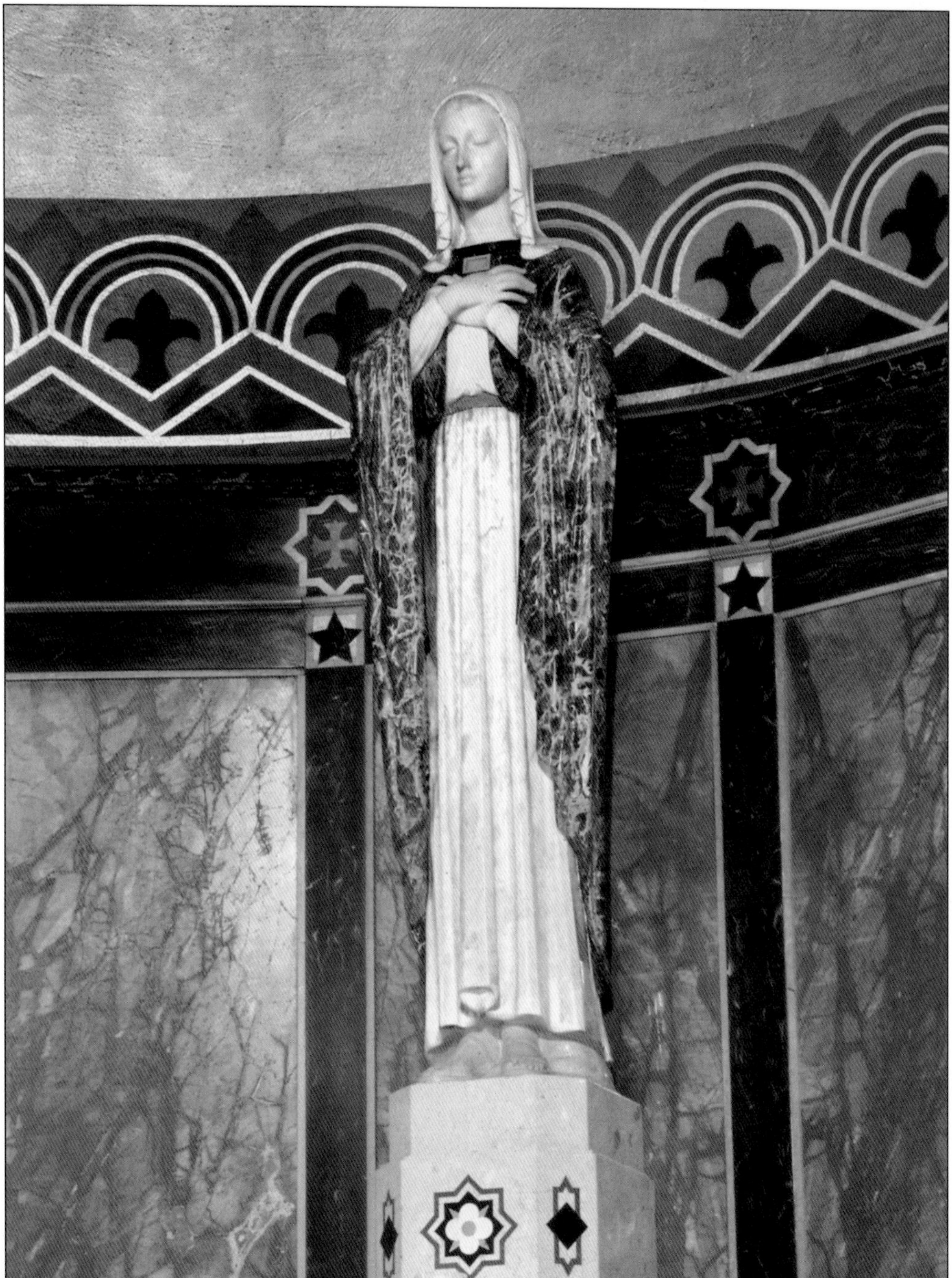

The statue of Mary above her altar was made from Italian Carrara marble. There are at least three different types of stone in this statue, each with a different color and texture. The same holds true for the statue of St. Joseph on the opposite side (not pictured).

The baptismal font is comprised of a beige limestone, also called Chiampo Perlato marble, from Vicenza, Italy. The Celtic cross and the serpentine ornamentation on the hood are probably a reflection of the Irish families that founded the church and possibly even Father Leahy himself.

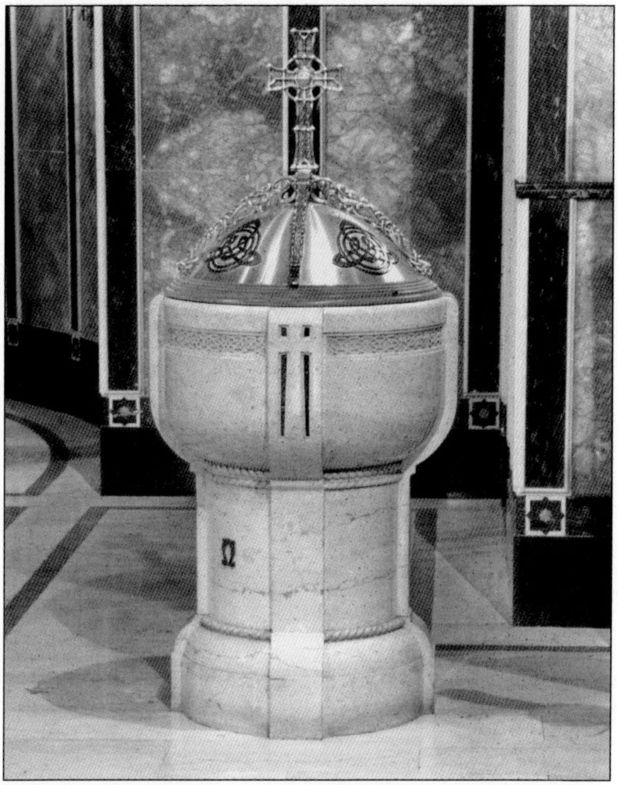

This 1957 photograph shows the crowd of people leaving St. James. It is indicative of how significant the church was to the community. For many years, Sunday Mass was one of the highlights of the week. (Cleveland State University, *Cleveland Press* photograph.)

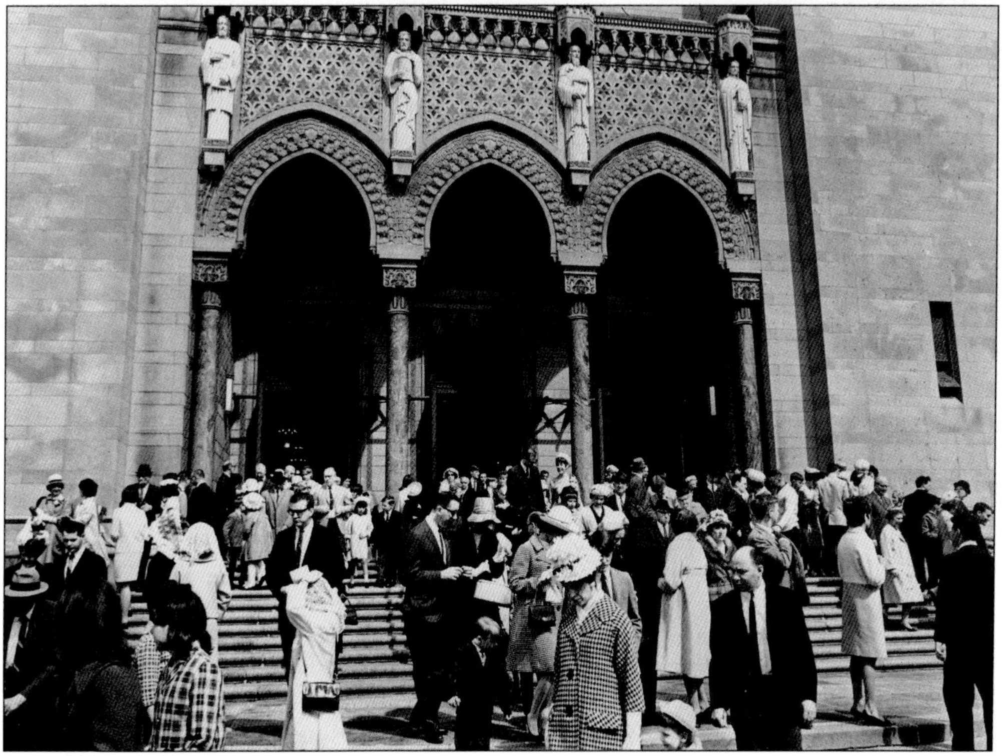

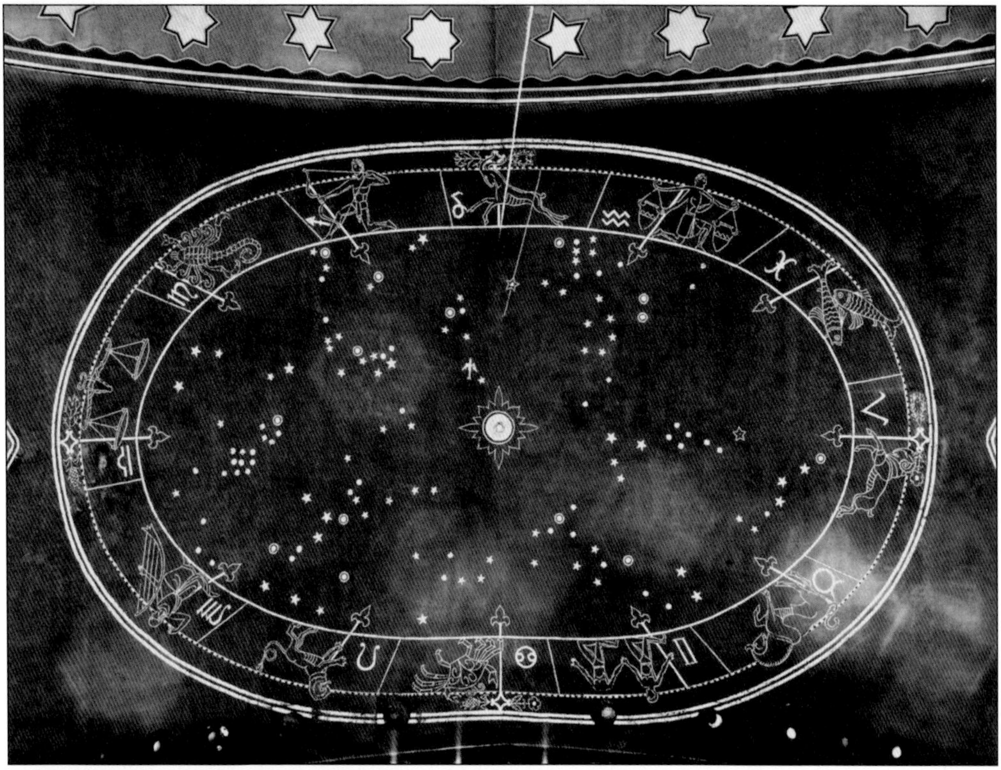

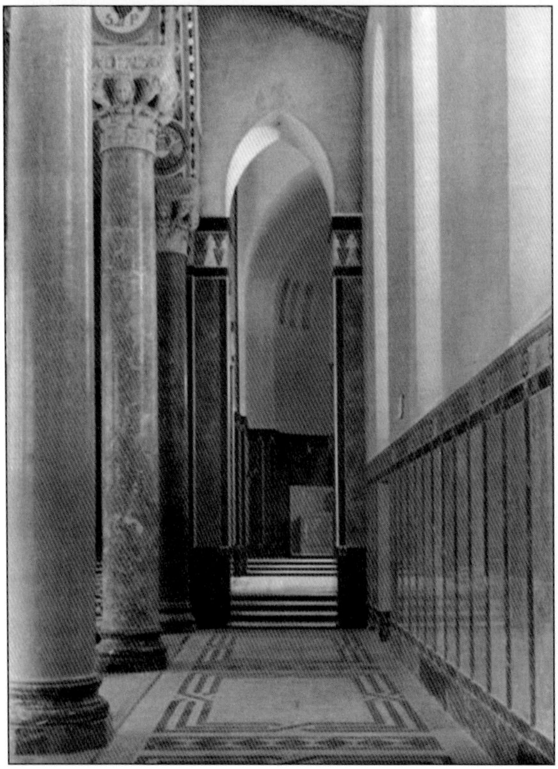

Between the pews and the sanctuary is the transept, or crossing. The ceiling of the transept is a dark blue and contains the 12 signs of the zodiac. In the center is the Epiphany star, and near it is a flying dove (symbol of the Holy Spirit). Between the concentric ovals is a third oval made up of a line composed of 365 divisions representing the days in a year. The entire panel represents the creation and presence of God.

The east-side isle leads to the St. Joseph altar, as seen here in this 1935 photograph. The floor is composed of Roman travertine and red Levanto marble. Three different marbles of the columns are clearly shown, but the walls are bare. The frescoes were not completed until 1944. (Cleveland State University, *Cleveland Press* photograph.)

The famed St. James Chalice is a highly jeweled, gold gift from the parishioners given to the parish on May 21, 1935, in conjunction with the dedication of the church. The gold and jewels came from the personal property of the parishioners who had the chalice made by the Potter and Mellon Company at the height of the Depression. (Ed Ferrall/Walter Grossman photograph.)

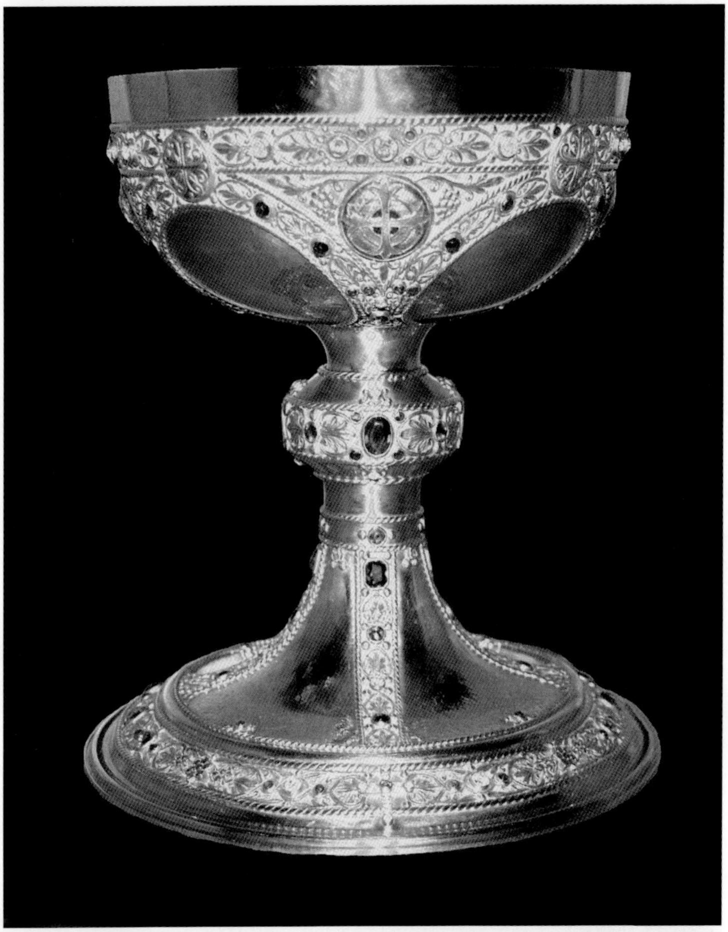

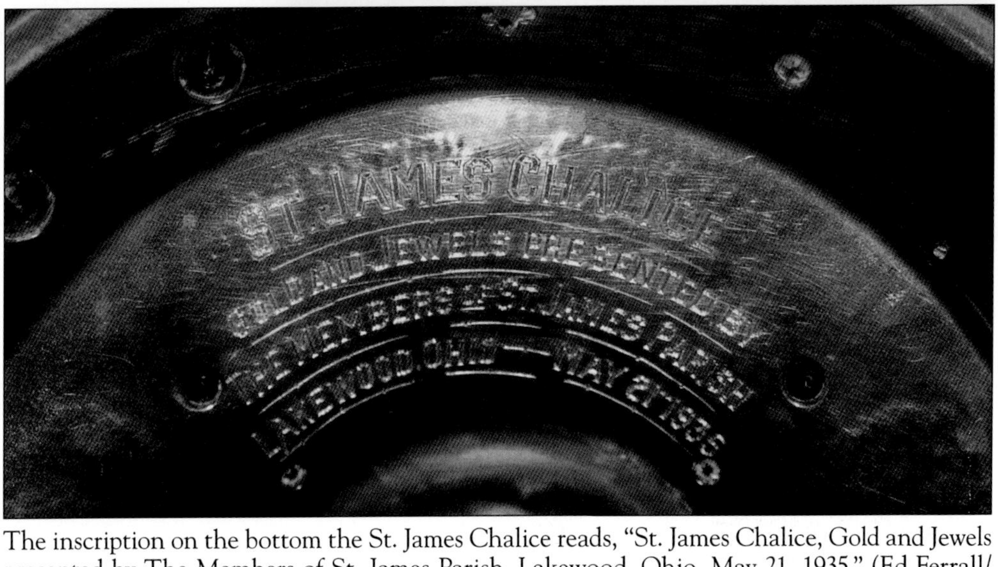

The inscription on the bottom the St. James Chalice reads, "St. James Chalice, Gold and Jewels presented by The Members of St. James Parish, Lakewood, Ohio–May 21, 1935." (Ed Ferrall/Walter Grossman photograph.)

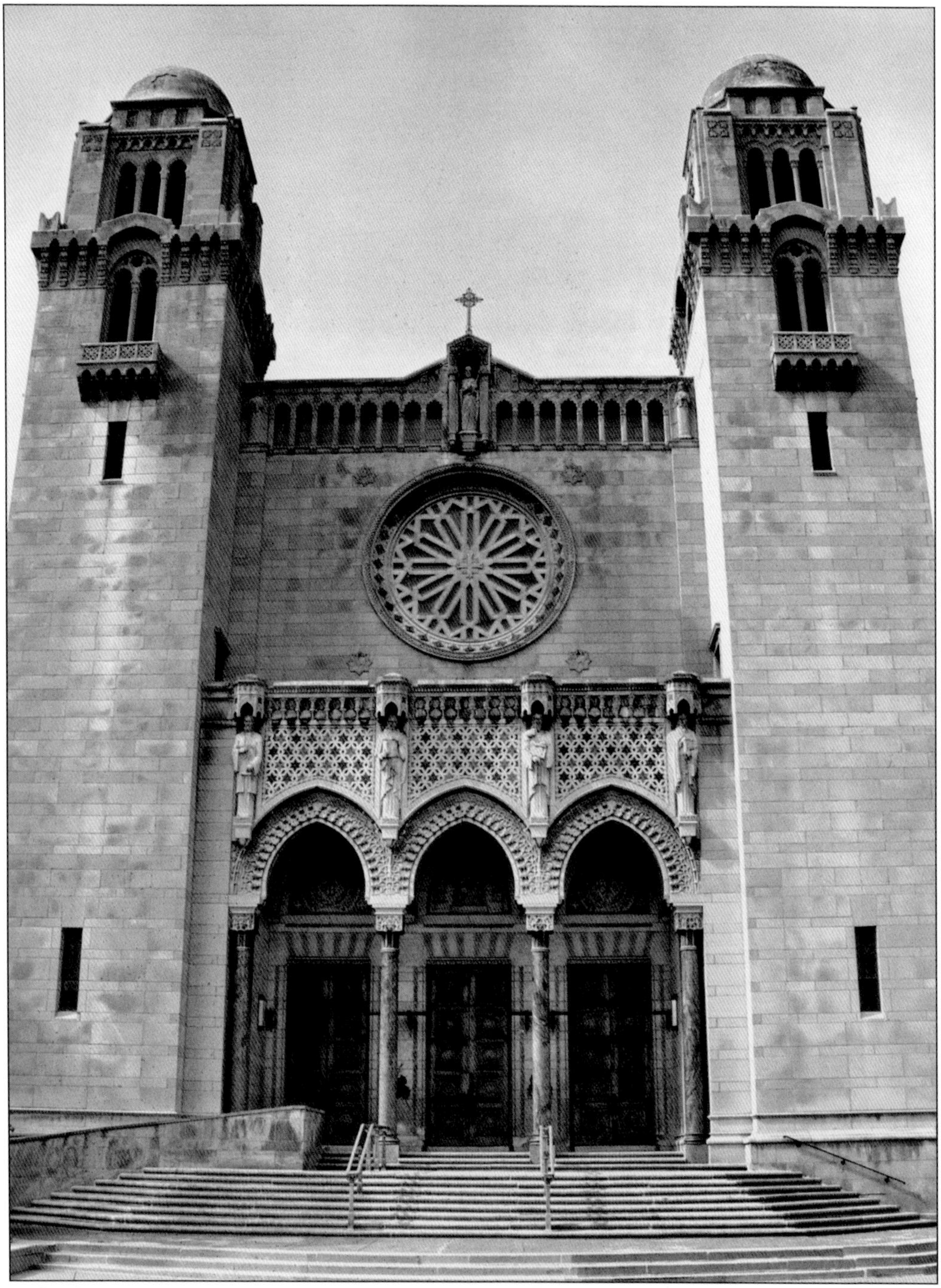

Before leaving St. James, one must take in this exotic and magnificent structure, a rare blending of the architecture of the East and the West. St. James was the main inspiration for this book, and it is hard to fathom its closing. The book's cover and the lead chapter are dedicated to St. James and hopefully give a representation of the beauty and timelessness of the structure. It will be gone by the time of this publication, a clear example of "Cleveland's Vanishing Sacred Architecture."

Two
St. Adalbert

The Bohemian parish of St. Adalbert at 2353 East 83rd Street was founded by Fr. Anthony Hynek in 1883 as a daughter church of St. Wenceslas Parish. The facility was opened in 1884 and served its members in a modest church until the present church was constructed in 1911, with the rectory having been completed in 1906. The architect for the new church was William P. Ginther of Akron, and the design was loosely patterned after the Cathedral of Salzburg in Austria. The total cost of the project was $60,000.

The namesake of the parish, St. Adalbert (939–997), was the bishop of Prague who subsequently became a missionary to the countries of Hungary, Poland, and Prussia. Although hostile tribesmen martyred him in Prussia, he was considered a great hero in Hungary and Poland.

In 1922, Our Lady of the Blessed Sacrament Church was established just three blocks west of St. Adalbert and served the needs of African American Catholics in the neighborhood. In 1961, the Bohemians left St. Adalbert, and the parish of Our Lady of the Blessed Sacrament, which was administered by the Missionaries of the Precious Blood, merged with St. Adalbert to form the first Catholic African American congregation in Cleveland.

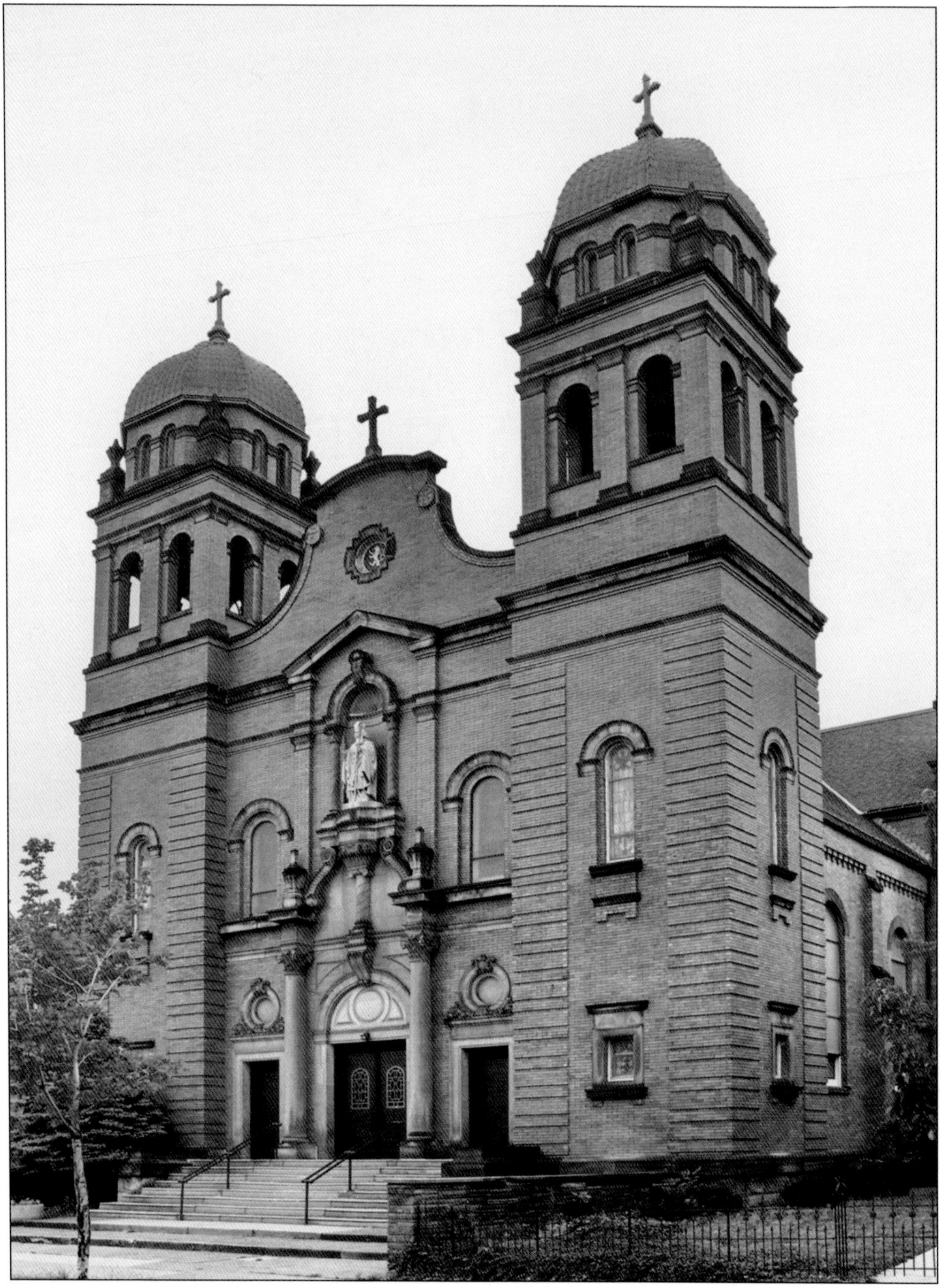

Since its construction, the church has been a landmark in the area. The twin bell towers are roofed in copper and stand above and beside a niche with a magnificent statue of St. Adalbert. Below the statue are three entrance doors leading to the narthex (vestibule) within.

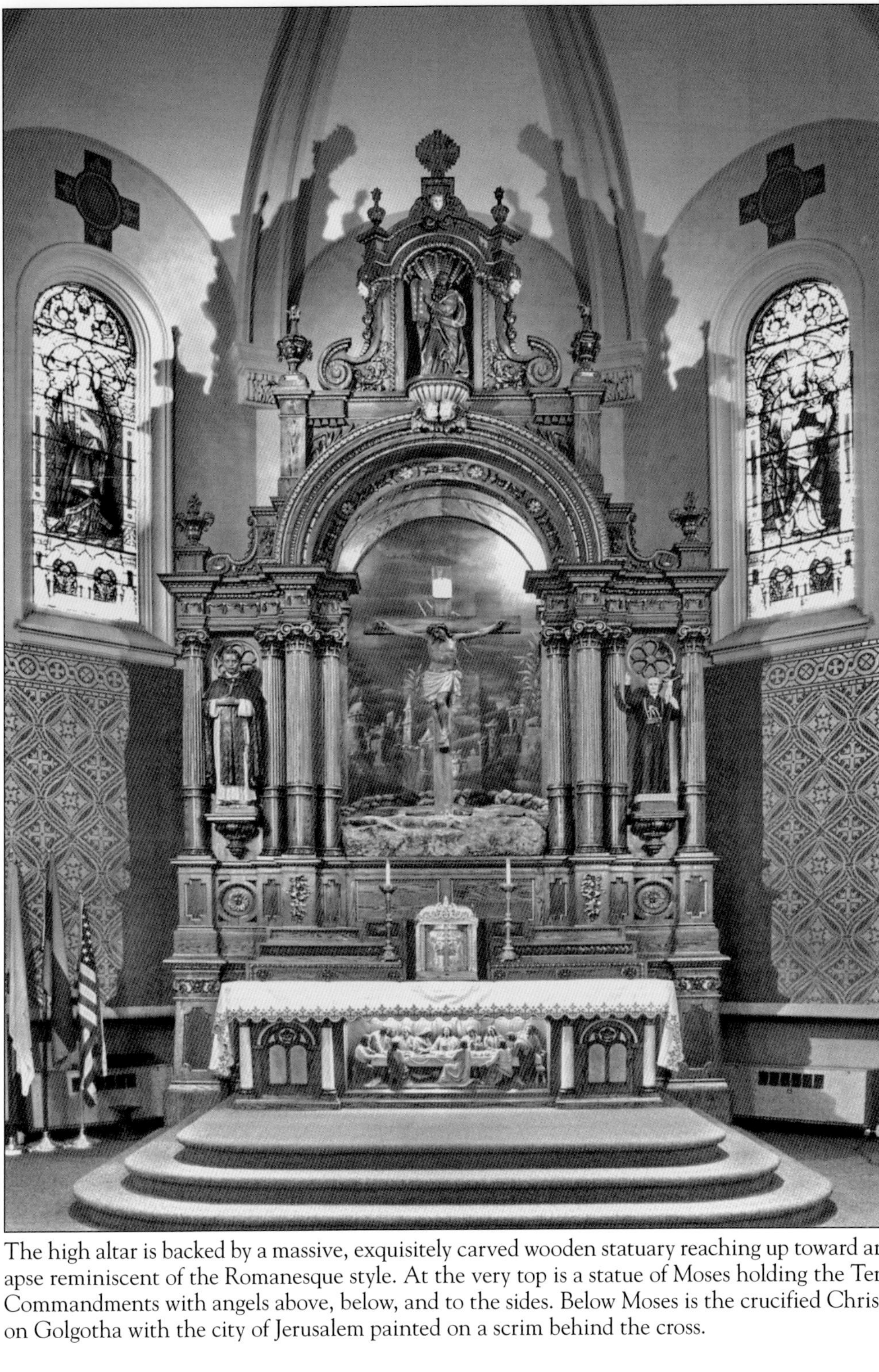

The high altar is backed by a massive, exquisitely carved wooden statuary reaching up toward an apse reminiscent of the Romanesque style. At the very top is a statue of Moses holding the Ten Commandments with angels above, below, and to the sides. Below Moses is the crucified Christ on Golgotha with the city of Jerusalem painted on a scrim behind the cross.

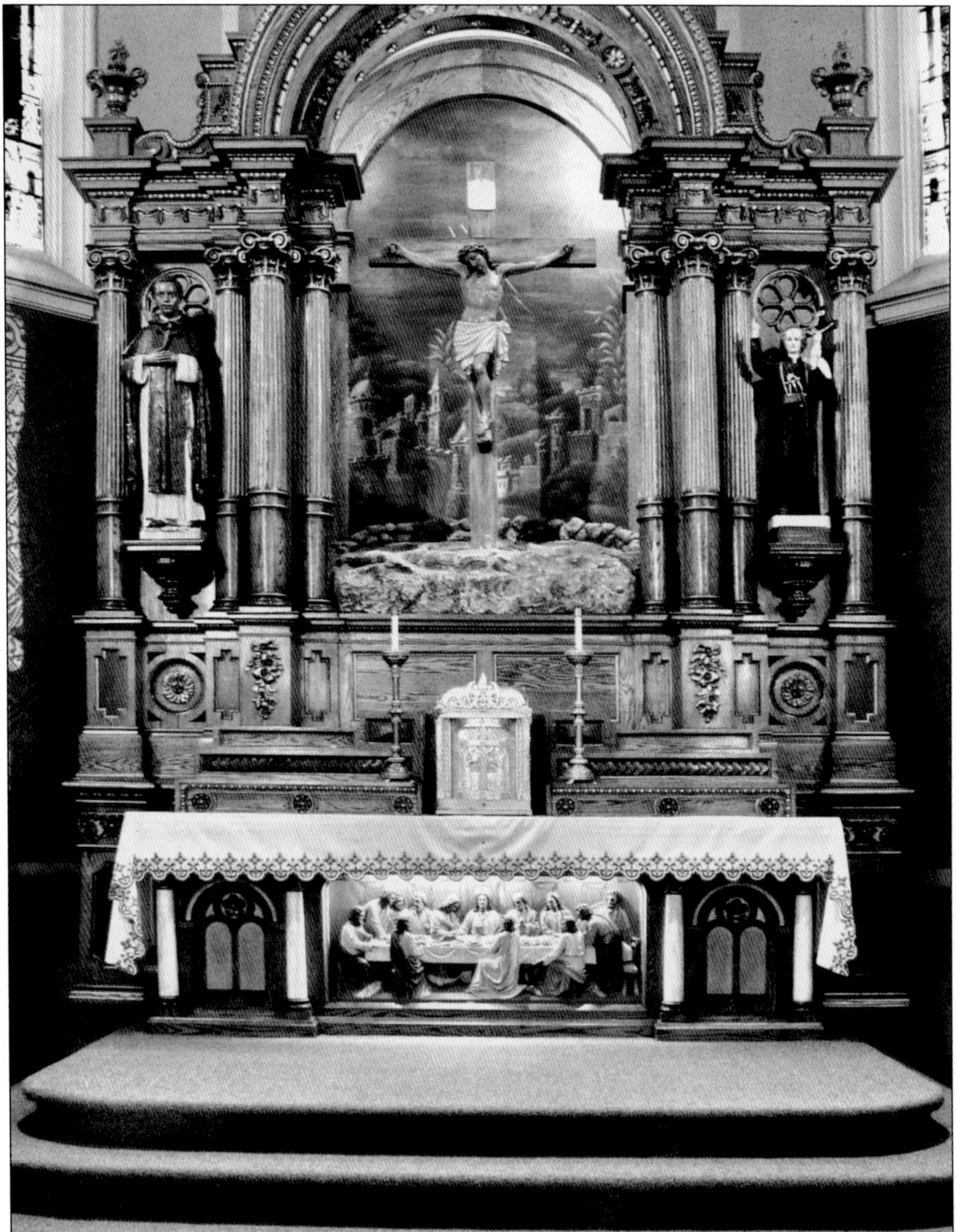

A closer view of the altar and statuary shows two very significant images at the sides of the crucifix. The image to the right is that of St. Gaspar del Bufalo (1786–1837), the founder of the Missionaries of the Precious Blood who currently administer St. Adalbert (the same order that ministered to the congregation at Our Lady of the Blessed Sacrament). The statue to the left is that of St. Martin de Porres (1579–1639). This son of a Spanish noble and a former slave became well known for his work among the poor and as a patron of people of mixed race. As a result, he is highly revered by Catholic African American congregations. Note also the elaborate carving of the Last Supper on the front of the altar.

This panel shows the detail, textures, and grains in the altar and lower statuary. Even the design of the tabernacle is in keeping with the design of its surroundings.

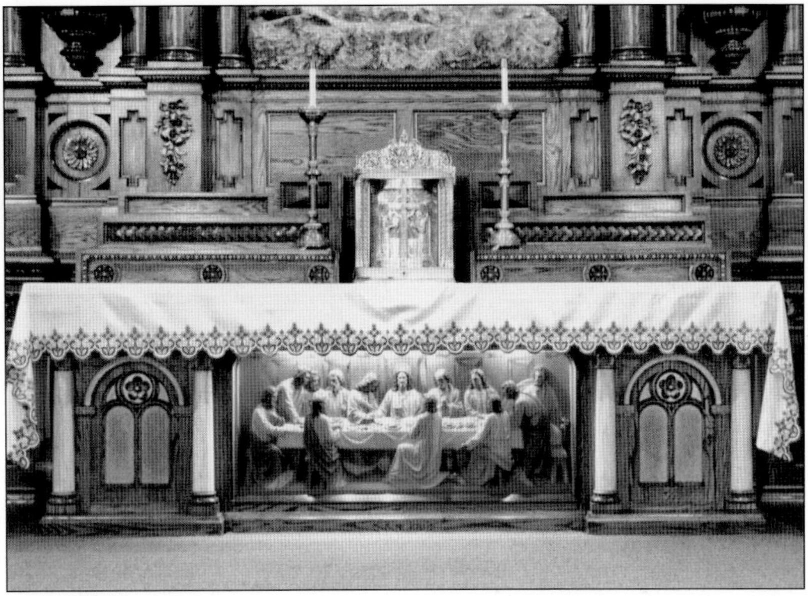

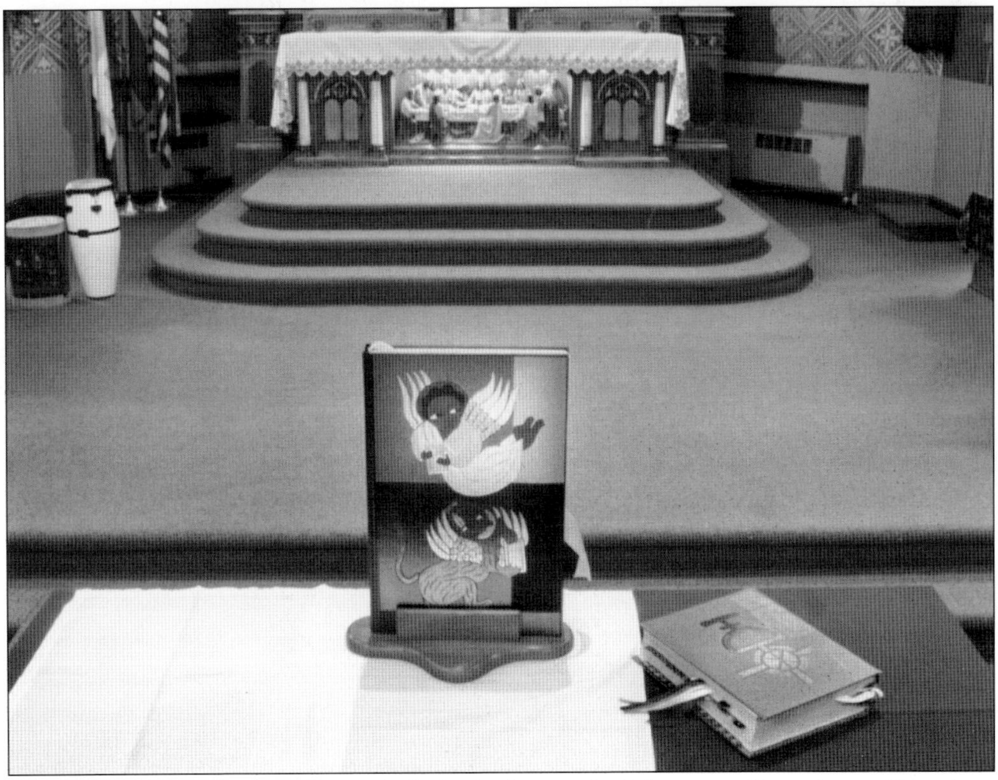

The Mass books on the low altar, with the high altar as a backdrop, as well as other artifacts show the cultural involvement and devotion of St. Adalbert's congregation.

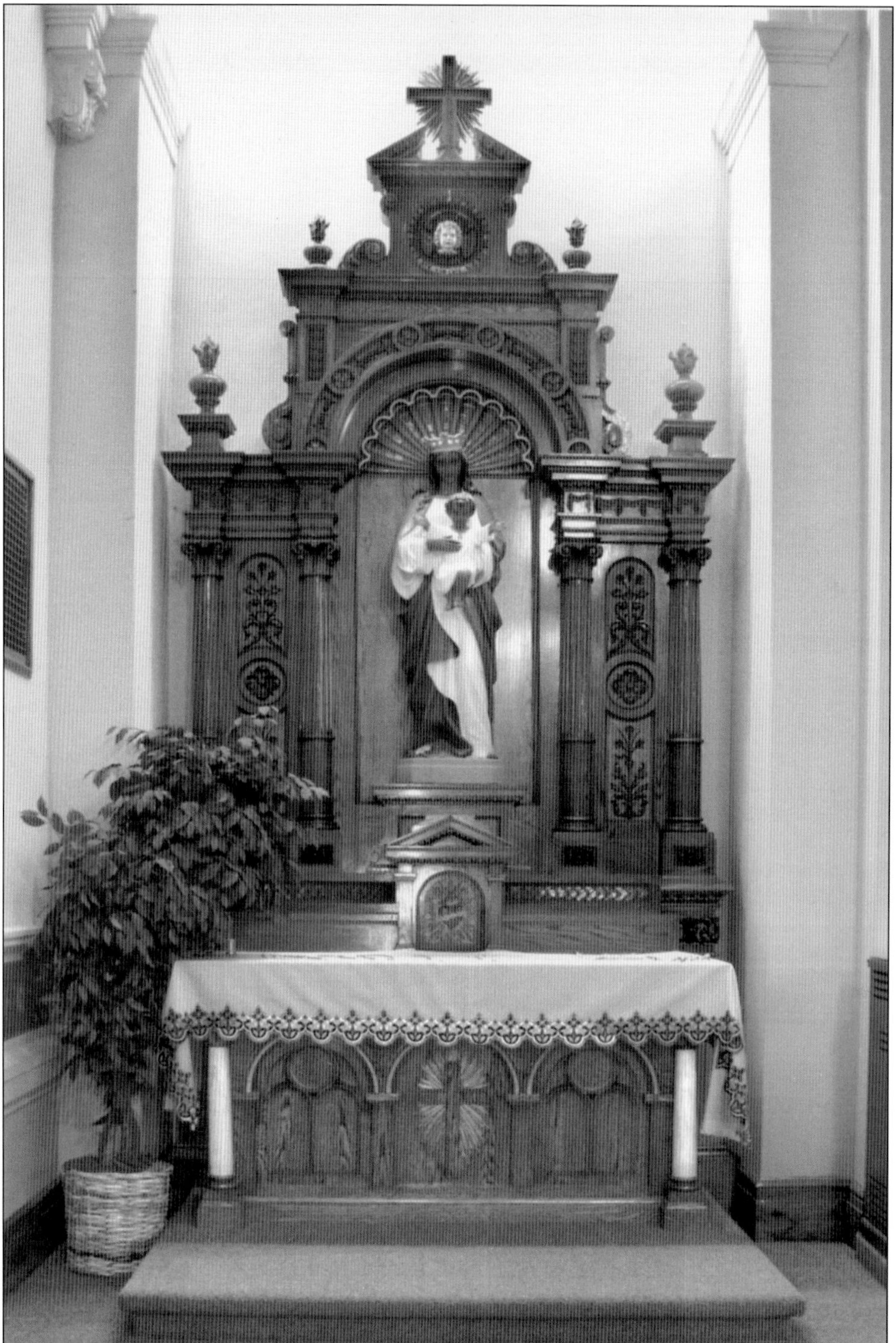

The theme and the structure of the main altar are carried over to the design of the Blessed Mother's side altar with its gorgeous carved wood. It is a blend of elegance and simplicity. The St. Joseph altar is similar.

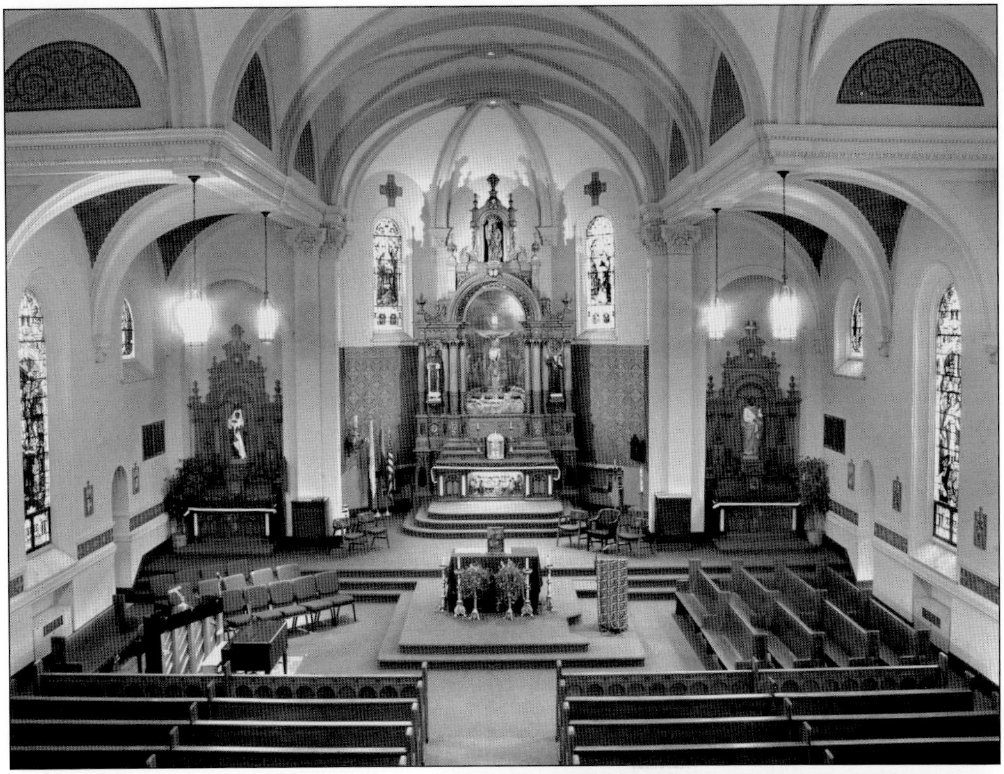

This view of the front of the church shows the balance of grandeur and aesthetics in the neoclassical and is a fine example of the Romanesque style.

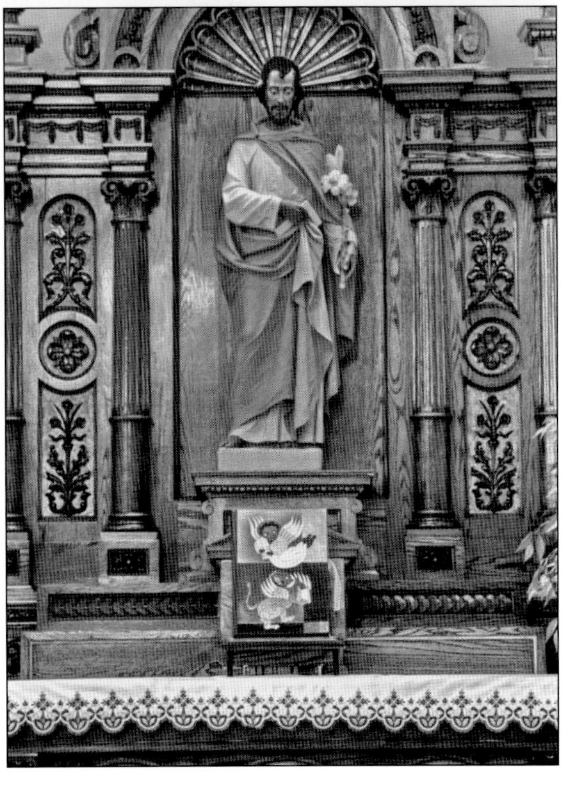

A closer view of the altar of St. Joseph reveals all the fine workmanship that went into these artifacts. The neoclassical theme of the church is reflected clearly in the columns, caps, and fringe above.

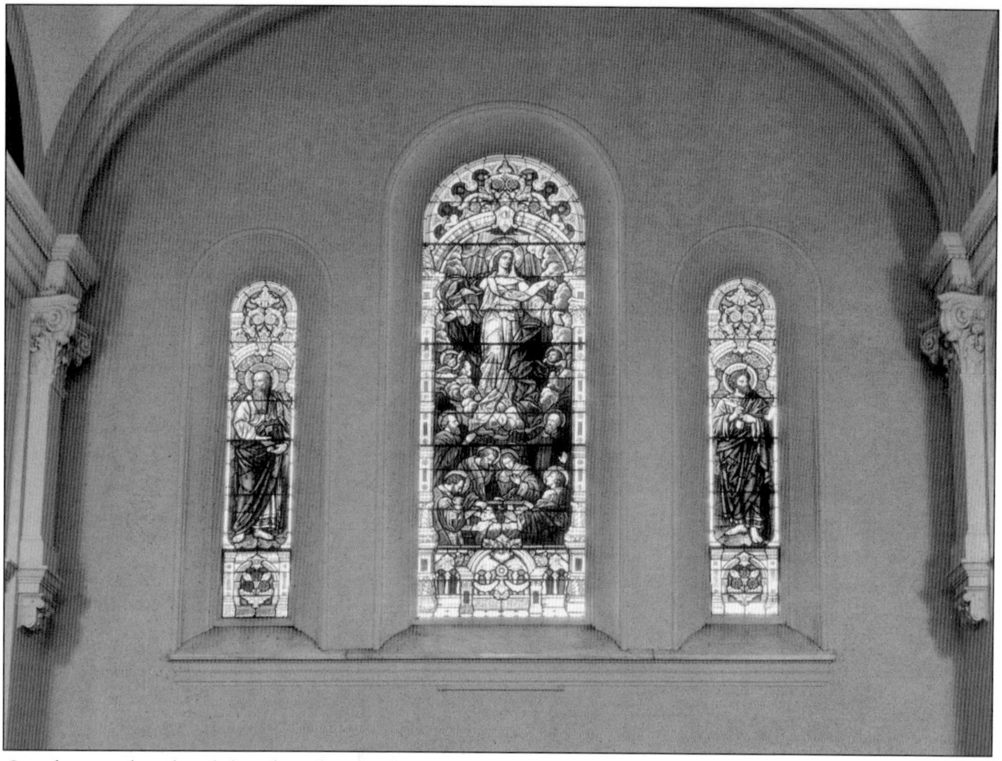

On the north side of the church is a three-window array showing the Assumption of Mary. The Munich Stained Glass Company of Chicago made the windows of St. Adalbert. It is unknown whether the glass was made in Germany and shipped to St. Adalbert, or if it was actually created in Chicago. In either case, the quality of the color and clarity of the image in these windows is remarkable.

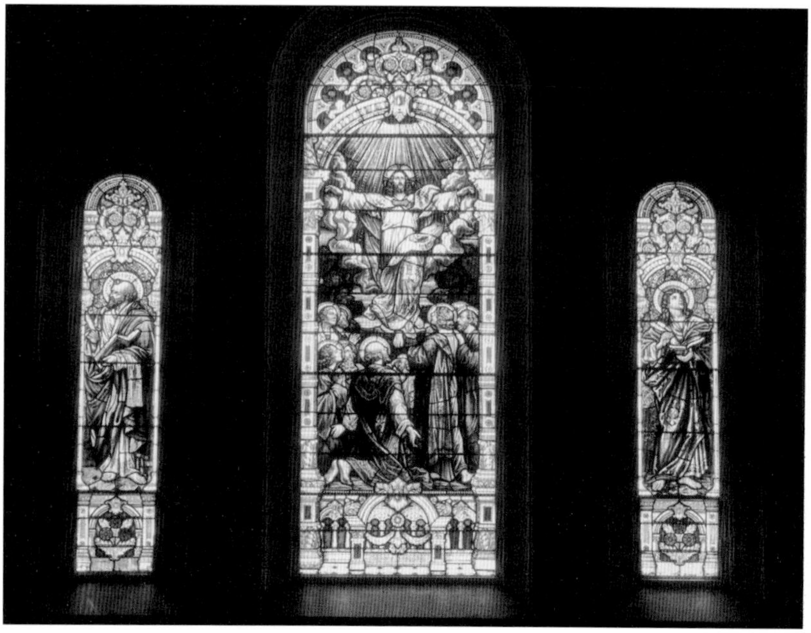

On the south wall is a similar set of windows depicting the Ascension of Christ. The painting in these windows is dynamic, and the detail is remarkable.

The altar is a true study in neoclassical style. Note the modified classical columns with the elaborated capitals supporting the Romanesque arch.

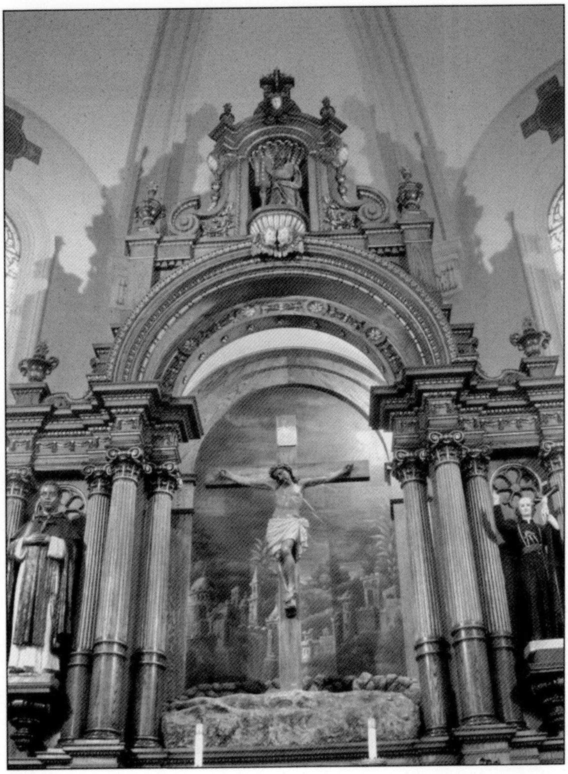

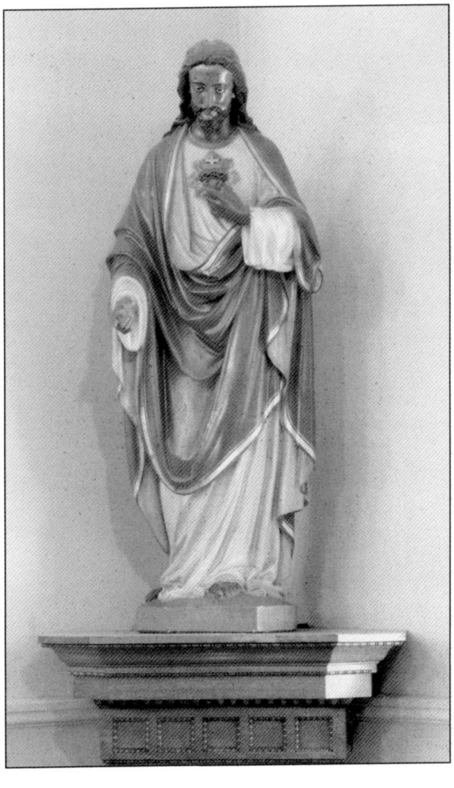

Below the windows on the church's south side is a statue of the Sacred Heart of Jesus. The Christ figure is depicted as a person of African descent.

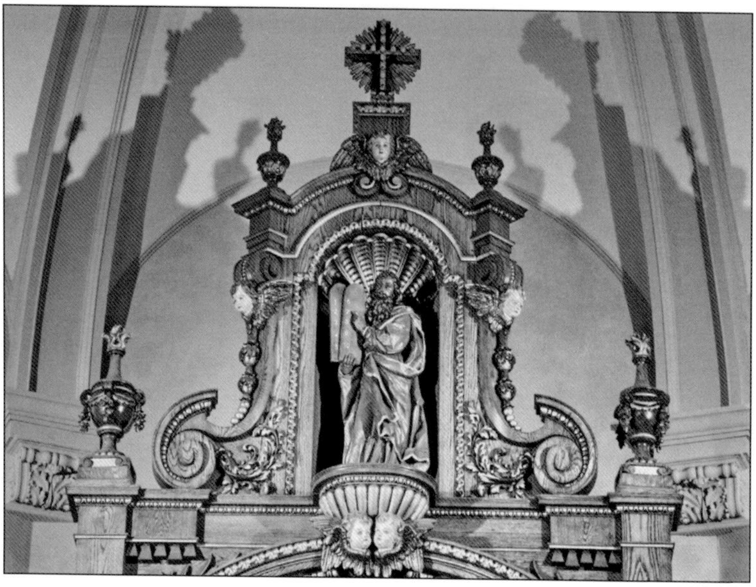

An exquisitely carved statue of Moses, also portrayed as an African, stands atop the statuary. In his hands are the Ten Commandments.

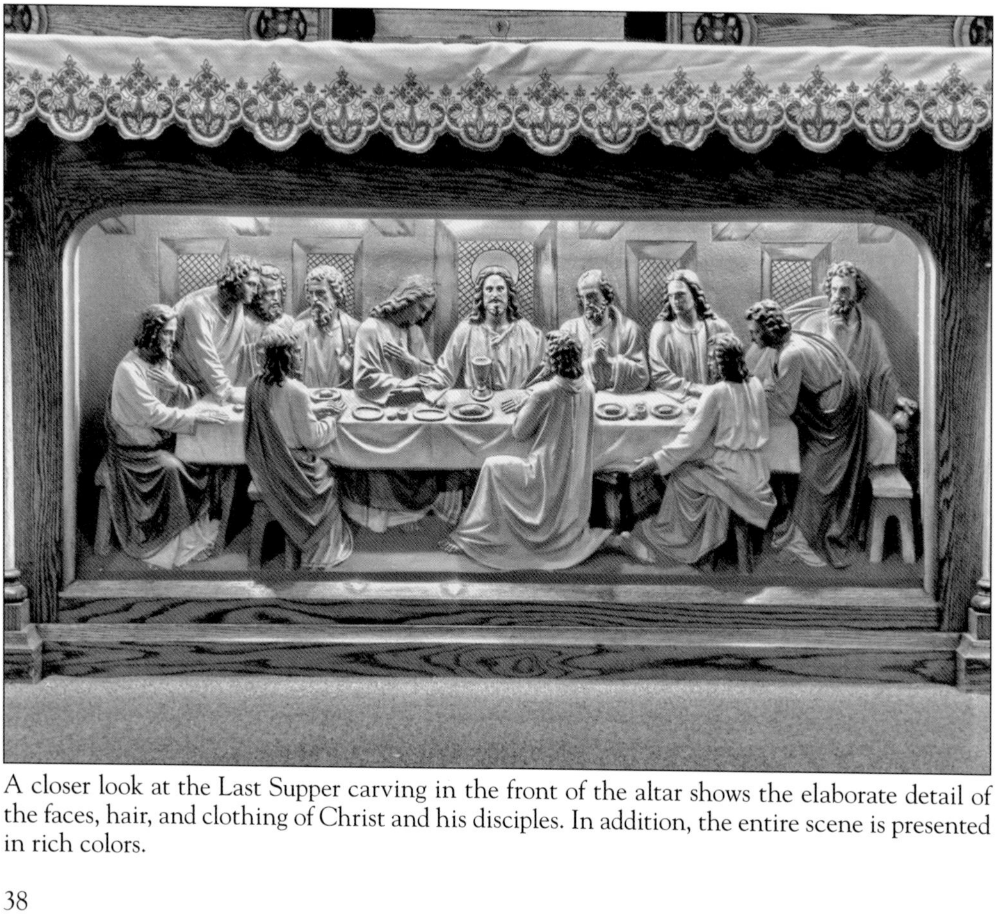

A closer look at the Last Supper carving in the front of the altar shows the elaborate detail of the faces, hair, and clothing of Christ and his disciples. In addition, the entire scene is presented in rich colors.

Three

St. Emeric

Located on the western edge of the Cleveland Flats at 1860 West Twenty-Second Street, St. Emeric Church stands as a citadel of the Hungarian Catholic community. The parish was founded in 1904 for the purpose of serving the Hungarian immigrant population. It prospered at its location on West Twenty-Fourth Street until 1916, when the church was destroyed by a fire. At that point, St. Emeric purchased St. Mary of the Annunciation Church, which had been a French church but suffered from a dwindling congregation. The new church was located east of the present-day church and, as it turned out, had been constructed upon land needed for the building of the Terminal Tower. Consequently the Van Sweringen brothers (builders of the Terminal Tower) purchased it, erected the current St. Emeric Church building in 1924, and moved the parish there. Many of the artifacts from the former St. Mary of the Annunciation, such as the altars, confessionals, statues, and bell, were transferred to the new location.

Although the architect of the new church remains unknown, the design of the building reflects the Gothic style in both the exterior and interior. Since the present church was built, St. Emeric has been the center of Hungarian culture on Cleveland's west side. Even today the parish supports a Hungarian School, provides a major center for the Scouts program, and is active in various neighborhood community programs.

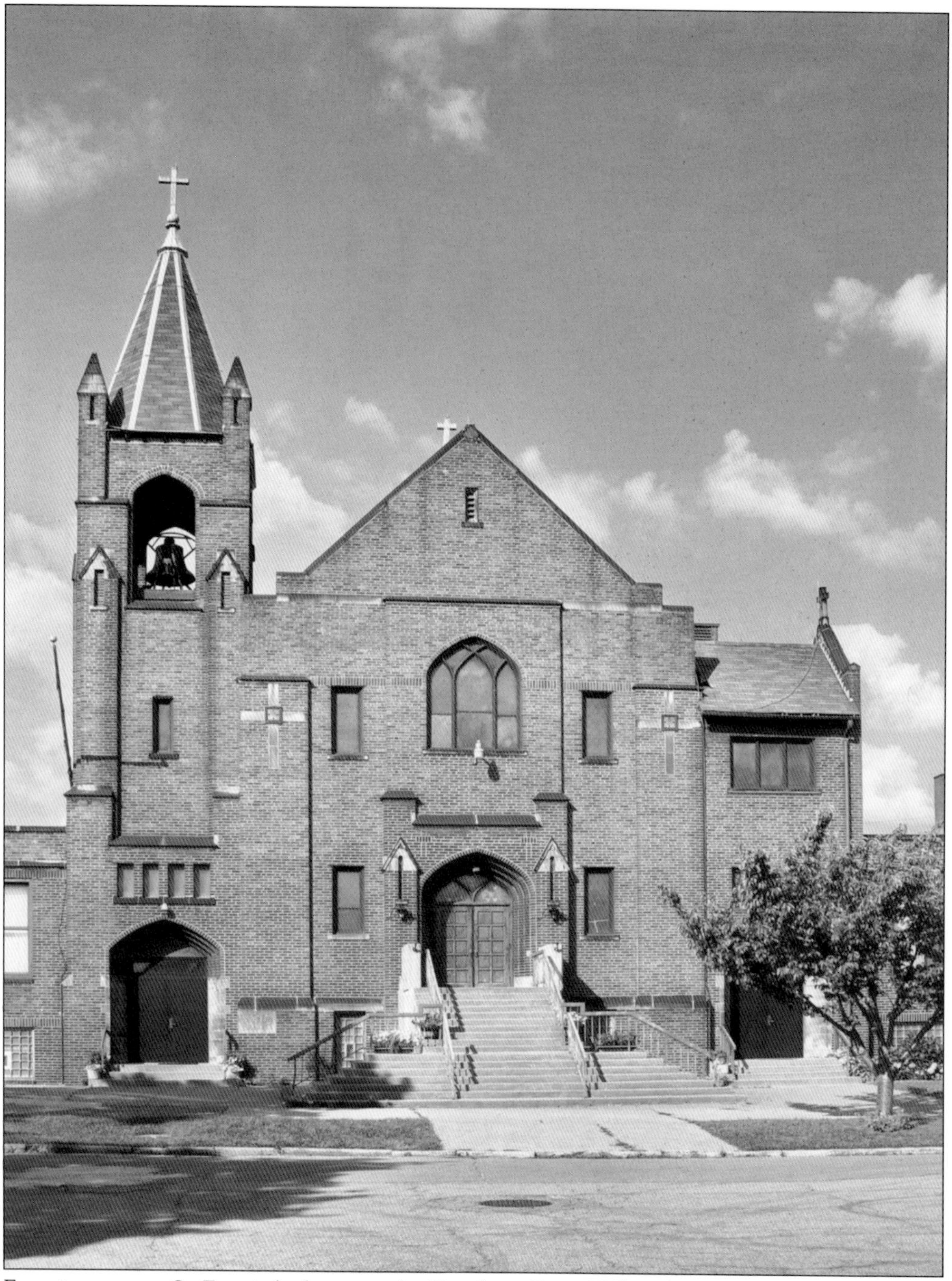

From its vantage, St. Emeric looks across the Cuyahoga River Valley Flats to the Cleveland skyline. The bell tower is definitely of Gothic design and houses the bell of St. Mary.

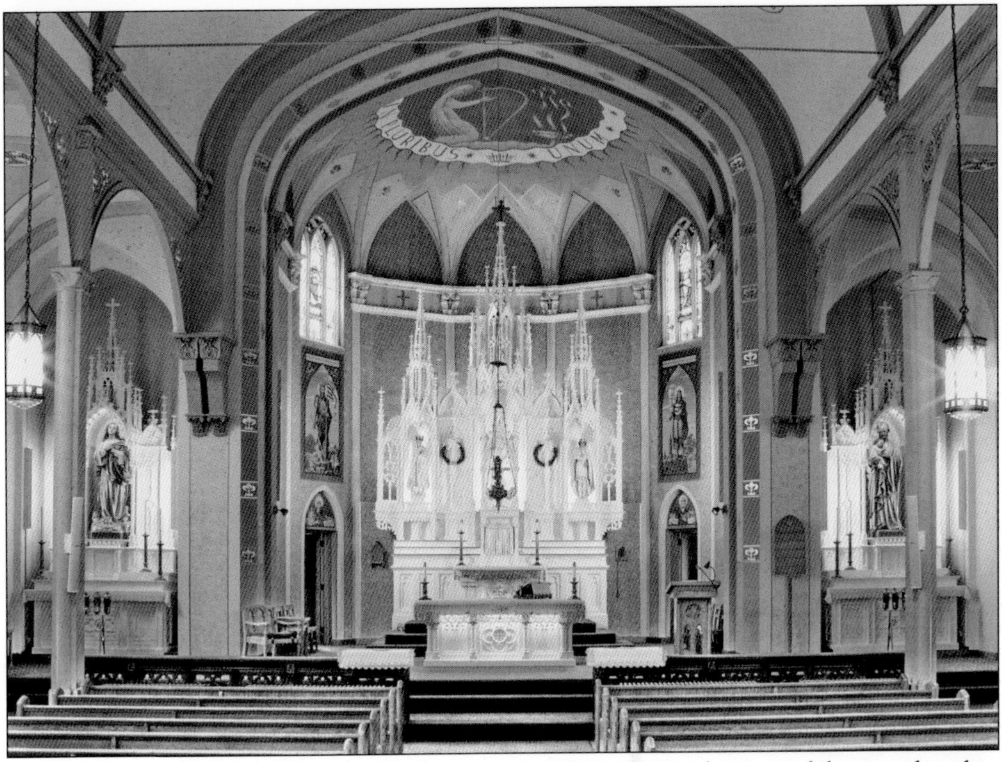

A view of the front of the church reveals an ornate white altar with spires of the type found in many Gothic churches. The side altars are a scaled-down version of the main altar. The ceiling and sanctuary are clear modifications of the Gothic tradition. The frescoes and ceiling paintings were originally done by Romeo Celleghin, an Italian immigrant who became known as the "Michelangelo of Cleveland." His frescoes and church paintings became nationally known through the years, and his work appears in many American churches.

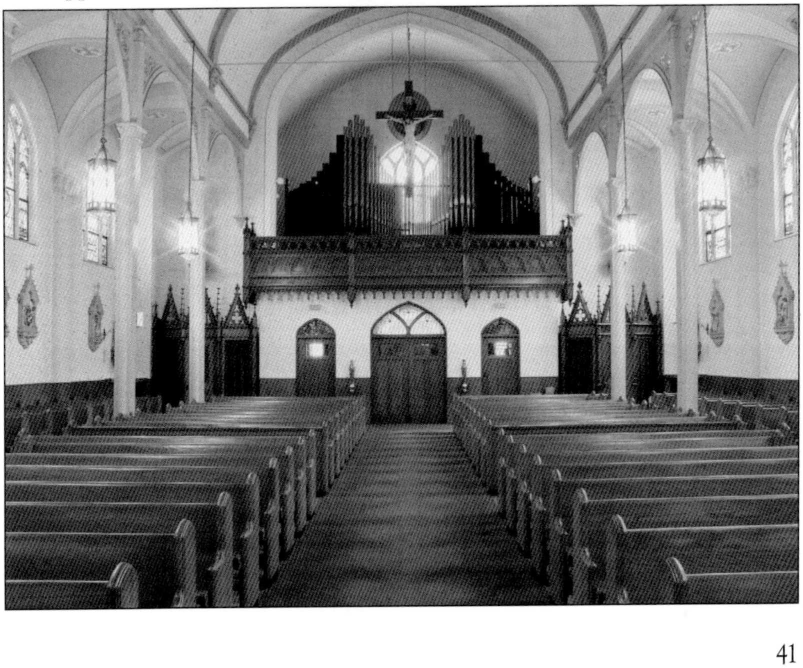

These Gothic columns and arches are seen at the back of the church. Notice the ornately carved confessionals and wood of the choir loft. There are six windows on each side.

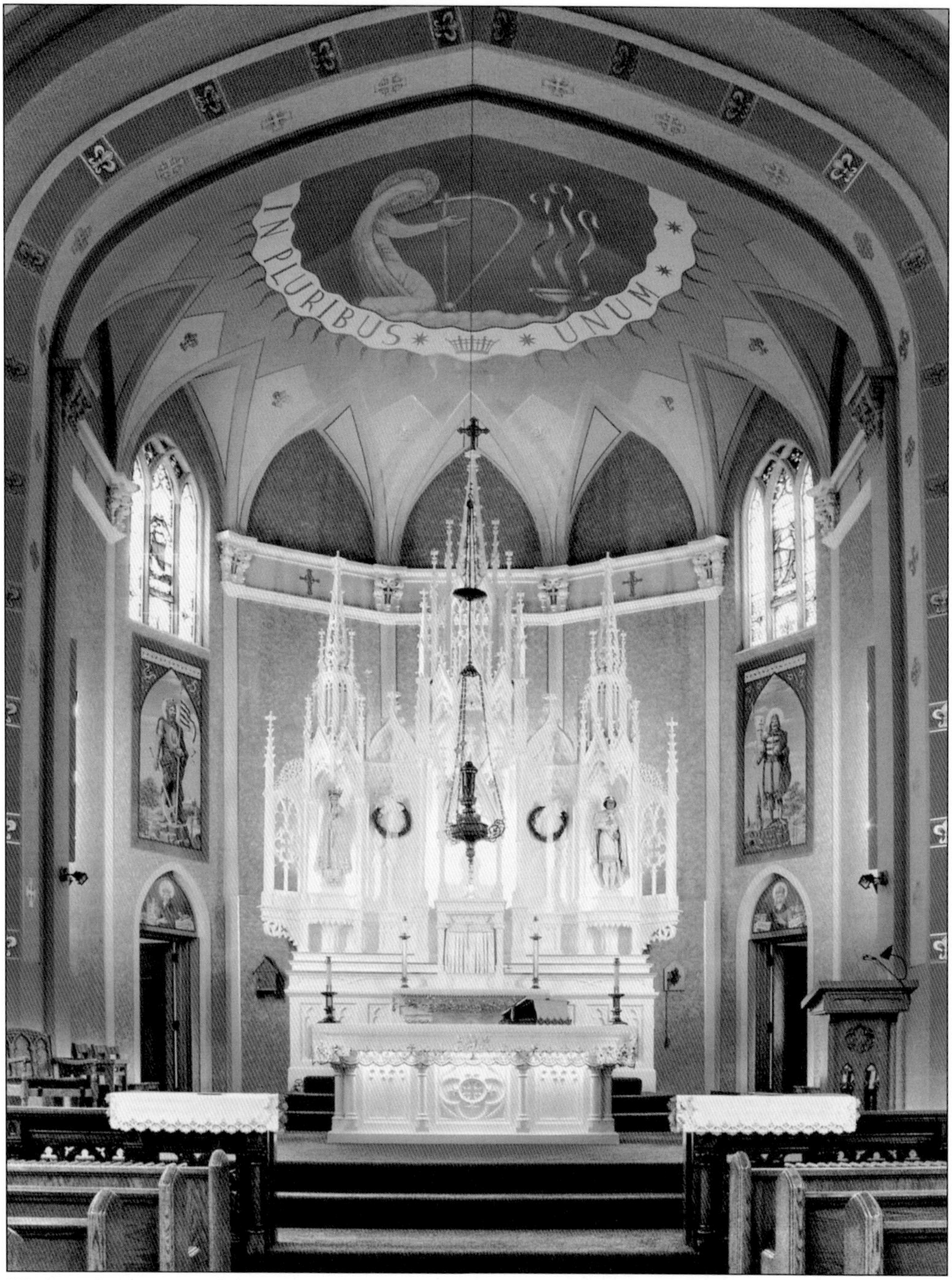

With a closer view of the sanctuary, a part of Hungarian history can be seen. Below the high window on the right is a portrait of St. Stephen (975–1038), the first Christian king of Hungary and father of St. Emeric. Above the sacristy door below is a portrait of St. Gerard, the spiritual advisor to St. Emeric. On the left side is a portrait of St. Ladislaus, the beloved king of Hungary from 1077 to 1095. Below this panel is a portrait of Blessed Gizella, the wife of St. Stephen and mother of St. Emeric. These portraits, as well as the *Millennial Mural*, were created by Romeo Celleghin or one of the artists associated with him.

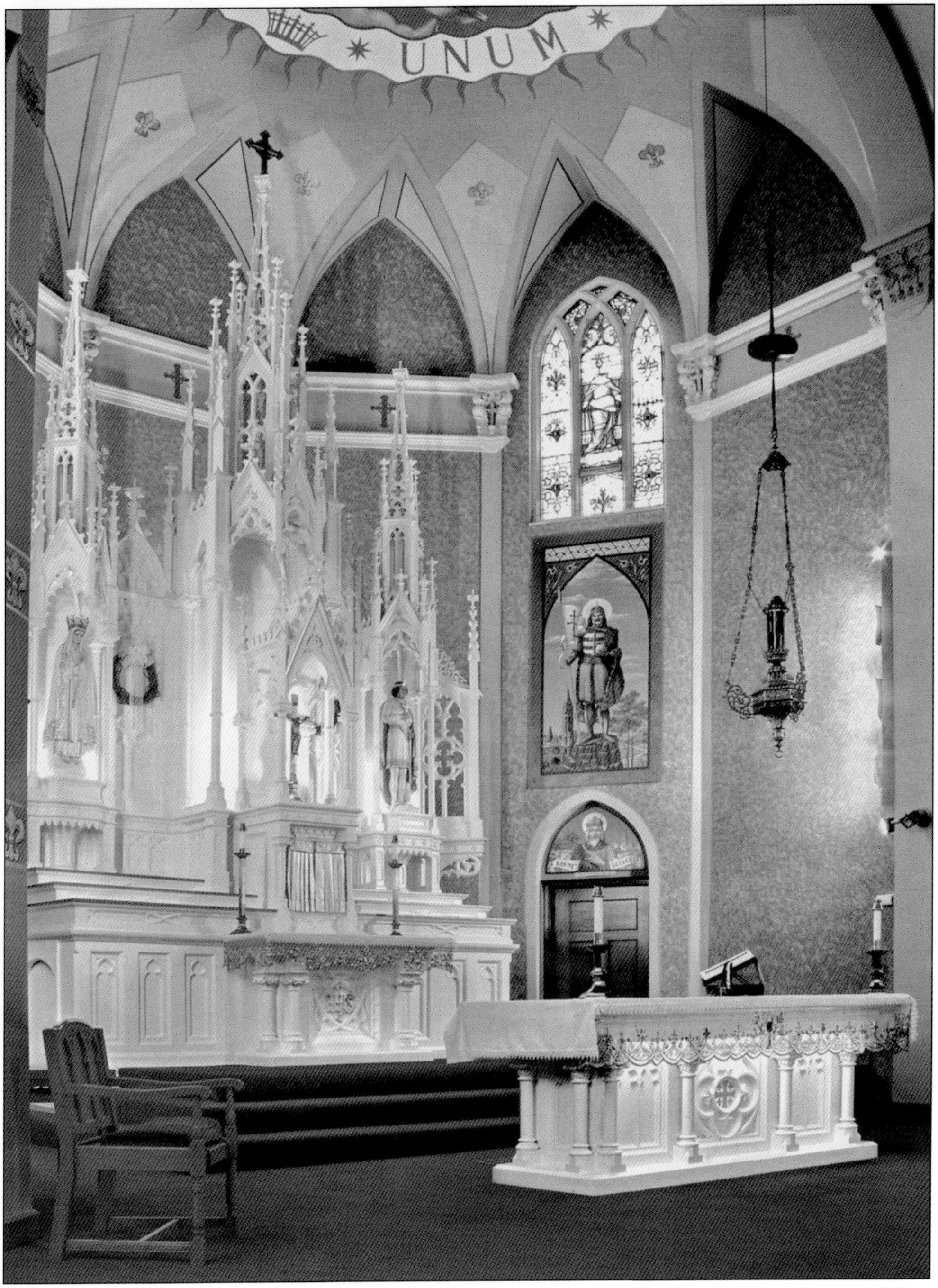

This view of the sanctuary from the south shows the portraits of St. Stephen and Gerard. Note the ornate details of both the high and low altars.

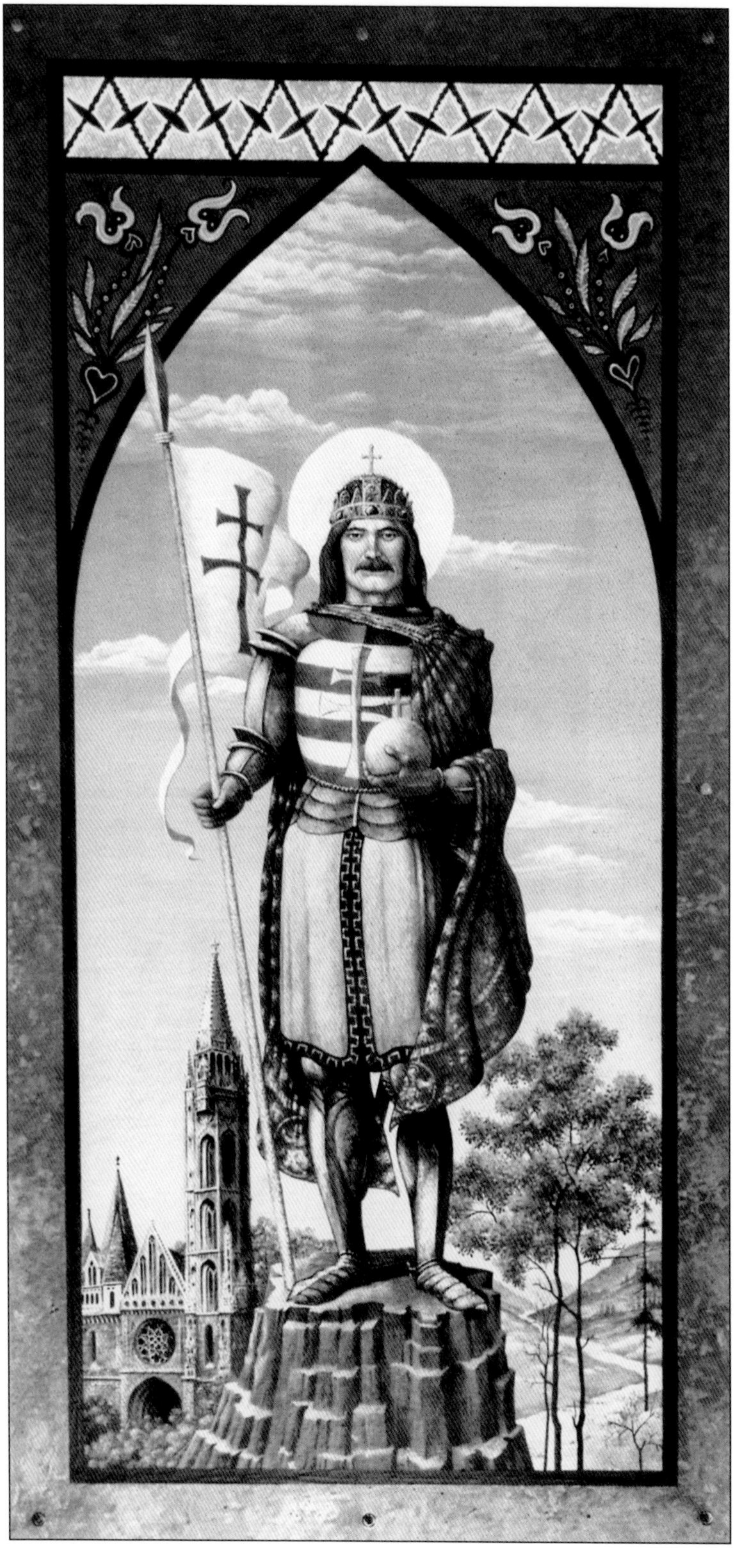

Detail of the King Stephen portrait shows the strong facial features and determination of this great king. In his left hand is an apple, a reference to the story of his being forced to shoot an apple from his son's head with an arrow.

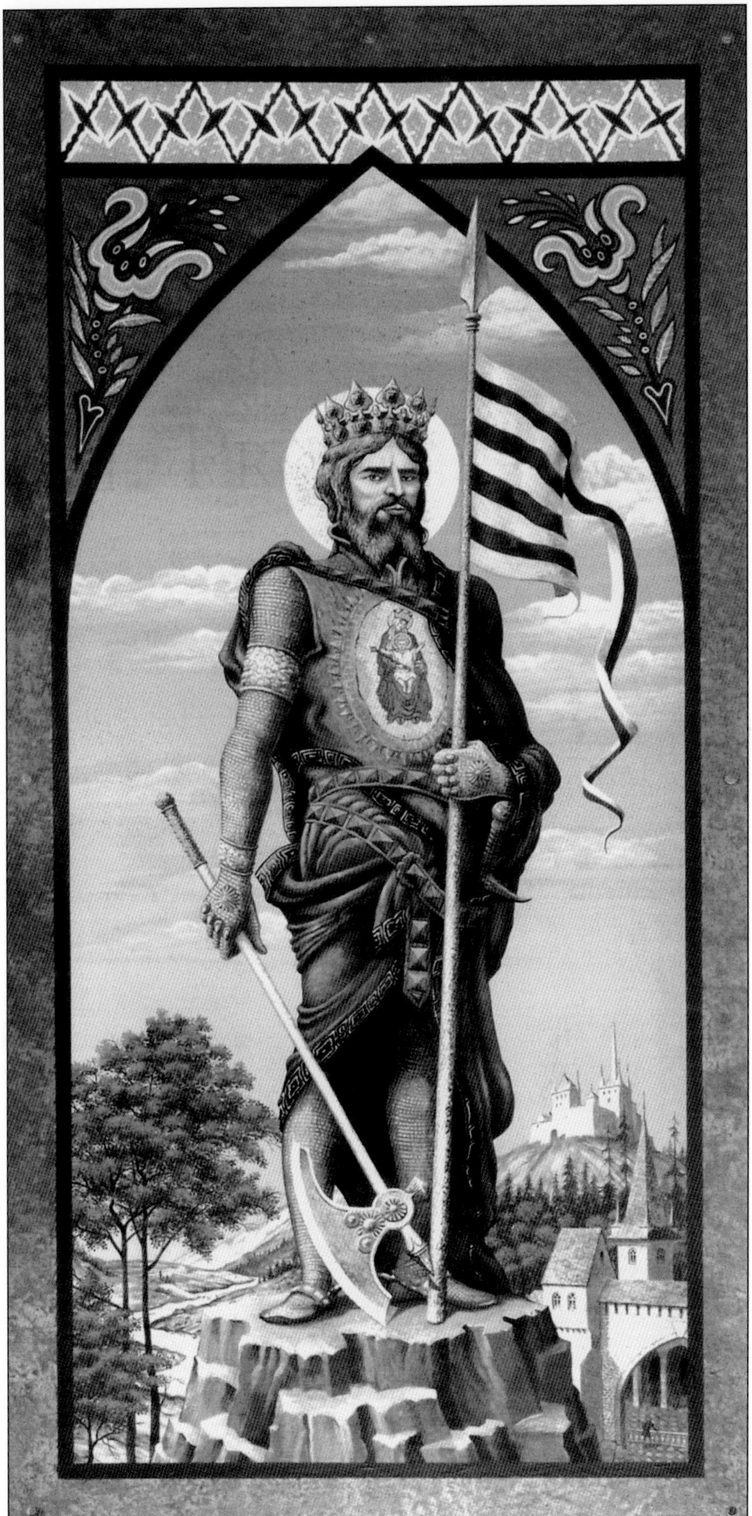

Detail of the portrait of St. Ladislaus also shows strong facial features and contains symbols of his position as King of Hungary. He was a distant relative of King Stephen and was the most beloved of Hungarian kings. He expanded Hungary's boundaries and solidified the country from within. Ladislaus also helped reorganize the Catholic Church in Hungary and Croatia.

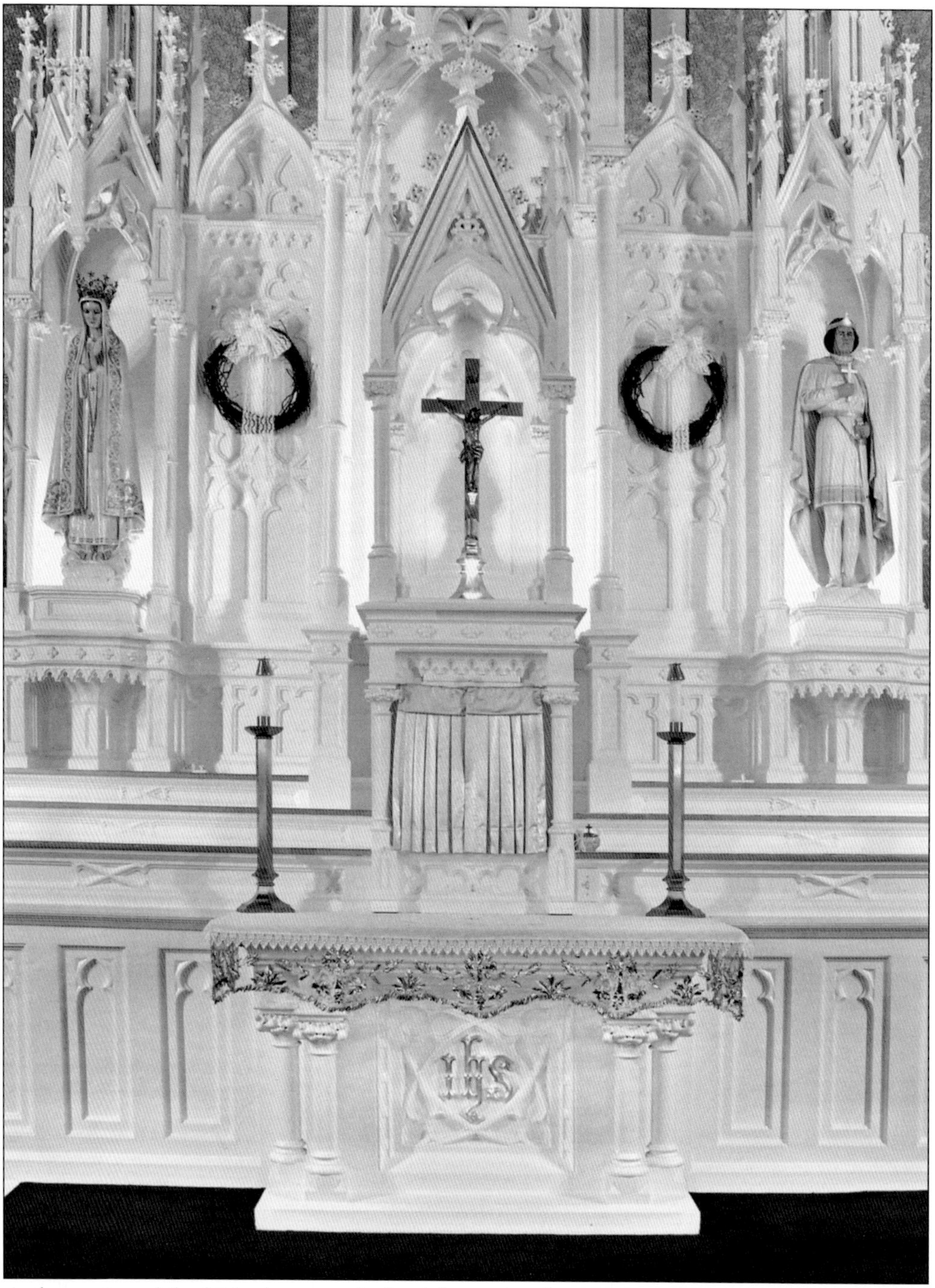

A closer view of the high altar reveals the delicate detail it contains. The statue on the right is that of St. Emeric (1007–1031), the namesake of the church. He was the son of King Stephen of Hungary and Gizella of Bavaria. This crown prince of Hungary never held the throne, as his father intended, due to his death in a hunting accident. There are many reports of healings and conversions at his grave site, however. He, his father, and Bishop Gerard were canonized together by Pope Gregory VII. To the left is a statue of Our Lady of Fatima.

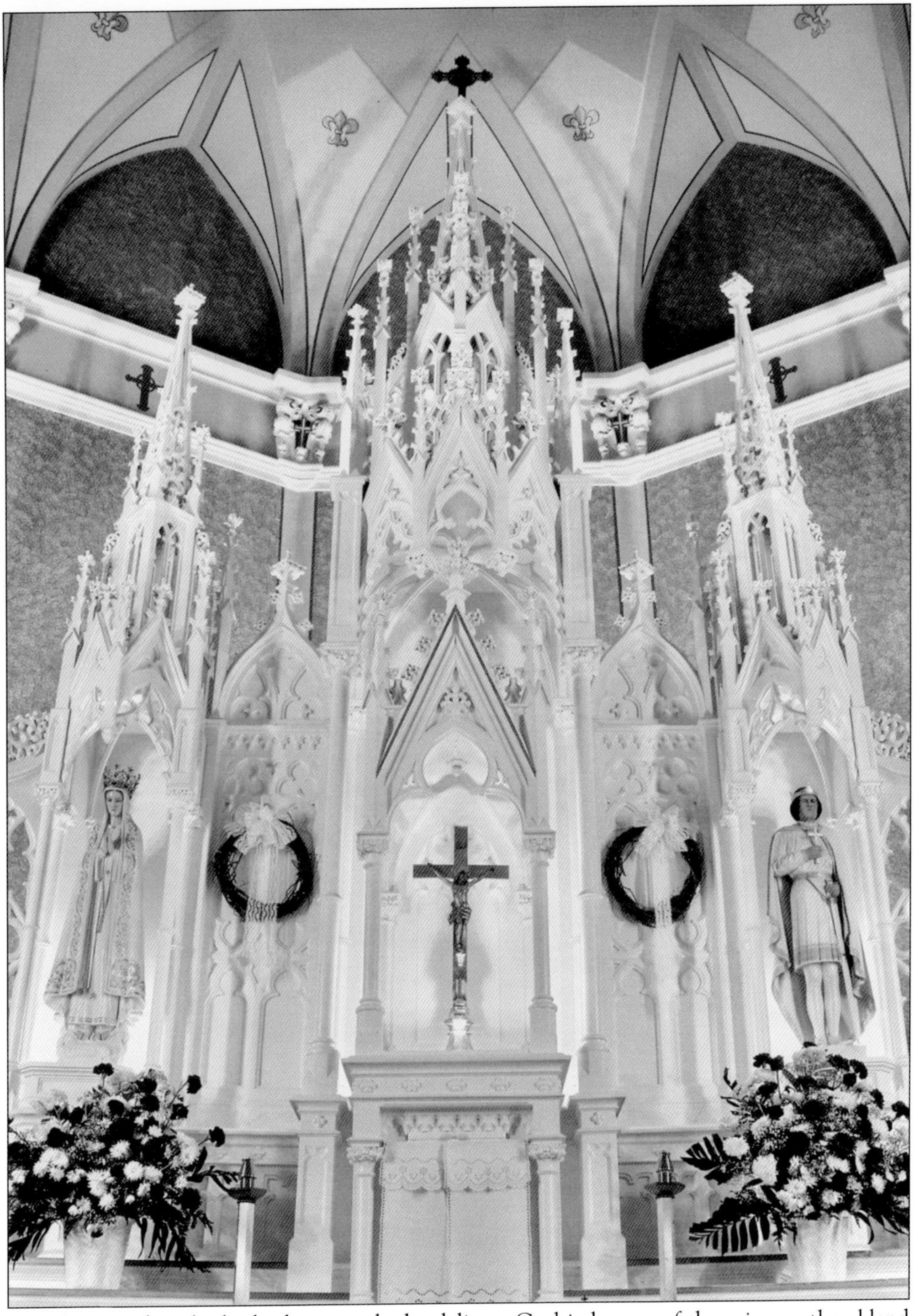

A look upward at the high altar reveals the delicate Gothic beauty of the spires as they blend with the arched ceiling above.

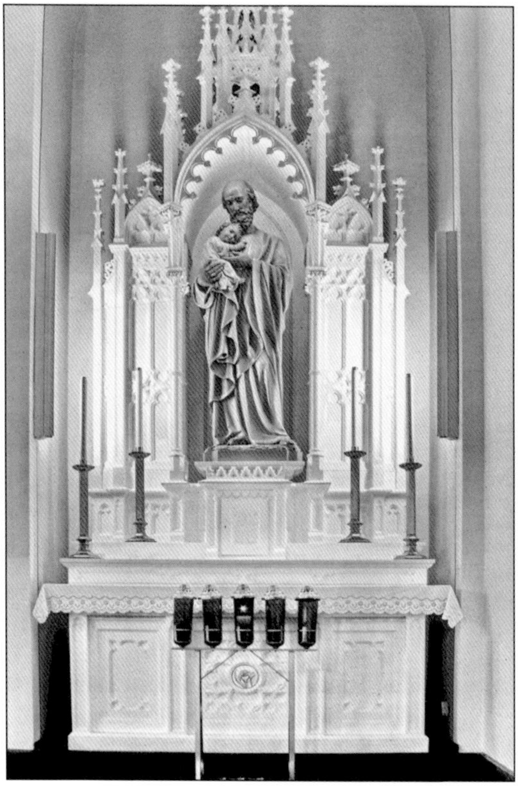

The side altars at St. Emeric are particularly interesting. To the north is the altar of St. Joseph. The statue is unique in that both the saint and the Christ Child are depicted in a very lifelike fashion.

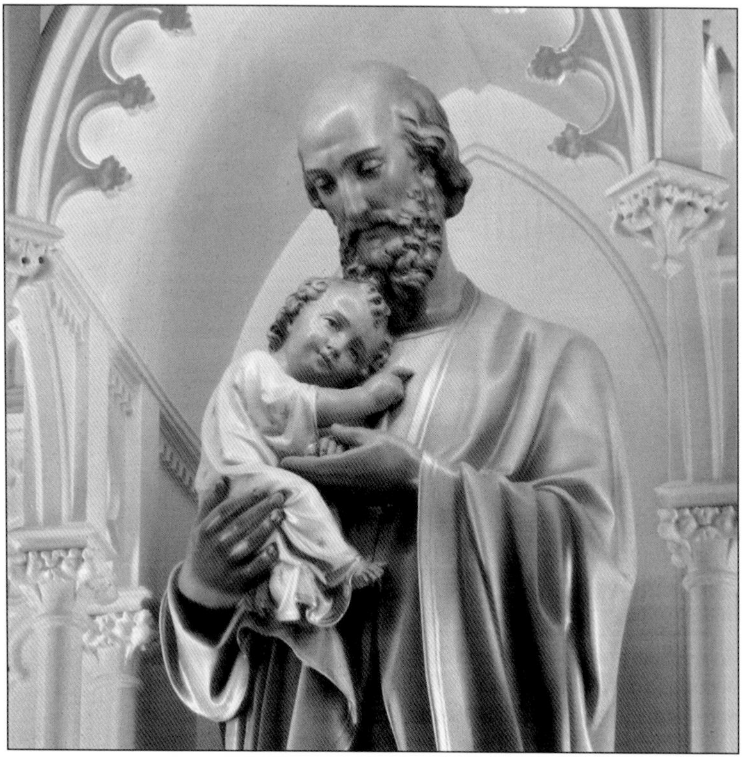

The expression on Joseph's face is one that only a father could display. The Christ Child's face, head position, and raised finger are very convincing.

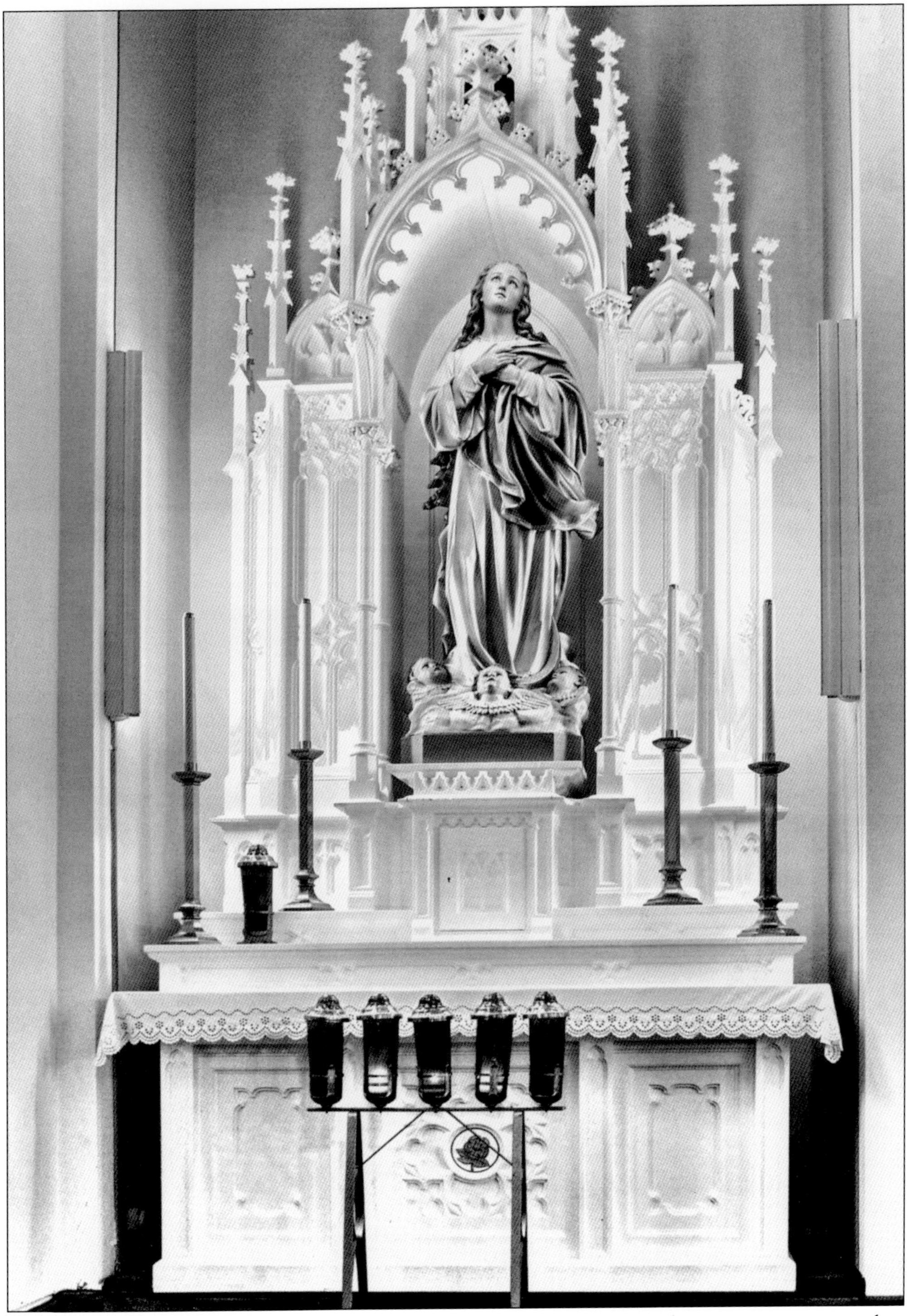

On the Blessed Mother altar, the statue possesses the same artistic quality as its counterpart but is more dynamic and emotional in its presentation.

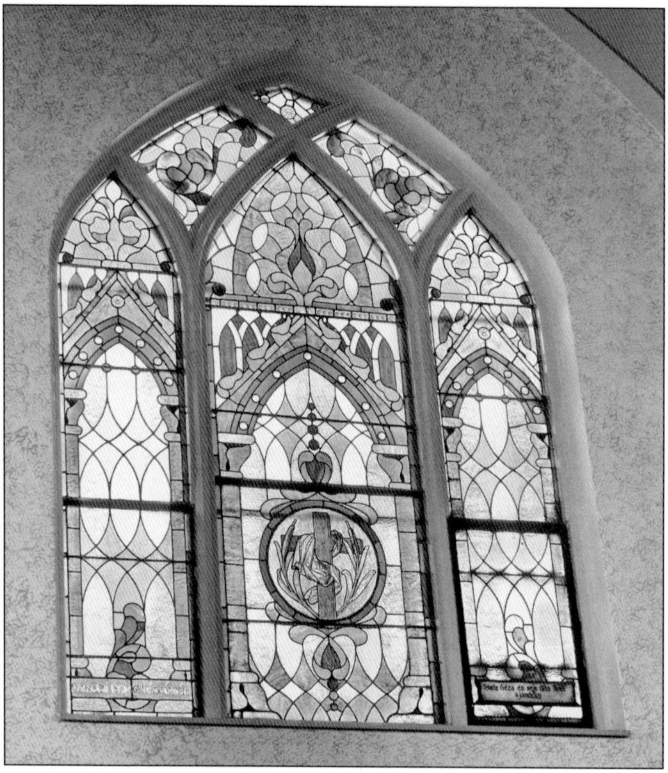

The first three pairs of windows have a different appearance than the last three. The window to the left is typical of the last three pairs. Notice the mostly geometric patterns in the design and the light, airy mood the window creates; the colors are pastel. This is typical of the windows that came from the "French" church. Pictured below is one of the first three pairs of windows. It is very obvious that the center section is different from the rest of the window. This section is dynamic and has vivid color. At some time, these sections were removed and replaced to make the window look more "Hungarian." It appears that the upper three sections of the window have also been replaced.

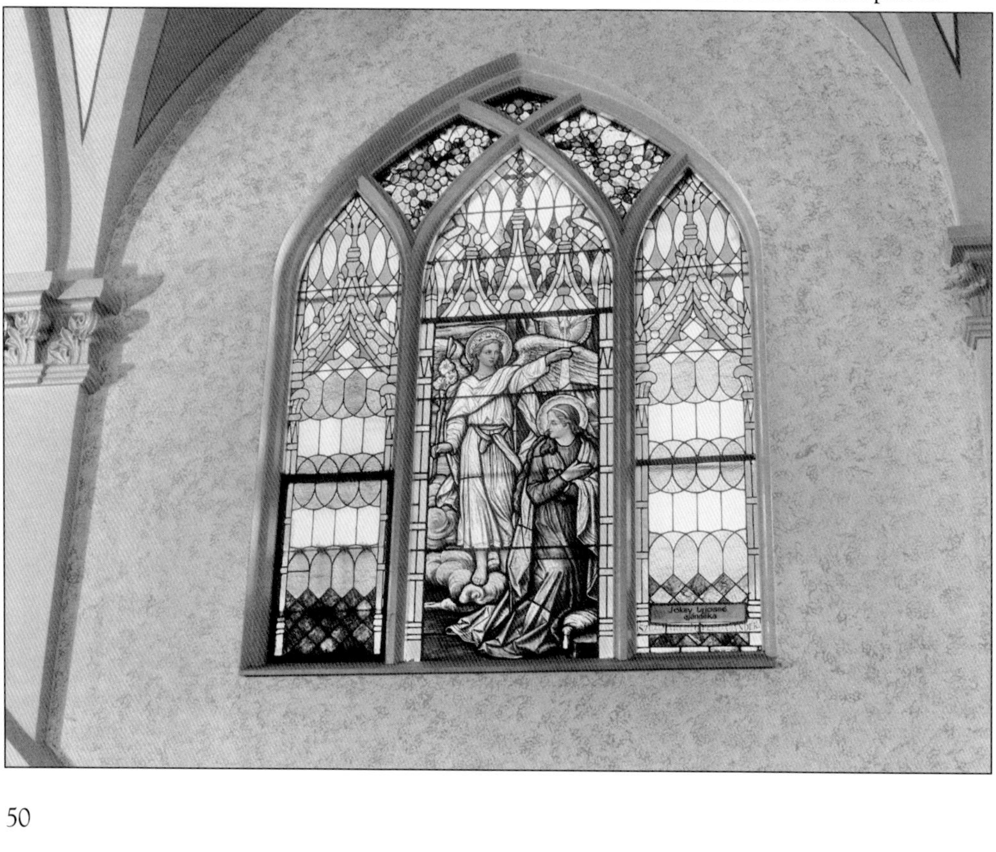

On the south wall of the church is the *Millennial Mural* depicting the essence of St. Emeric Church, a Hungarian-Catholic people of the United States. It refers to the thousand years of Christianity in Hungary since the birth of St. Steven and extending to the present (1970s). At the top are symbols of the U.S. and Hungary. Between them is an icon of Christ and below is a symbol of the most historic event in the United States at the time, the moon landings.

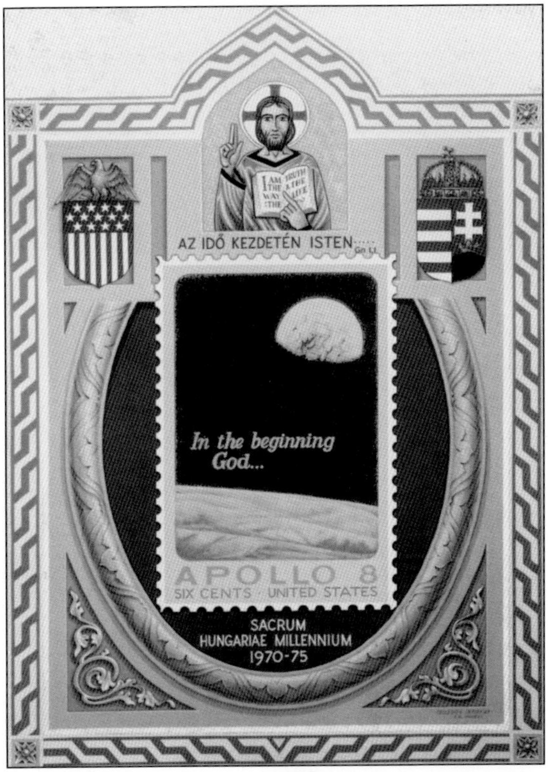

Along the walls of the church are the beautifully carved Stations of the Cross with inscriptions written in Hungarian.

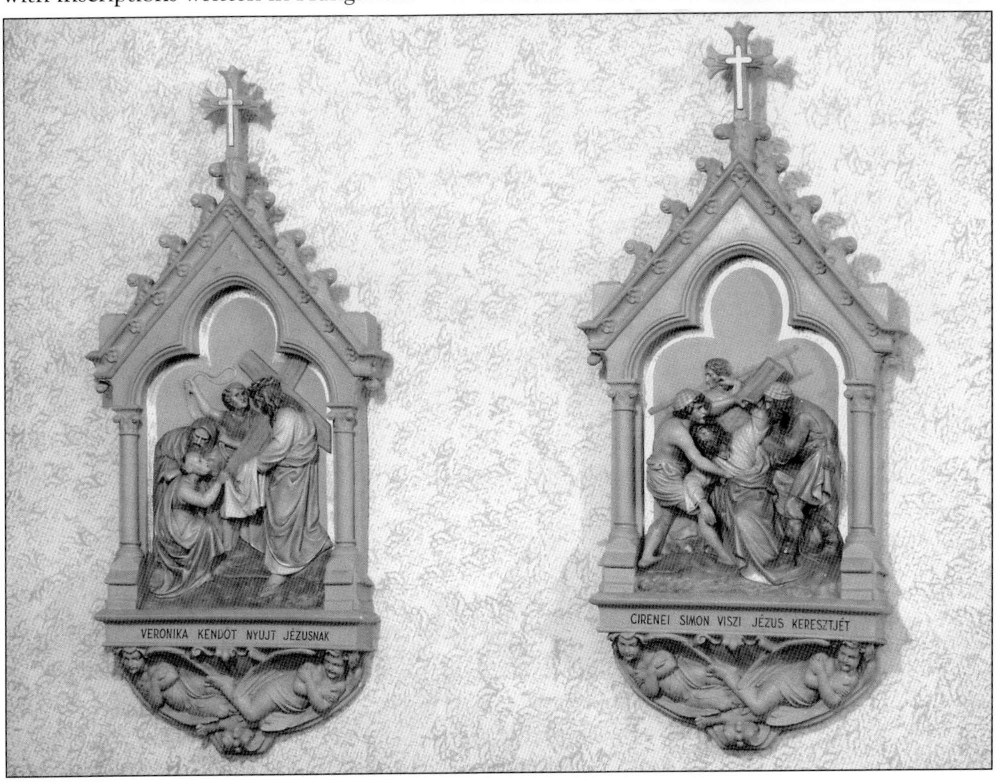

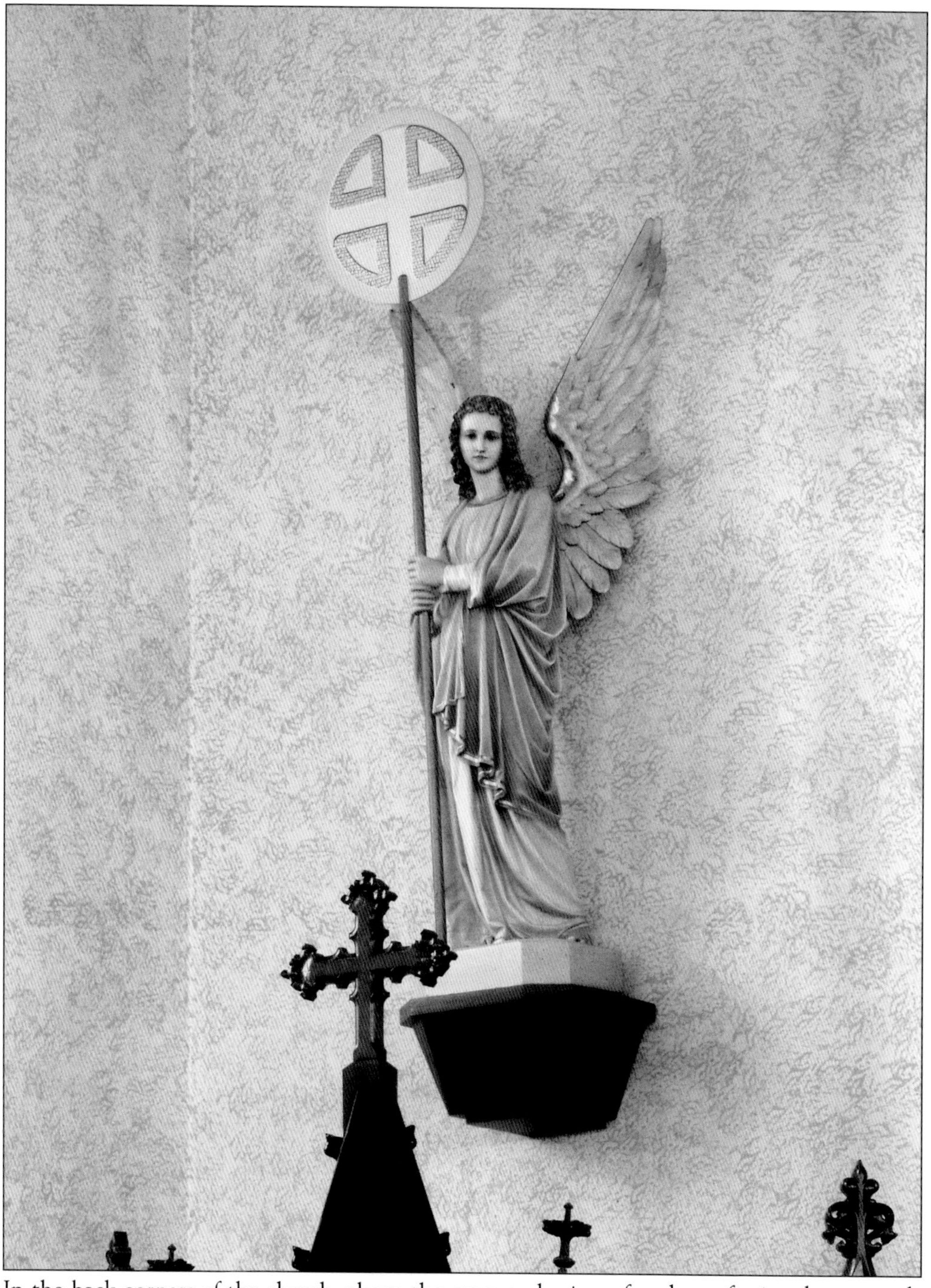

In the back corners of the church, above the cross and spires of each confessional, are angels looking over the congregation from above.

Four

St. Rose

In the 1890s, with the population of the neighborhood growing rapidly, Fr. Ignatius J. Wonderly established the Parish of St. Rose. Initial services were held in a local hall until 1900, when a frame church was built on the corner of West 114th Street and Detroit Avenue. This location was common to the more affluent neighborhood on the Lake Erie shore to the north as well as the working-class neighborhoods to the south.

This church became inadequate for the size of the congregation by 1930. As a result, it was razed and replaced by a larger building. The new church lasted until 1957, when it was replaced by the present one.

The new church was designed by Anthony Ceresi, a Cleveland architect, and had seating for 1,100 parishioners. It is a simple but effective design comprised of yellow brick with a sandstone block facade. There is a lower level, which houses an auditorium, and the church itself is on the upper level. The main entrance to the church is protected by a flat canopy above, which holds a very large statue of St. Rose. Behind the statue is a deep blue background with metallic symbols of early Christianity. On the east side of the building is a monolithic, 125-foot-high bell tower.

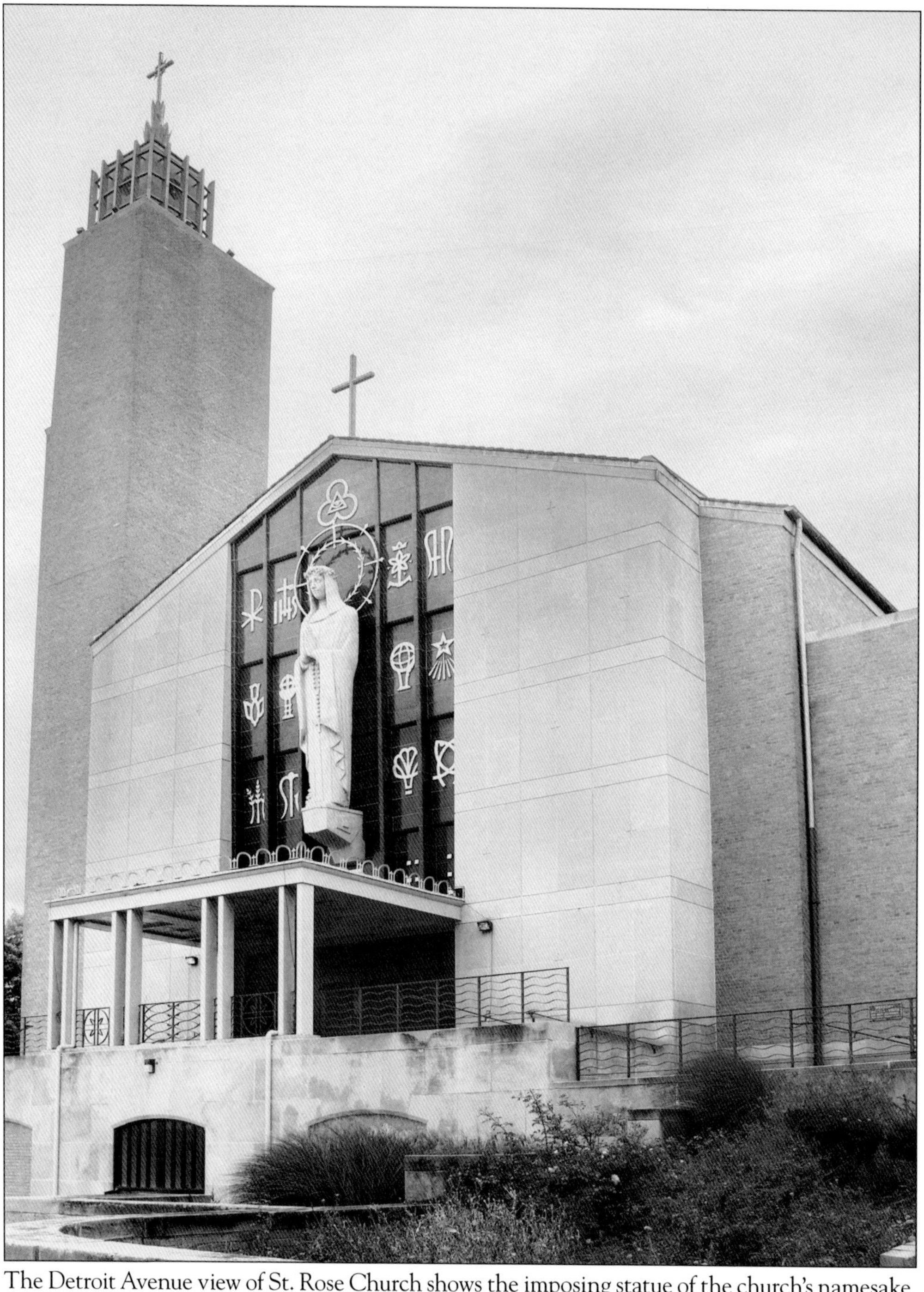

The Detroit Avenue view of St. Rose Church shows the imposing statue of the church's namesake. The figure, sculpted by Joseph Motto in Florence, Italy, is 20 feet high and weighs 10 tons.

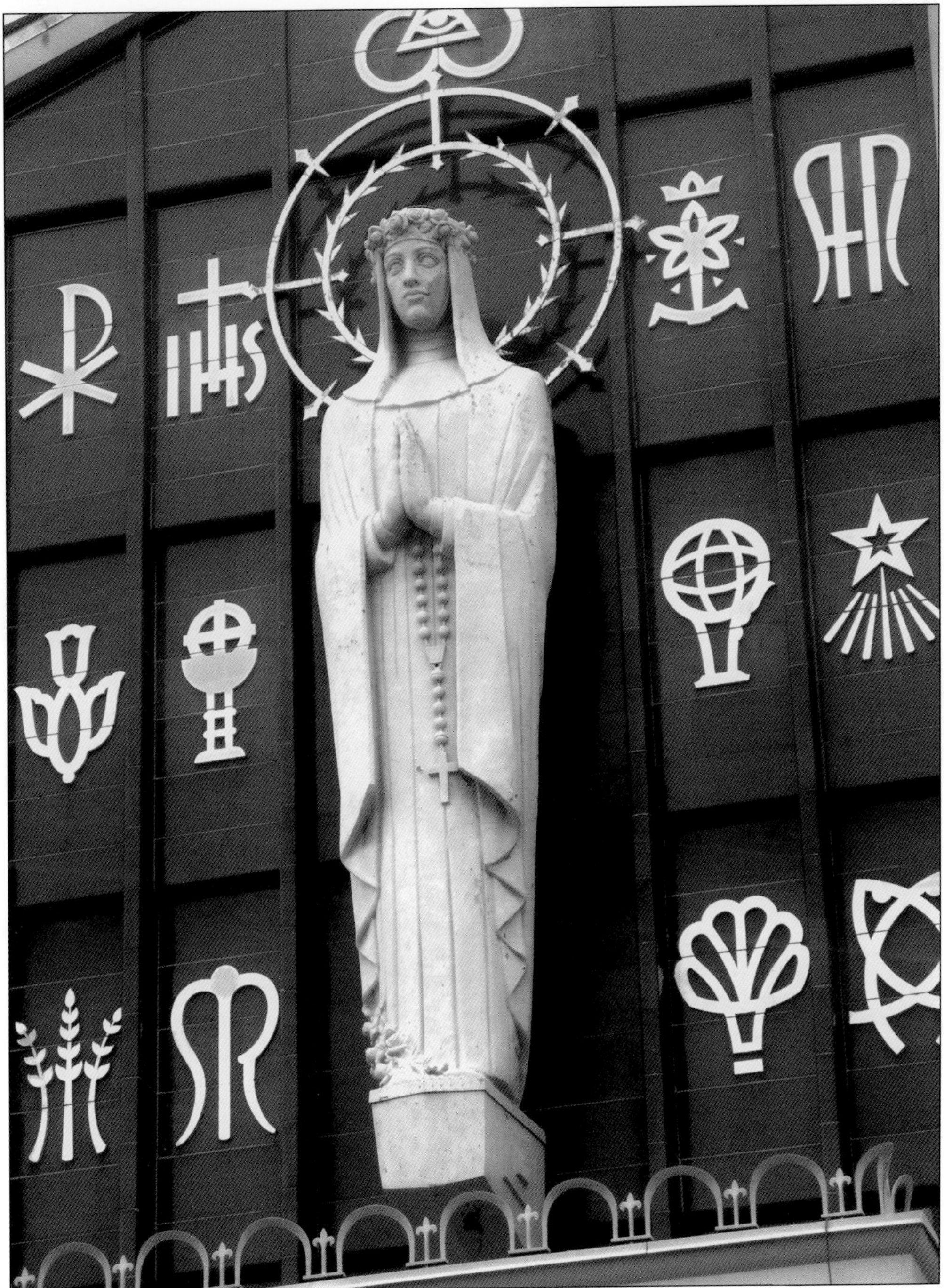

Here is a closer view of this very impressive statue. St. Rose (1586–1617) was born of Spanish parents who had immigrated to the new colony of Lima, Peru. She was devoted from an early age to a life of prayer and mortification and ultimately took a vow of virginity inspired by "supernatural love." This view shows the Christian symbols on the backdrop of the statue very clearly.

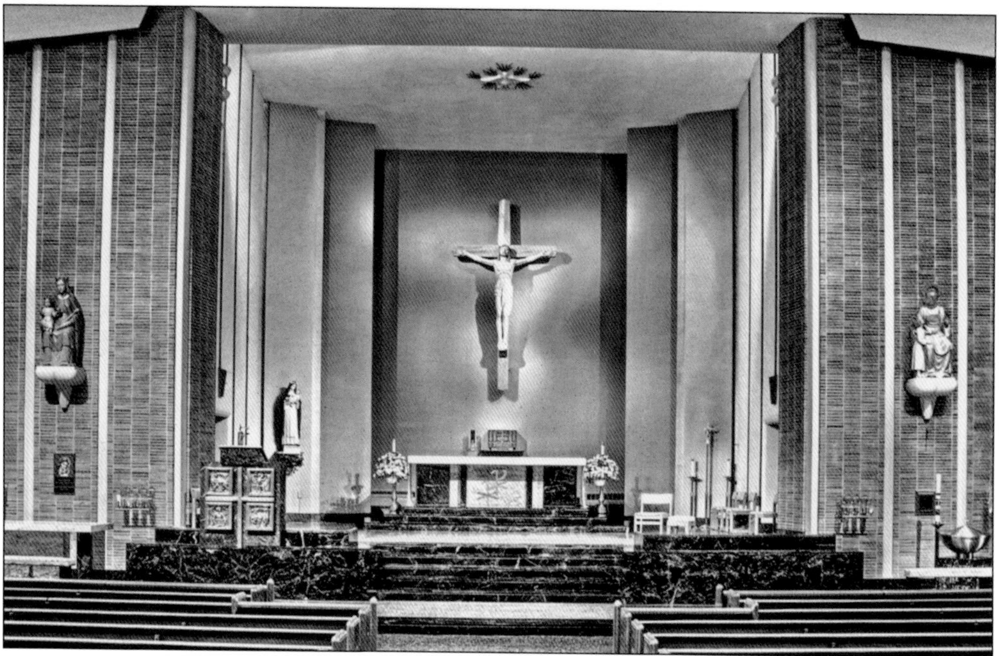

The interior of the church features a large sanctuary with walls and a ceiling developed from many planar surfaces, some large and some smaller. The high brick sidewalls open to reveal the center sanctuary and a single altar. A very large crucifix dominates the center of attention, and a dove (the Holy Spirit) dominates the ceiling above the altar. Of particular interest is the abundant textured black marble that comprises much of the center sanctuary.

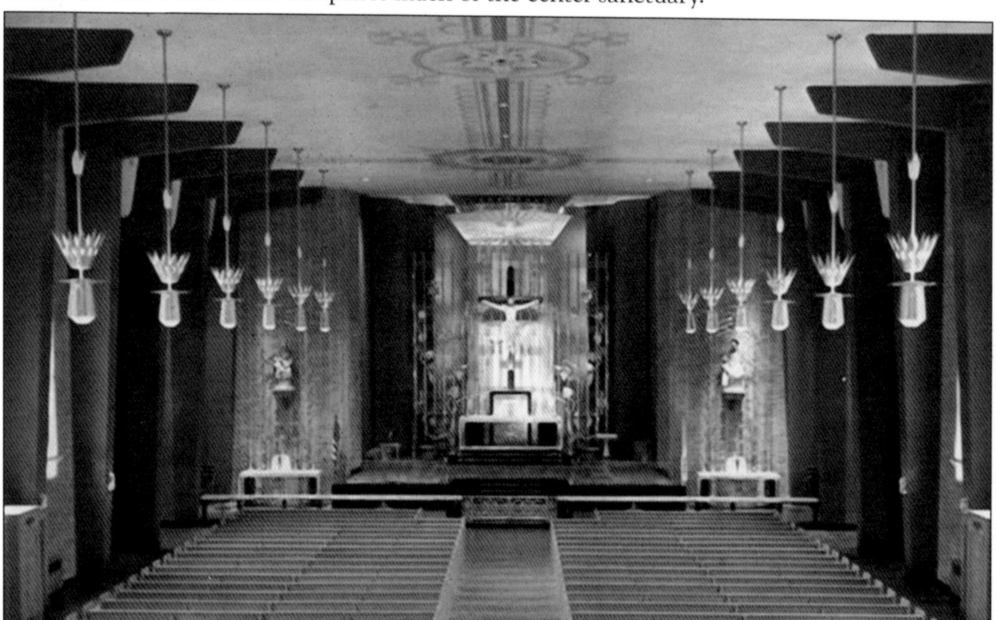

In 1957, when the church was built, the sanctuary was more ornate than it is today. The icon screen, the tester (the lowered ceiling over the altar), and the St. Joseph altar were removed at some point. Also removed are the ceiling patterns over the nave. (Cleveland State University, *Cleveland Press* photograph.)

As one enters the sanctuary, passing a low wall, there are five steps of gorgeous, richly textured black marble. Beyond these is a distance of light floor, followed again by three more black steps leading to the altar.

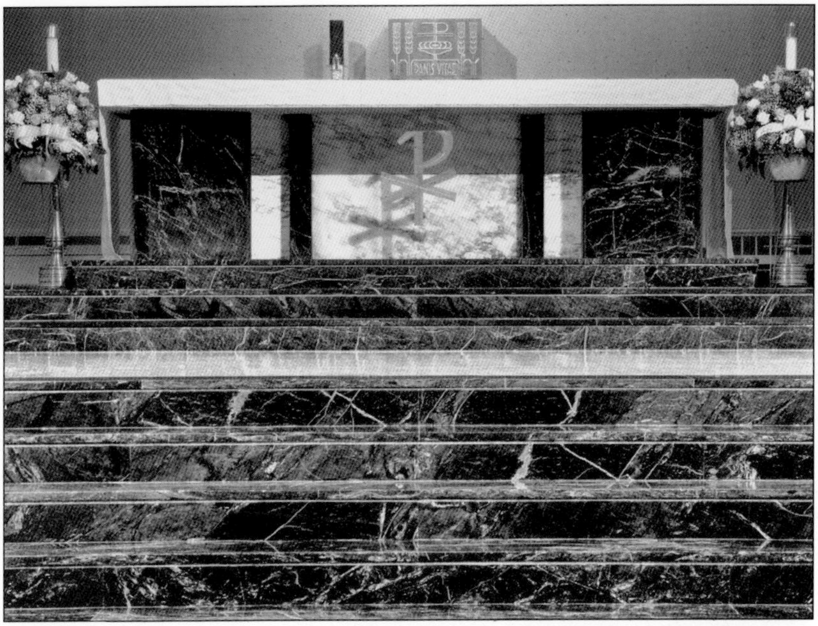

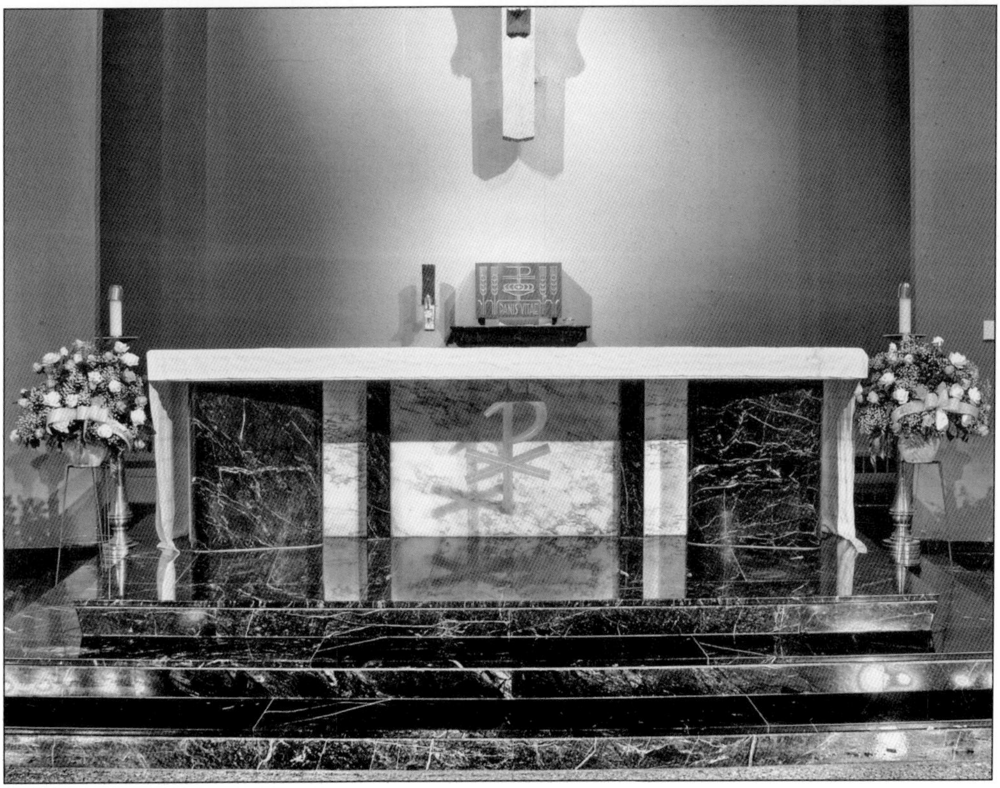

The altar itself is made up from alternating panels of black and white marble that is reflected in the mirror-like floor around it.

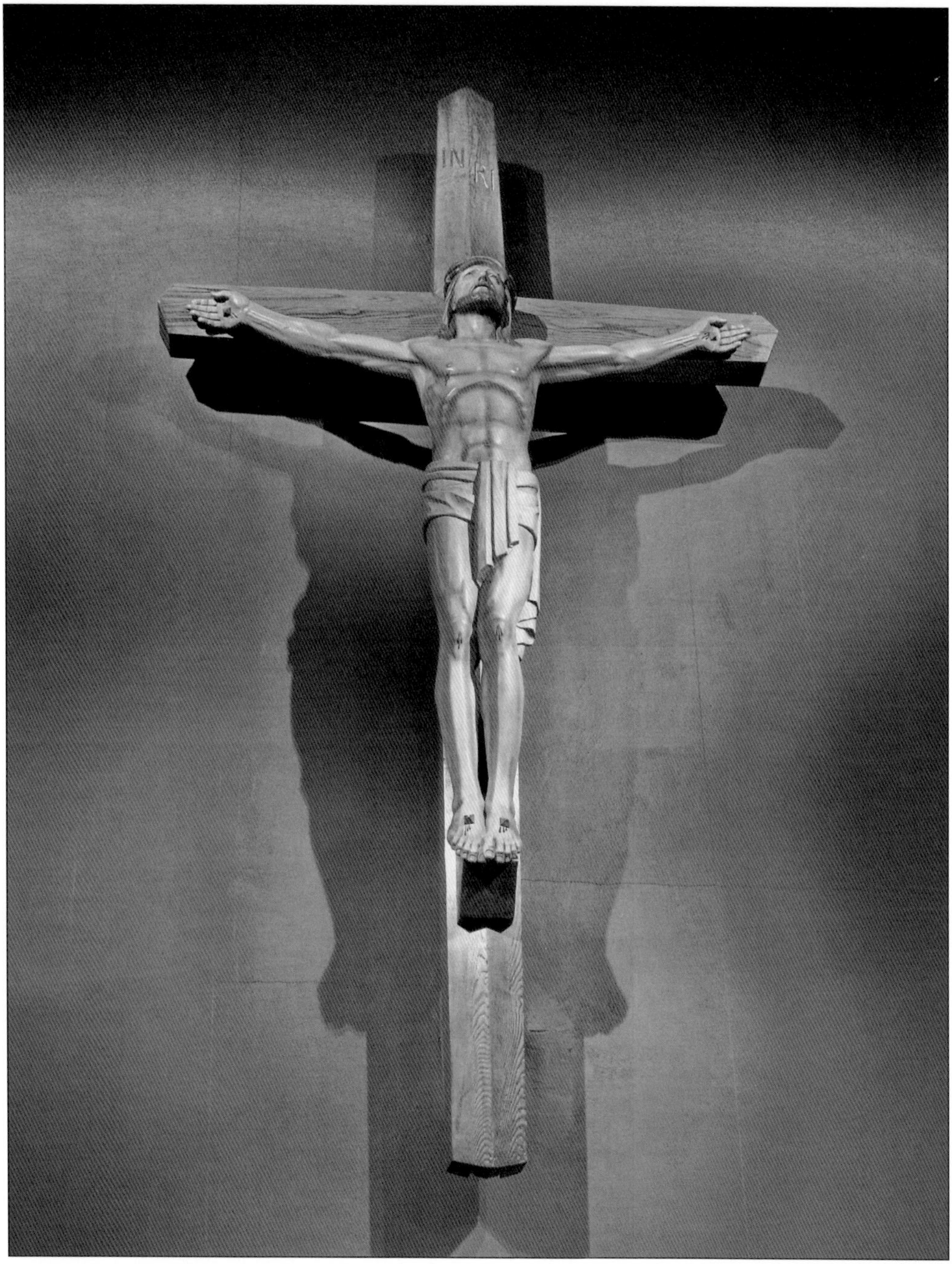

The extreme detail of the large crucifix over the altar is of particular photographic interest. The highly defined Body of Christ and the dramatic lighting above the altar provide the elements for a striking photograph.

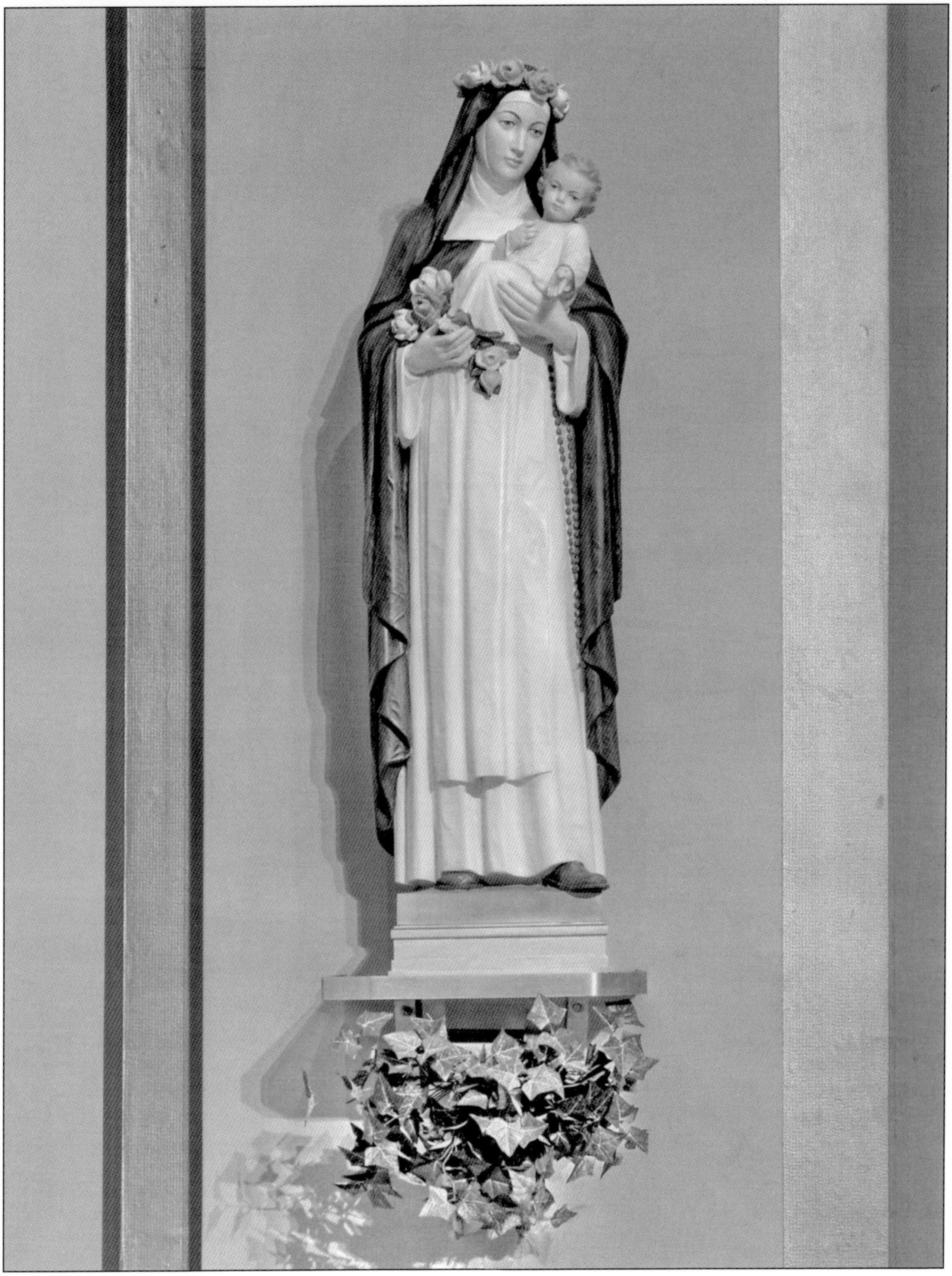

On the wall to the left of the altar is the statue of St. Rose. She subjected herself to many penances and mortifications, including wearing a spiked metal crown concealed with roses. Such things she did to atone for her country's (Peru) lack of faith and to petition for the conversion of sinners. All her sufferings were overridden by revelations of Christ, which left her in peace and ecstasy for long periods of time. Miracles were reported after her death, and Pope Clement X canonized her in 1671. The statue depicts her wearing her Dominican habit and showing her devotion to the Christ Child.

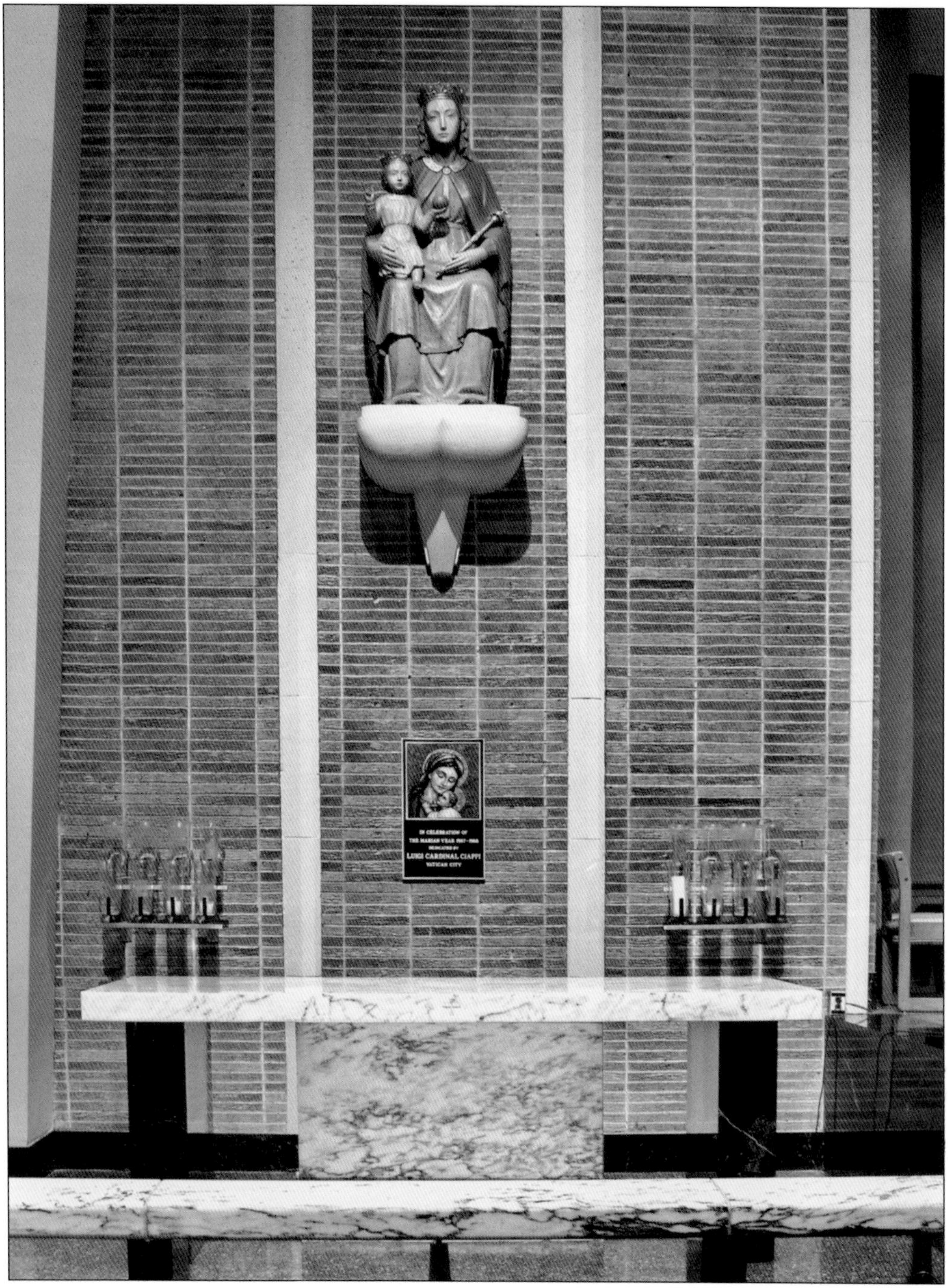

The Blessed Mother side altar to the east of the high altar portends an unusual design. The statue of Mary is high on the wall, and the altar itself is a simple white marble table that can be accessed from either side. The white marble communion rail can be seen in front. On the wall is a plaque commemorating the Marian Year of 1987–1988, which was dedicated by Card. Luigi Ciappi.

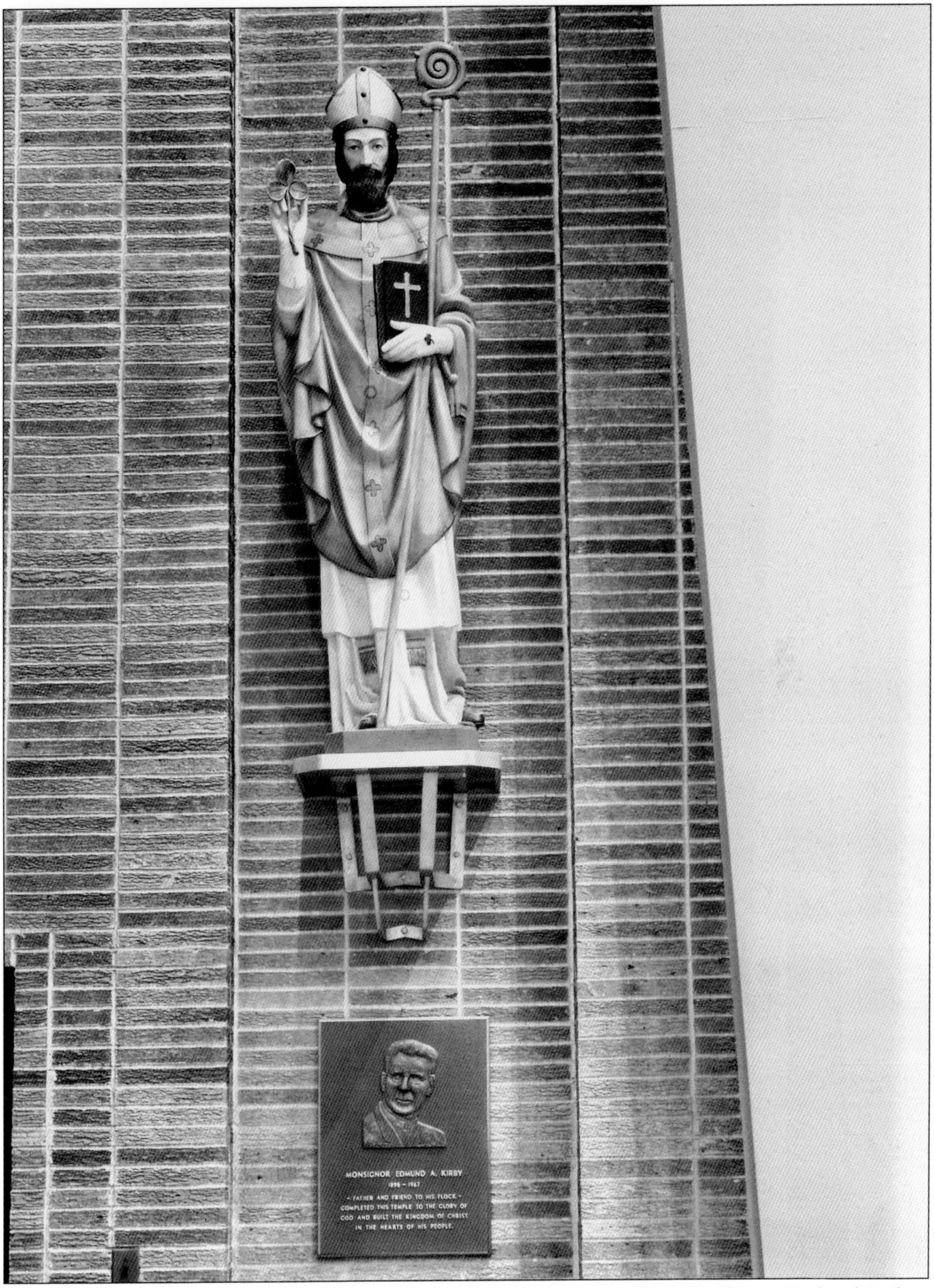

To the left (east) of the Blessed Mother altar is a statue of St. Patrick, the bishop of Ireland. Below this is a plaque of Msgr. Edmund A. Kirby, who directed the building of the new church.

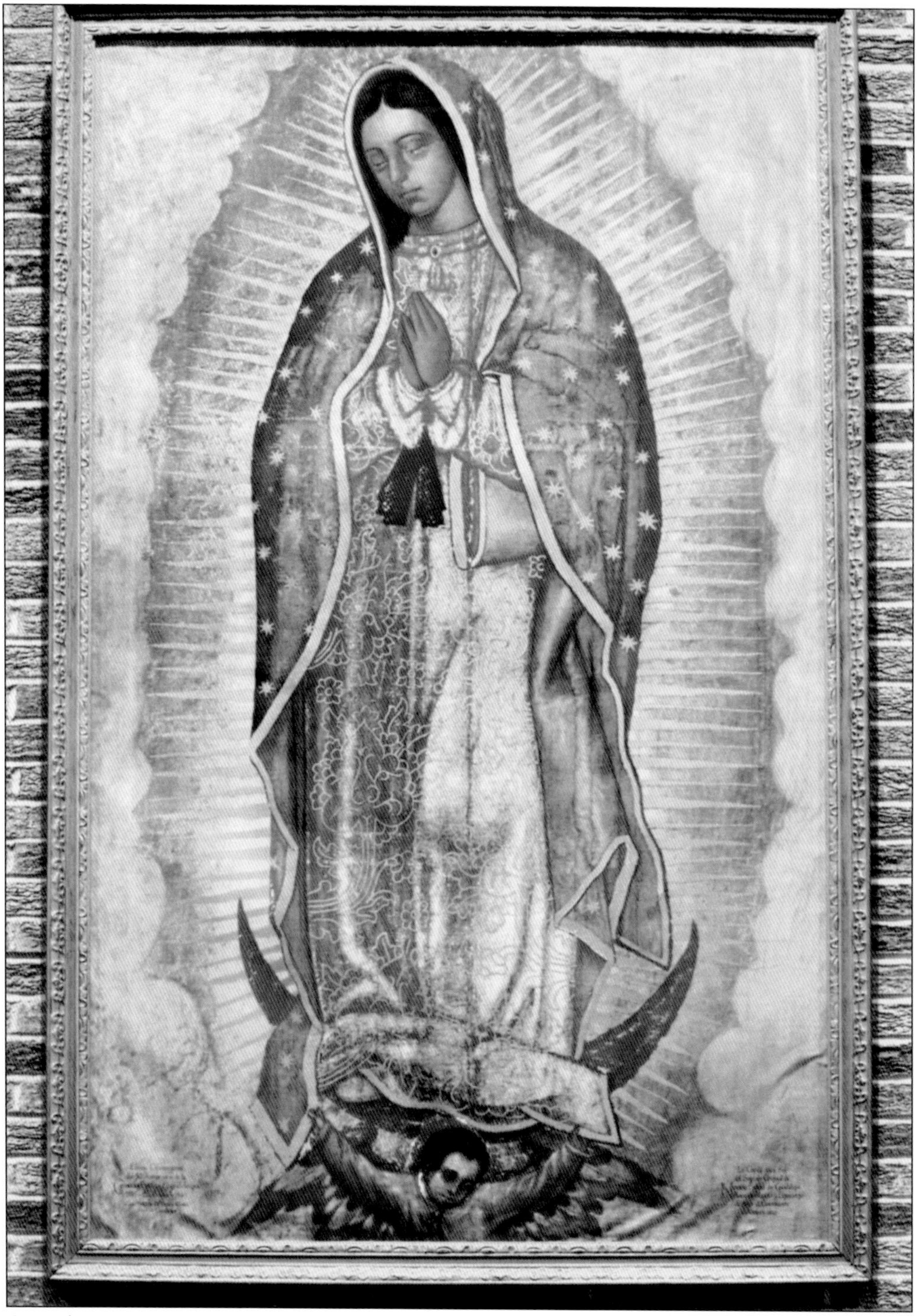

Over the east entrance of the church is a large replica of the image of Our Lady of Guadalupe as it miraculously appeared on the *tilma* (or cloak) of Juan Diego in 1531 in Mexico. The actual tilma is displayed in a shrine in Mexico City. Our Lady of Guadalupe is the patroness of the Americas.

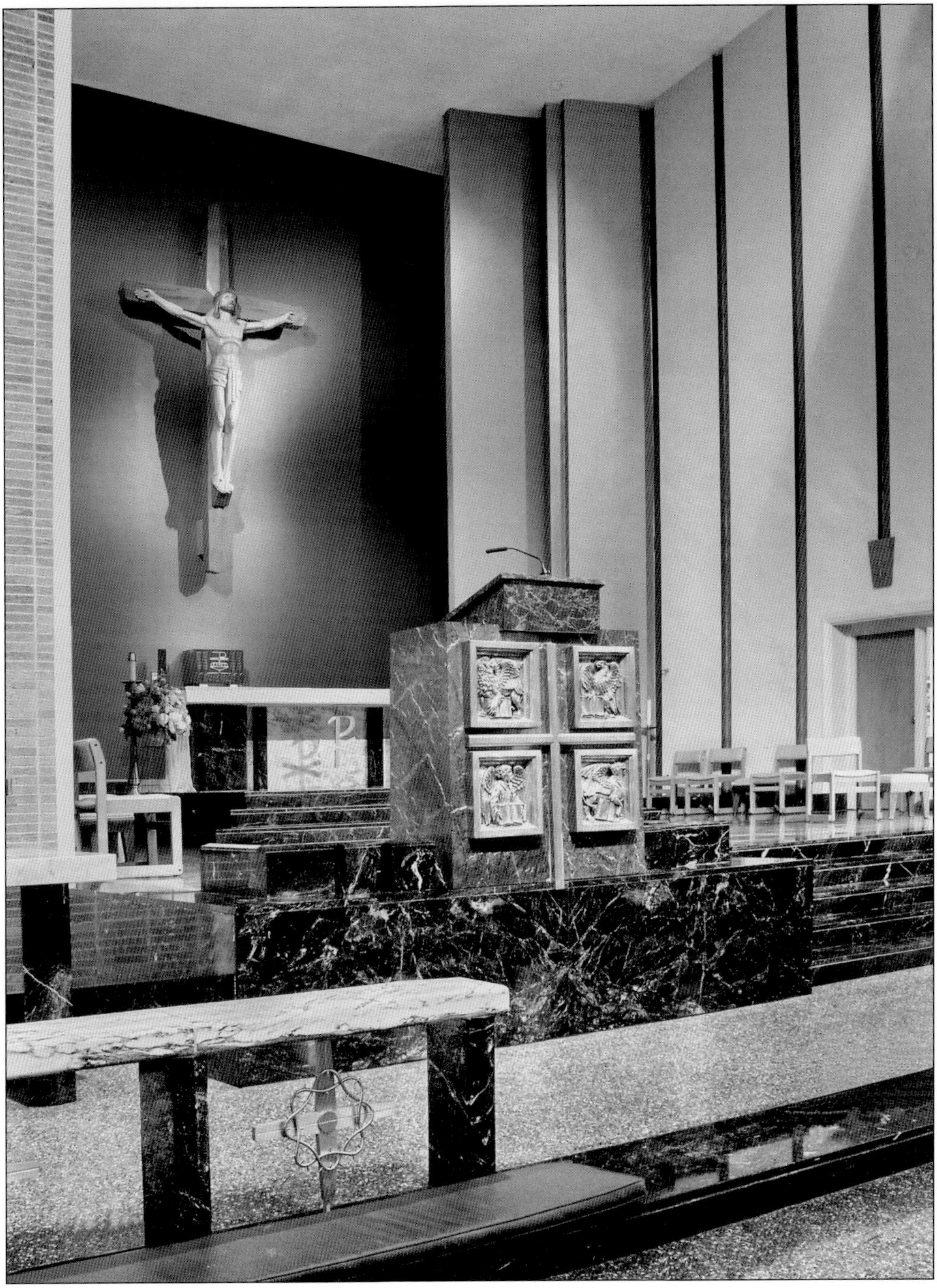

A view of the sanctuary from the east corner clearly shows its planar design. The pulpit is of a lighter black or gray marble and has a finer grain pattern than the darker marble around it.

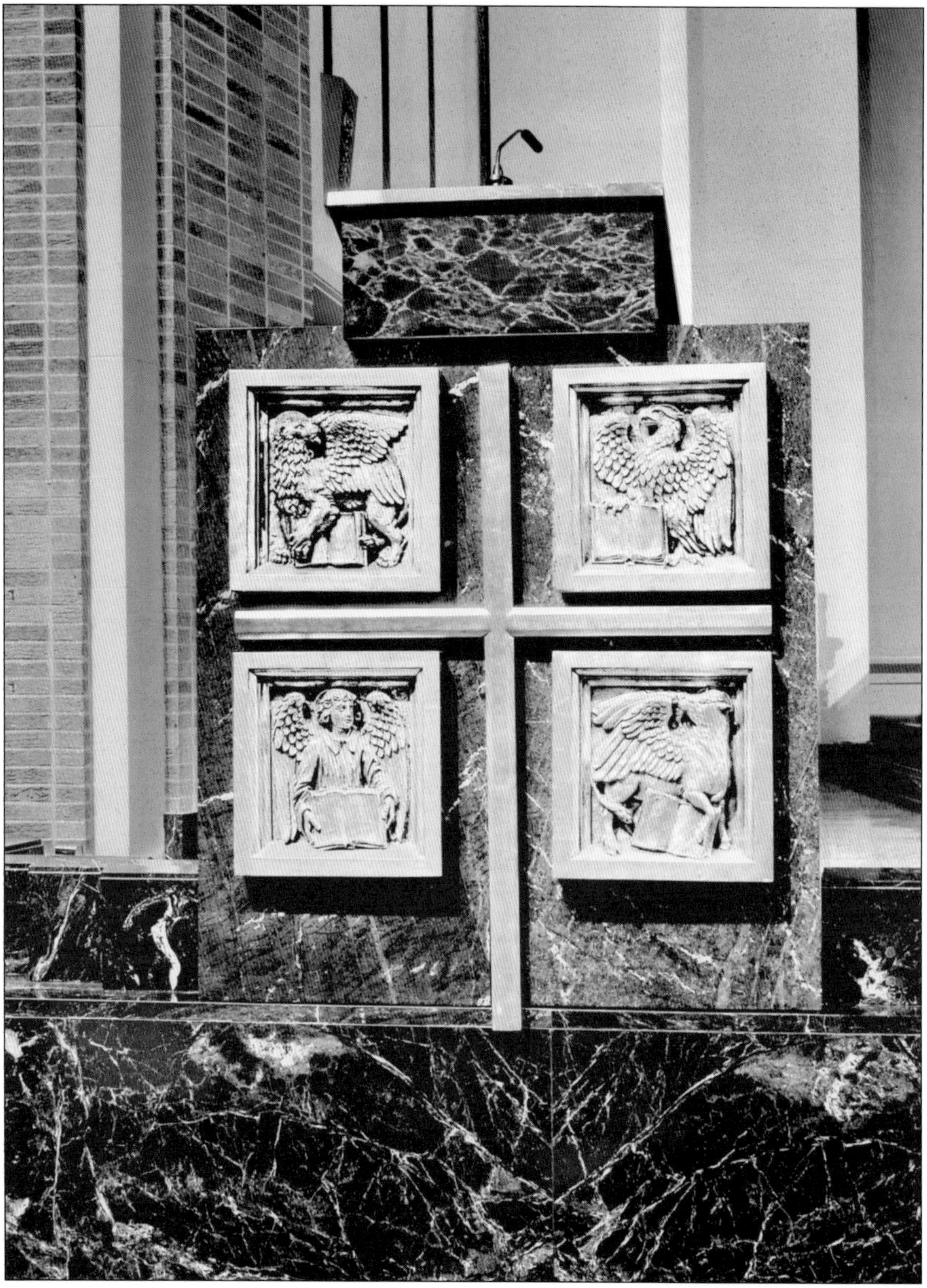

On the front of the pulpit is a polished brass cross, which separates four panels, each bearing a symbol of an Evangelist: St. Mark the Lion, St. John the Eagle, St. Matthew the Angel/Human, and St. Luke the Ox.

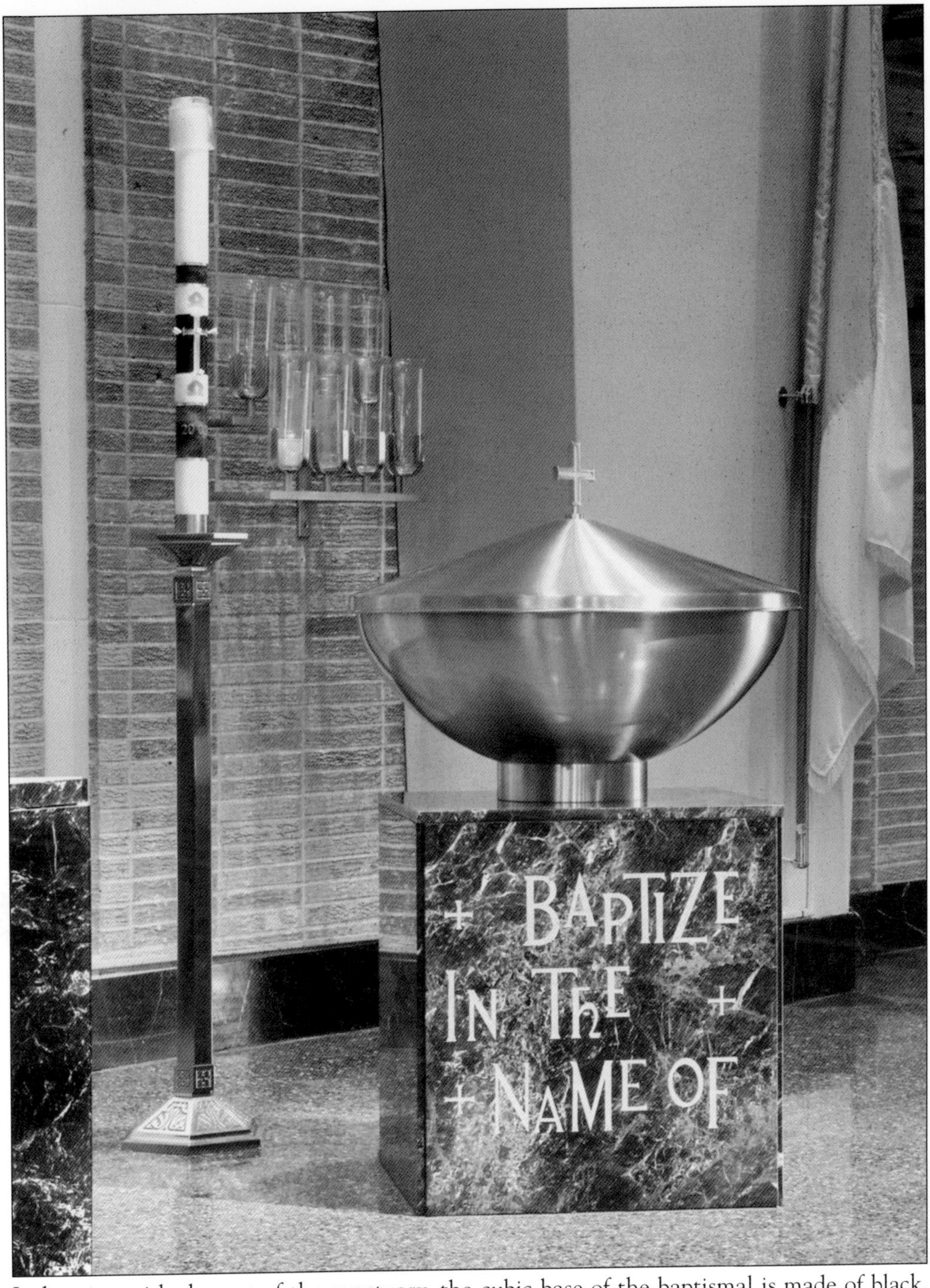

In keeping with the rest of the sanctuary, the cubic base of the baptismal is made of black, textured marble.

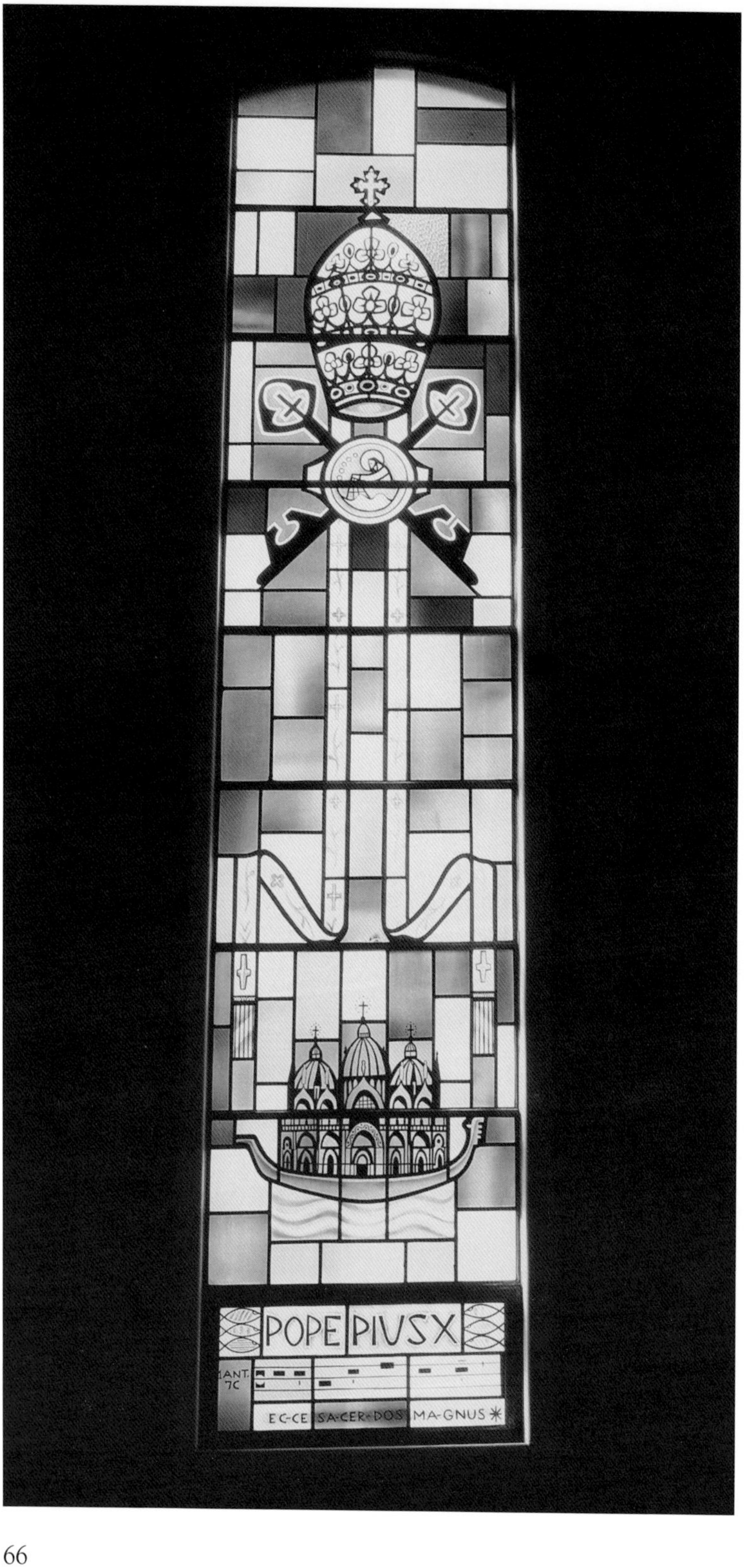

The stained-glass windows in the church are more geometric than pictorial. Each represents a saint or a saintly figure from more recent church history.

Five

Sacred Heart of Jesus

In the late 1800s, the Polish population of Cleveland's south side grew so fast that the new neighborhood of the Harvard Avenue area was too far from St. Stanislaus Parish (then 10 years old) for children to attend school there or for the faithful to be able to attend Mass and services. As a result, Fr. Kolaszewski, pastor of St. Stanislaus, received permission from Bishop Richard Gilmor to purchase property at East Seventy-First Street and Krakow Avenue for $2,500. In this way, Sacred Heart Parish was founded in 1889. The new church consisted of a two-story church and school combination, at a cost of $2,000, that was located at 6916 Krakow Avenue.

By 1908, the church and school became inadequate for the rapidly growing congregation, and the foundation of a new church was begun. The initial architect for the new church was W. P. Ginter, but his design was altered greatly through the years. Due to financial and internal problems, the basement was roofed and used as the church for a number of years. The ensuing years were met with continuous financial problems, so construction of the church was accomplished over an extended period of time. In the 1950s, the interior of the church was finally finished under the leadership of Pastor Francis Szczepanski.

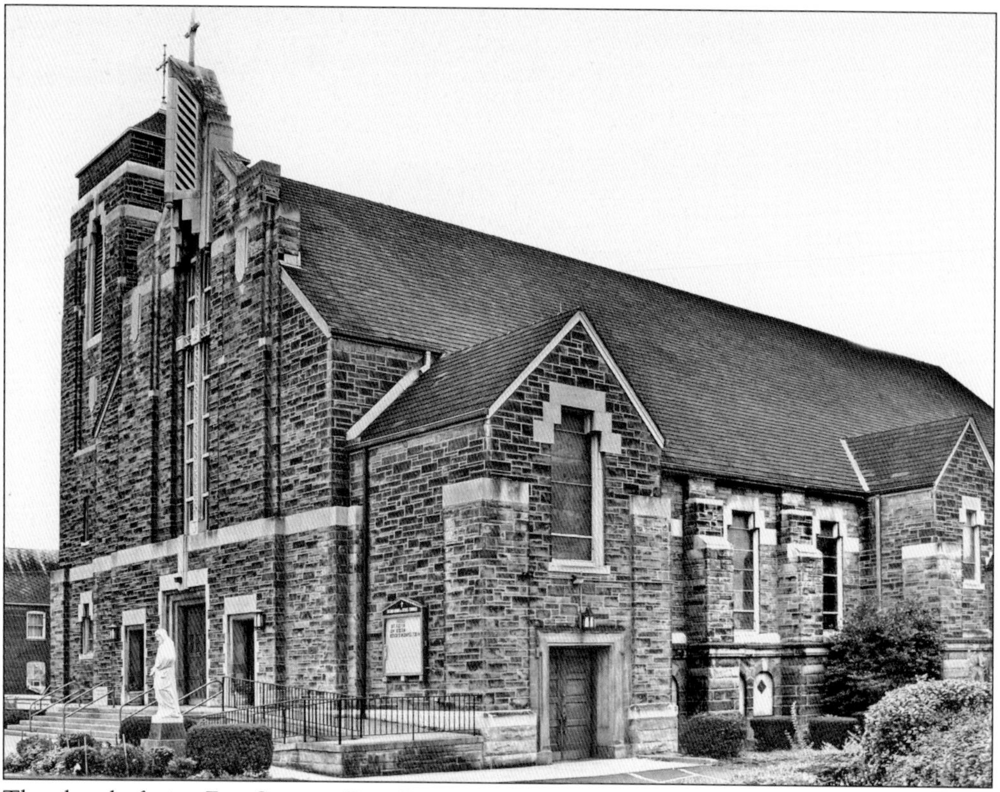

The church, facing East Seventy-First Street, is an impressive structure of sandstone block with sandstone trim. The basement, which was the former church sanctuary, is now the church hall.

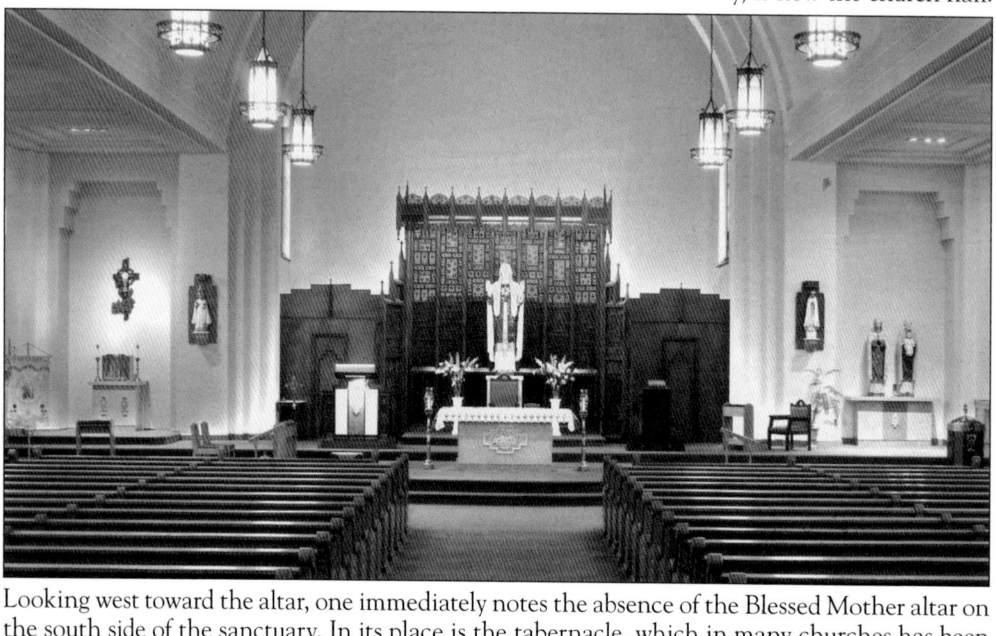

Looking west toward the altar, one immediately notes the absence of the Blessed Mother altar on the south side of the sanctuary. In its place is the tabernacle, which in many churches has been moved from the high altar to the side. On the north-side altar stand statues of both the Blessed Mother and St. Joseph with the Christ Child.

The center sanctuary is backed by an intricately carved wooden screen, possibly reminiscent of the icon screen found in most churches of the Eastern Rites. Before the screen is a magnificent statue of the Sacred Heart of Jesus, which is made from multiple types and colors of marble. It is the dominant structure, and namesake, of the church.

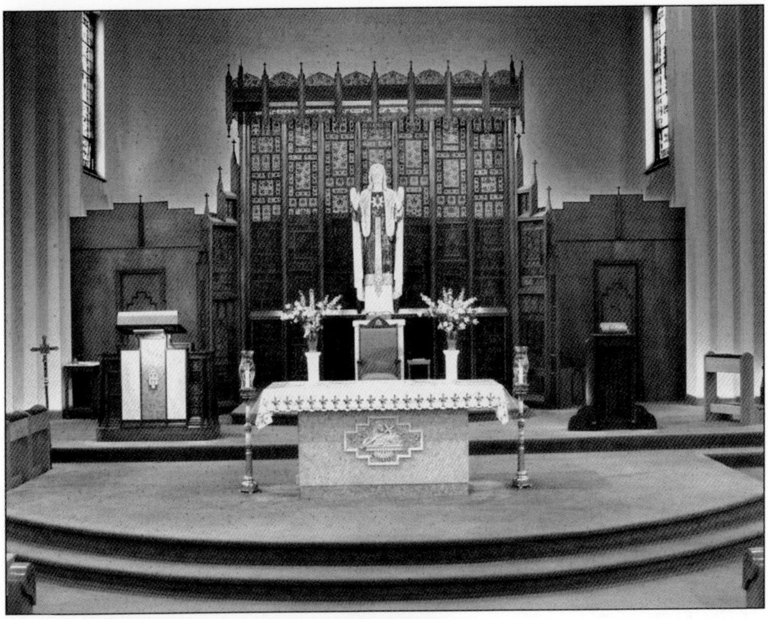

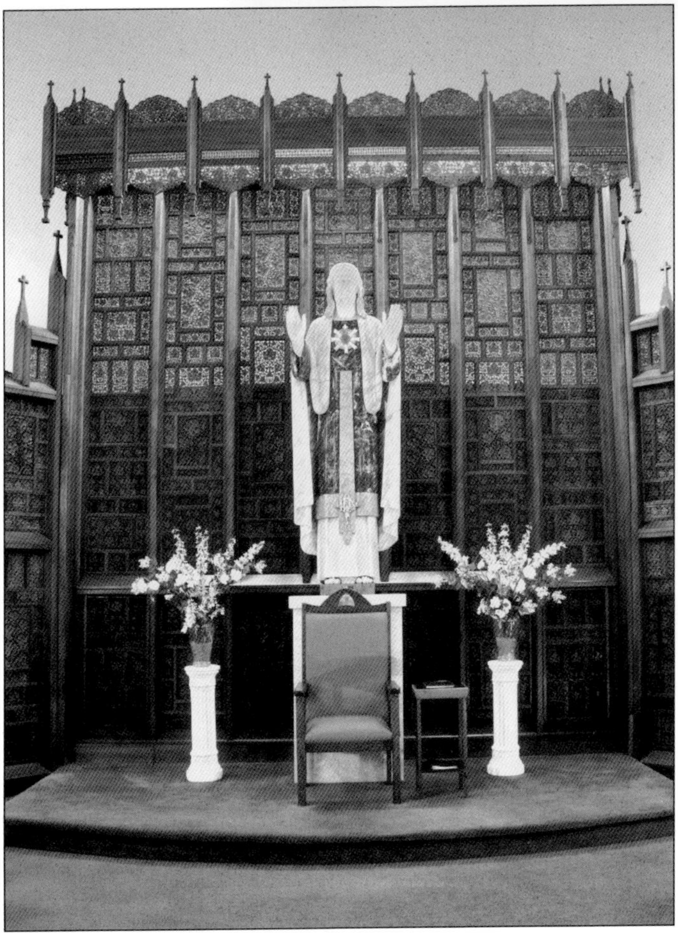

A closer view of the statue reveals that the marble of the face and hands has a translucent quality, which gives the image an almost supernatural appearance. Also visible here is the amazing detail of the wooden screen behind the statue.

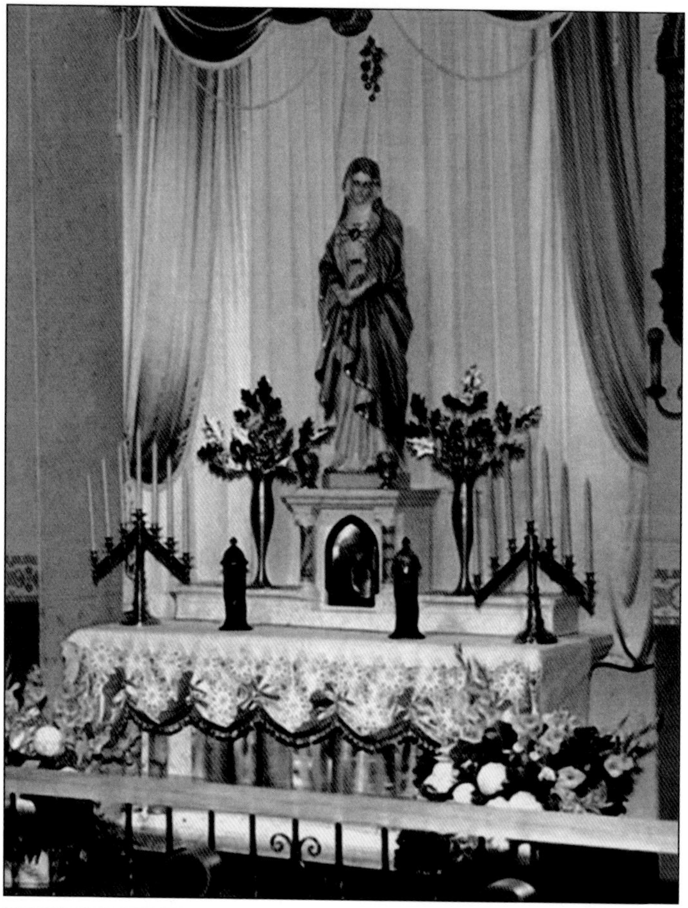

This 1941 image shows the first Polish shrine in Novena to Our Sorrowful Mother on the north wall of the church. (Cleveland State University, *Cleveland Press* photograph.)

A plaque containing the mission statement of the church, with its timeless message and etching of the church, appears on the wall at the rear of the church.

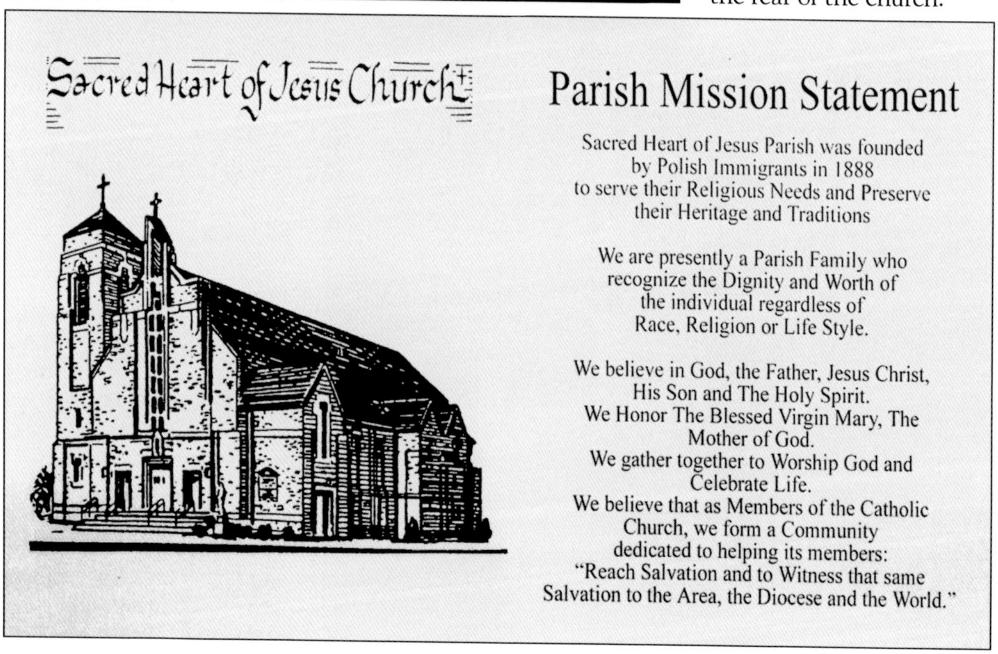

Sacred Heart of Jesus Church

Parish Mission Statement

Sacred Heart of Jesus Parish was founded
by Polish Immigrants in 1888
to serve their Religious Needs and Preserve
their Heritage and Traditions

We are presently a Parish Family who
recognize the Dignity and Worth of
the individual regardless of
Race, Religion or Life Style.

We believe in God, the Father, Jesus Christ,
His Son and The Holy Spirit.
We Honor The Blessed Virgin Mary, The
Mother of God.
We gather together to Worship God and
Celebrate Life.
We believe that as Members of the Catholic
Church, we form a Community
dedicated to helping its members:
"Reach Salvation and to Witness that same
Salvation to the Area, the Diocese and the World."

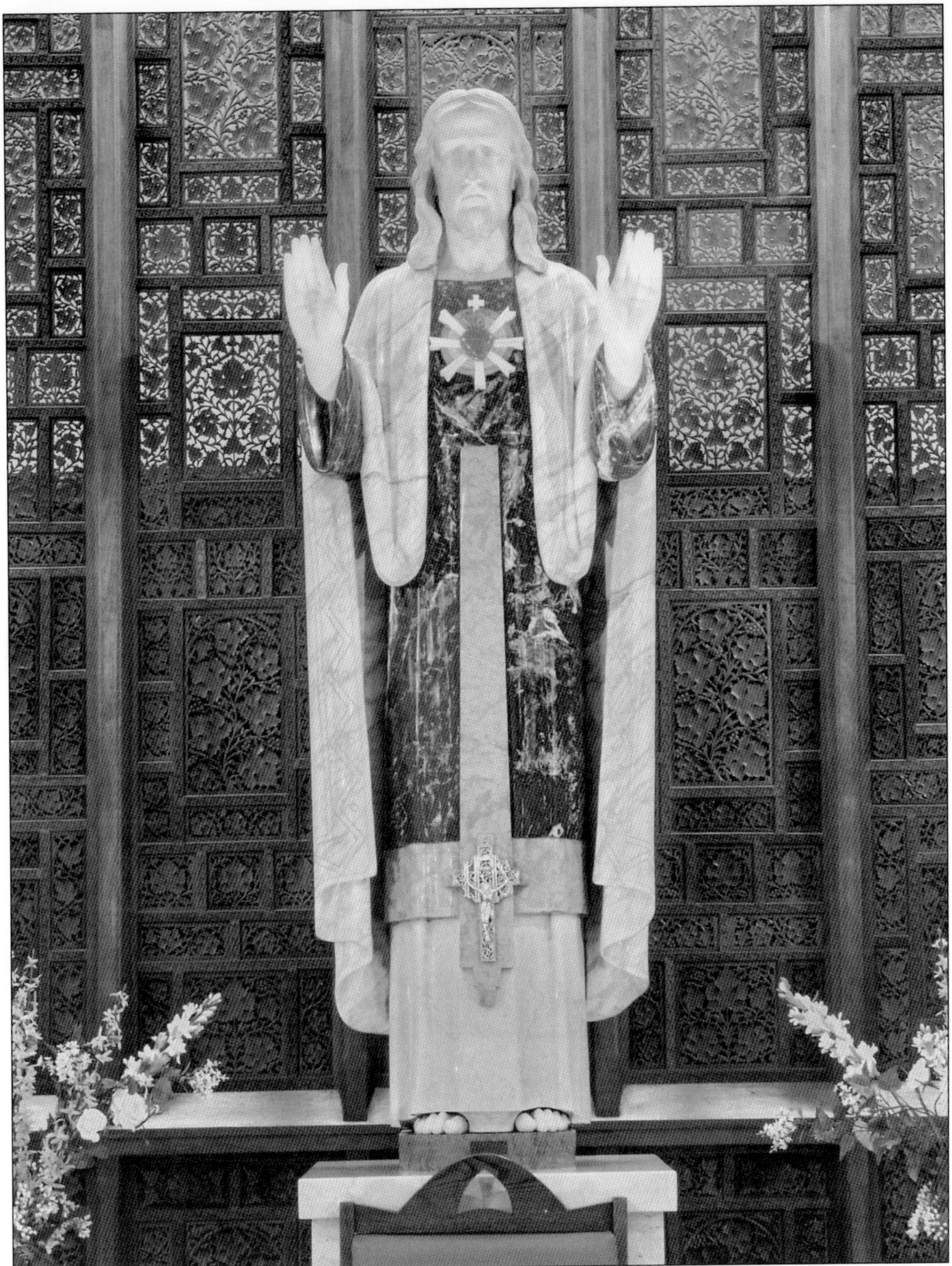

The blend of marbles and textures creates a unique version of this church icon. The Sacred Heart has long been a symbol of Christ's love and devotion to his people. Catholics believe that in visions to St. Margaret Mary, between 1673 and 1675, Christ made promises concerning anyone who practices devotion to his Sacred Heart. Among these was the promise to show special consideration at death to those who receive the Eucharist on the first Friday of nine consecutive months. Since 1856, Catholics have celebrated the Feast of the Sacred Heart on the Friday that falls 19 days after Pentecost.

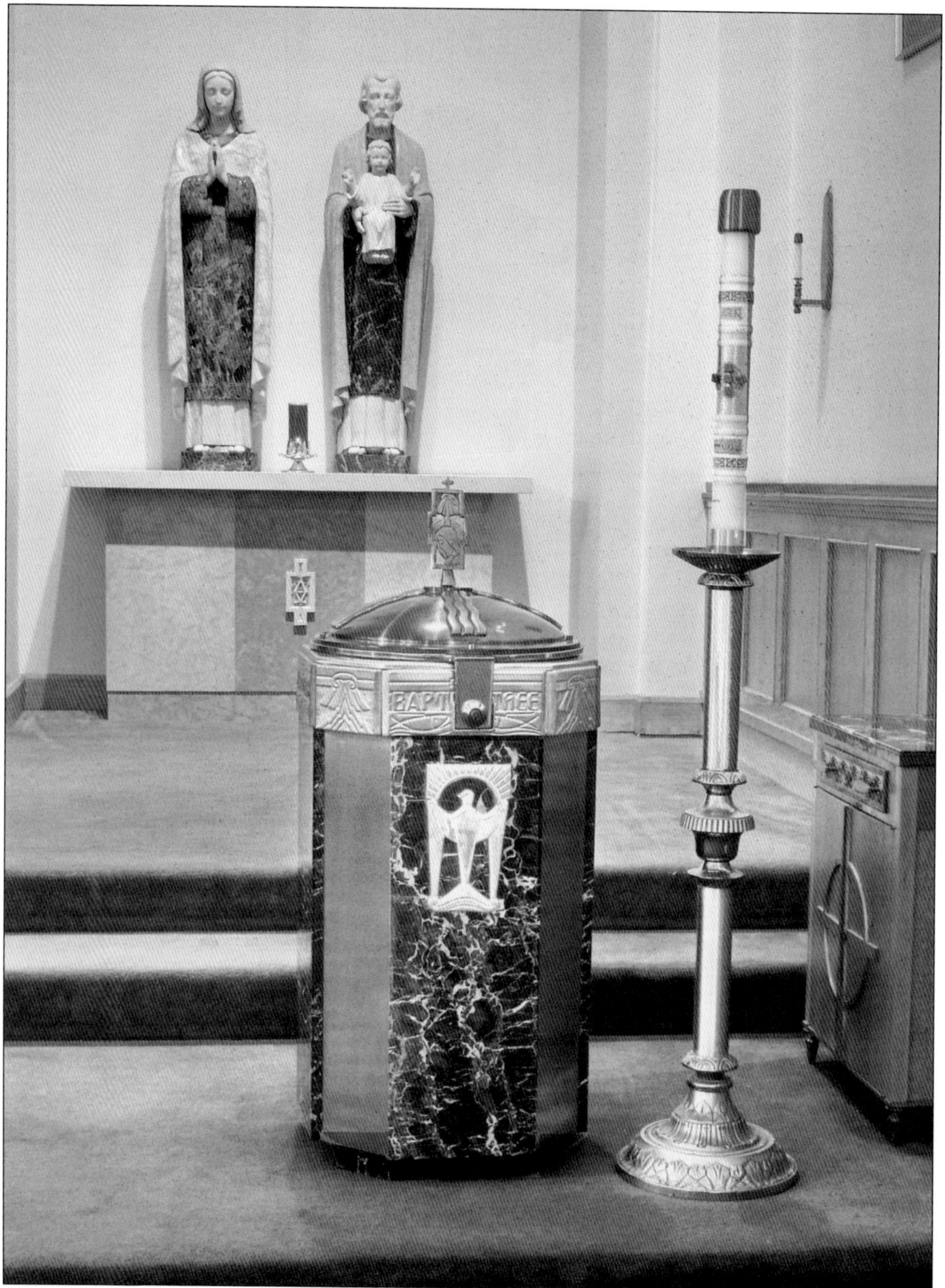

The baptismal occupies the north part of the sanctuary, with the side altar behind it. Rich black textured marble enhanced by both satin and polished brass comprises the font with the symbol of the Holy Spirit on the front.

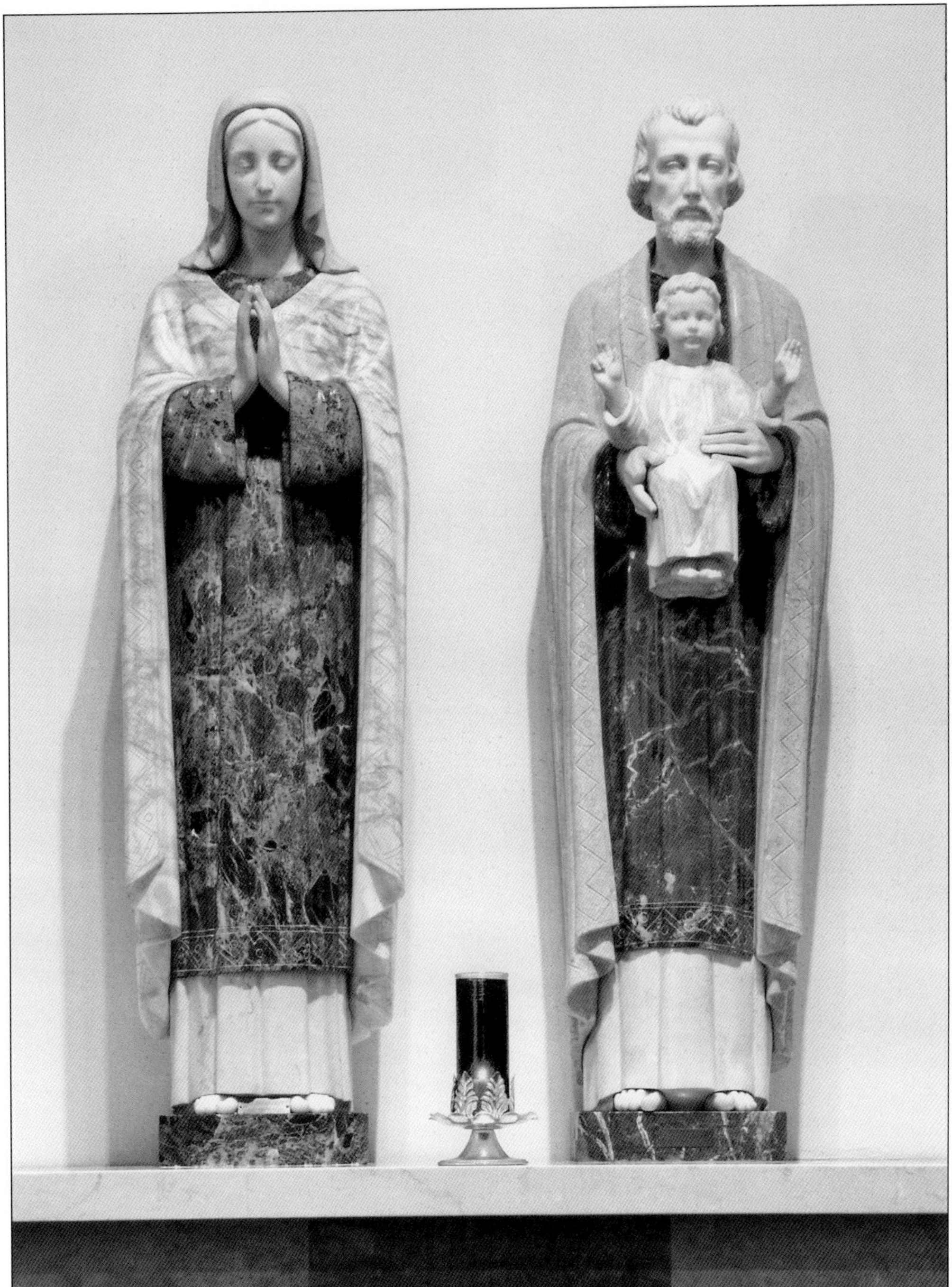

On the north-side altar are statues of Mary and Joseph with the Christ Child. These magnificent statues are two more examples of how multiple types of marbles are combined to create an unusual and appealing artistic result.

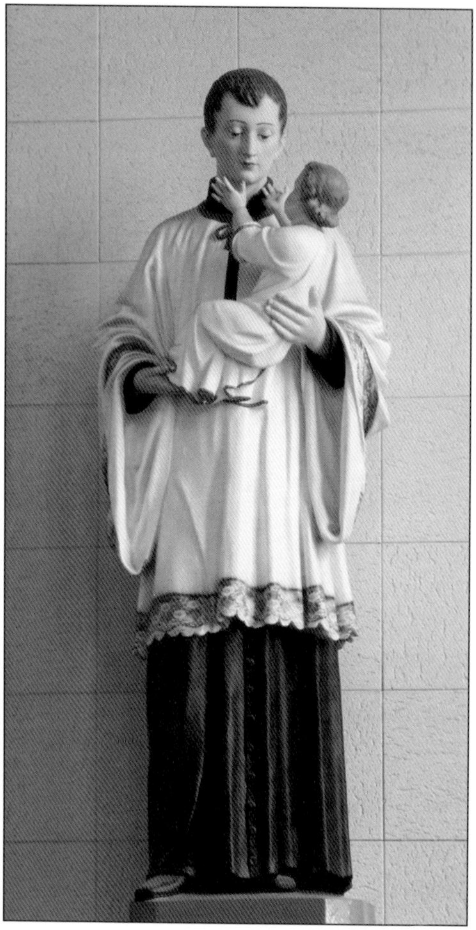

In the southeast corner of the church are two statues of saints of particular significance to the congregation. St. Stanislaus (1550–1568) is a very popular saint of Poland and is the namesake for many religious institutions. Traditionally his depiction in art is varied. One of these is his receiving the Baby Jesus from the Blessed Mother as presented here.

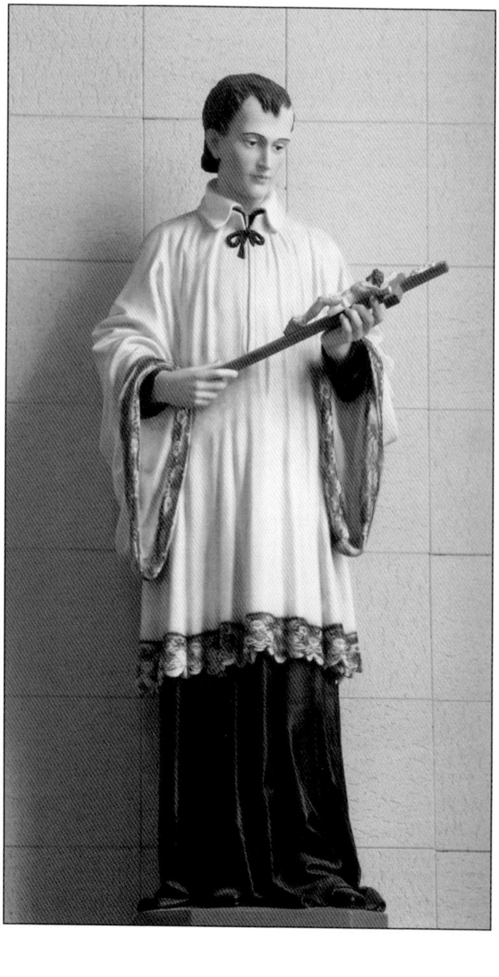

Next to St. Stanislaus is a statue of St. Aloysius (1568–1591), an Italian saint who devoted himself to caring for the sick—though he himself was in fragile health. Ultimately he succumbed to illness.

For 600 years, the Icon of Our Lady of Chestochowa has been a religious symbol of Poland. There are many legends regarding the icon. In each, the image saved its church from destruction from some peril, one of which was fire. Thus the faces in the image were charred, bringing about the icon's alternate name, the "Black Madonna."

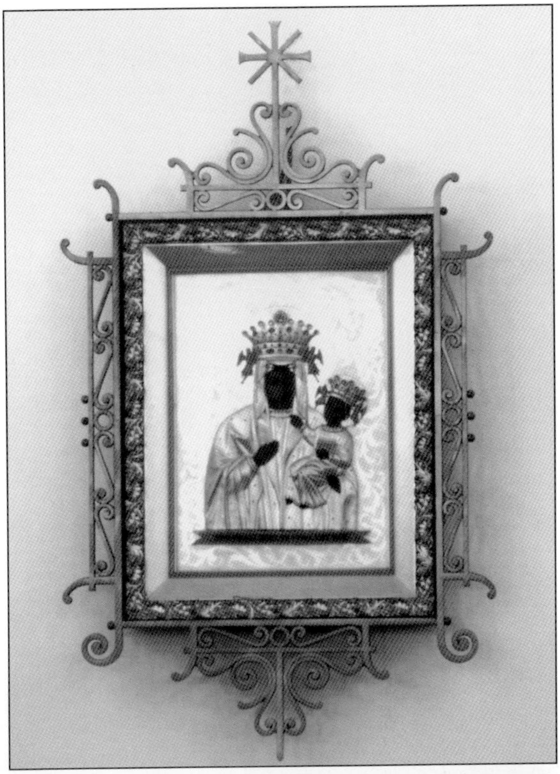

To the rear of the sacristy of Sacred Heart Church is a small chapel with a stained-glass mural of the church's namesake.

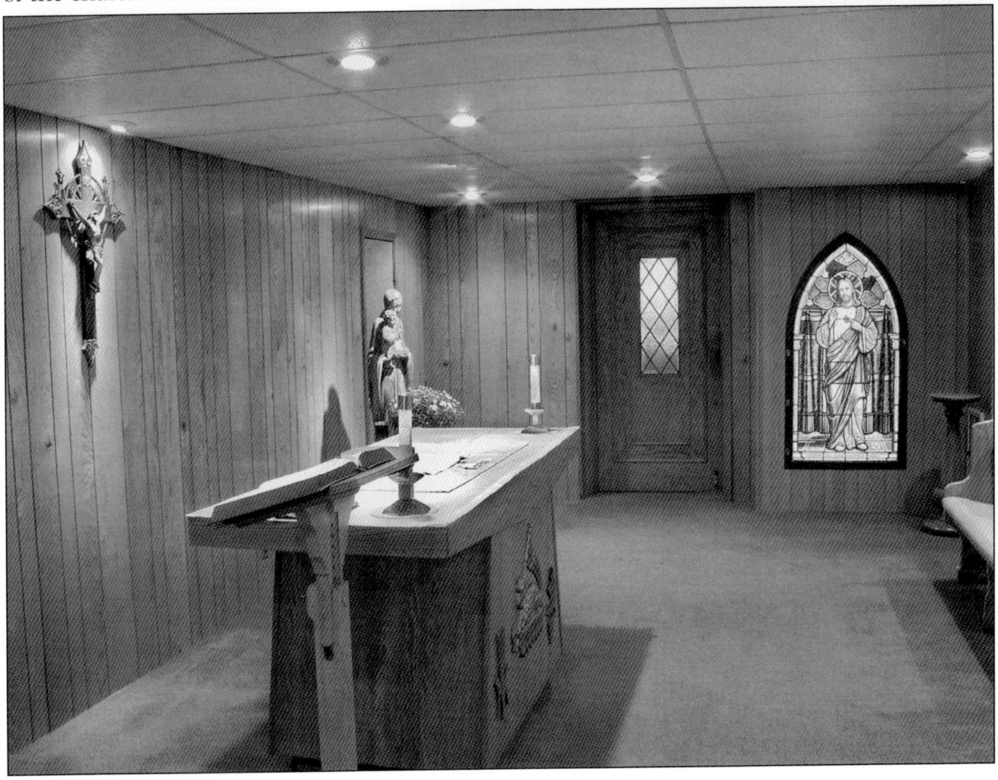

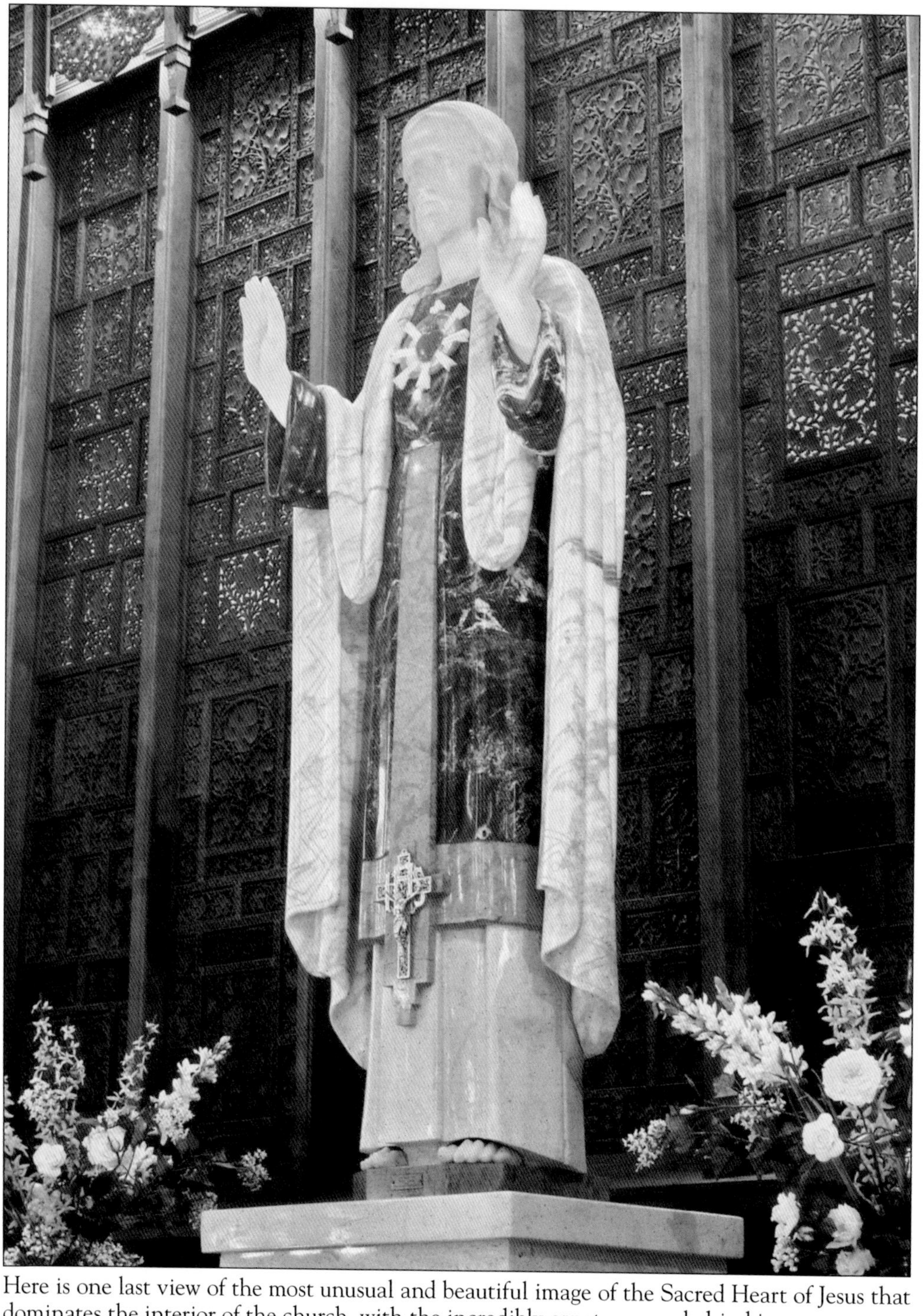

Here is one last view of the most unusual and beautiful image of the Sacred Heart of Jesus that dominates the interior of the church, with the incredibly ornate screen behind it.

Six

St. Procop

In 1872, Fr. Anthony Hynek established St. Procop Parish at 3182 West Forty-First Street to serve the spiritual needs of Bohemian Catholics living on the west side of Cleveland. For two years, another church was used as temporary quarters until a wooden church was built on West Forty-First Street. There ensued a tumultuous period when vast disagreements existed between parishioners, pastors, and the diocese, and it lasted for quite some time. Finally the new church, with seating for 1,200 people, was built in 1902 under the direction of Frs. Peter Cerveny and Wenceslas Panuska. The architects on the project were Emile Uhlrich and Godfrey Fugman.

In 1899, Emile Uhlrich entered into a partnership with fellow architect Godfrey Fugman. The partnership lasted until 1904, and it was generally believed that Fugman handled more of the engineering and business side of projects, while Uhlrich was the creative genius.

In 1903, St. Procop's Church was dedicated. *The Catholic Universe Bulletin* called it "one of the finest church buildings in the city." The architects were receiving rave reviews for setting a new standard in local church design. However, the disagreements within the church continued to the point that the bishop almost closed the new church down. Over the course of several years, the dust settled, and St Procop prospered.

Uhlrich and Fugman employed the newest technologies and techniques of the time. They engineered a structural frame of steel trusses, which allowed for a massive, wide-open interior space that was unobstructed by columns. They hid indirect lighting throughout the interior and slightly raked (sloped) the floor from the vestibule to the main altar, thus drawing the eye forward. The new St. Procop's was a highly designed, highly functional space worthy of being called the new standard.

Uhlrich went on to design the breathtaking Our Lady of Victory Basilica in Lackawanna, New York, as well as the Shine of Our Lady of Consolation in Carey, Ohio.

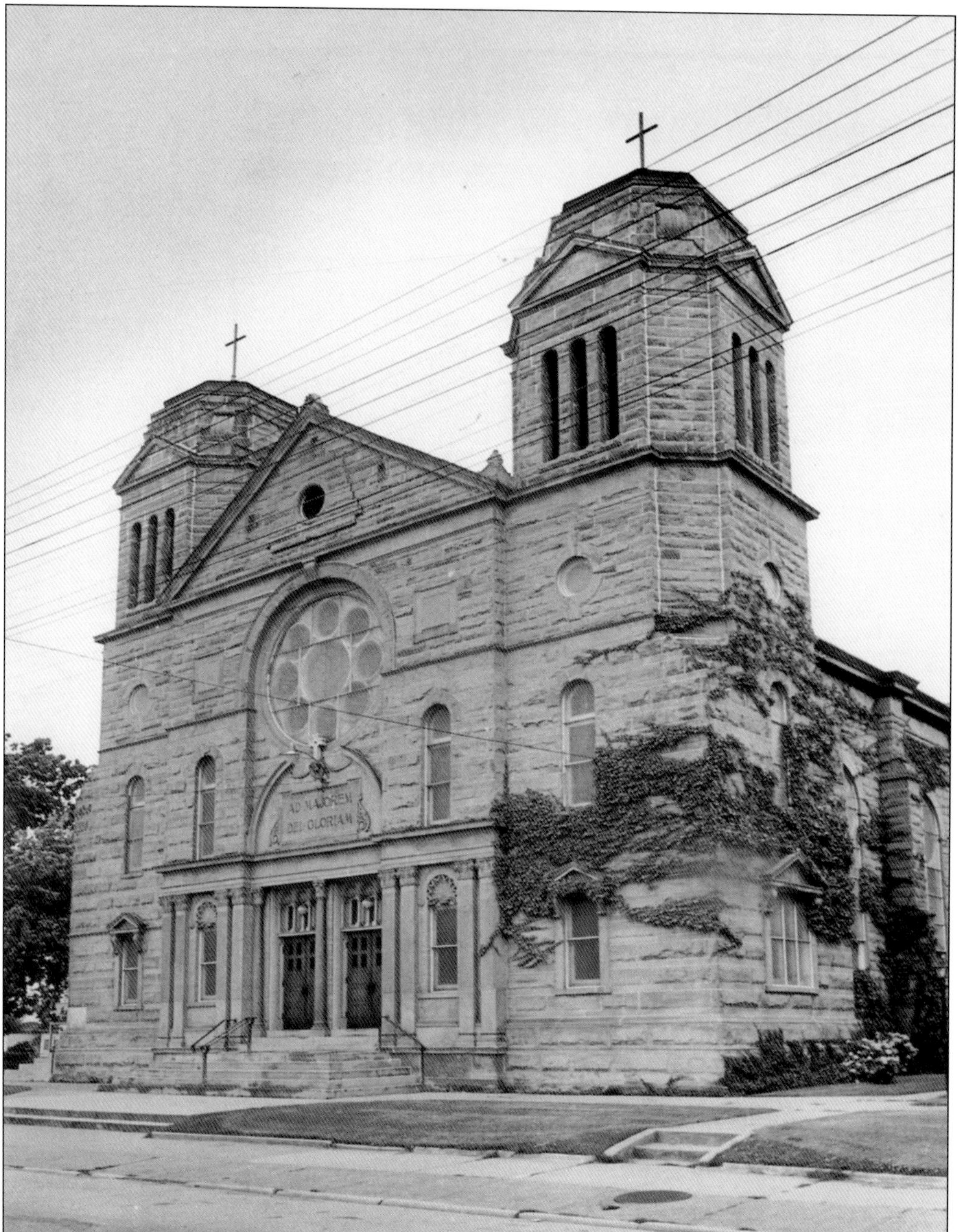

The exterior of the church is constructed of Berea sandstone block of varying size. There are two octagonal bell towers with a triangular pediment between them. Two windows on the facade and the side entrances also have pediments, while the remaining windows are round at the top. The basic style of the church is Italian Renaissance. (Cleveland State University, *Cleveland Press* photograph.)

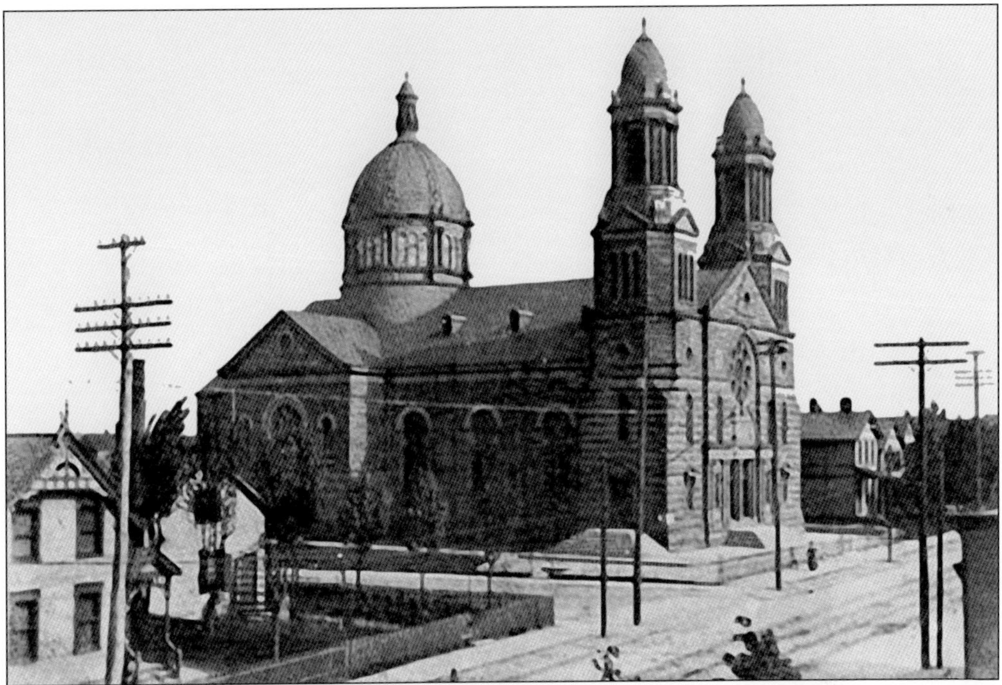

A 1920 picture of St. Procop shows the original twin towers and dome. In 1962, these structures were dismantled due to a deteriorating condition and prohibitive repair cost. (Cleveland State University, *Cleveland Press* photograph.)

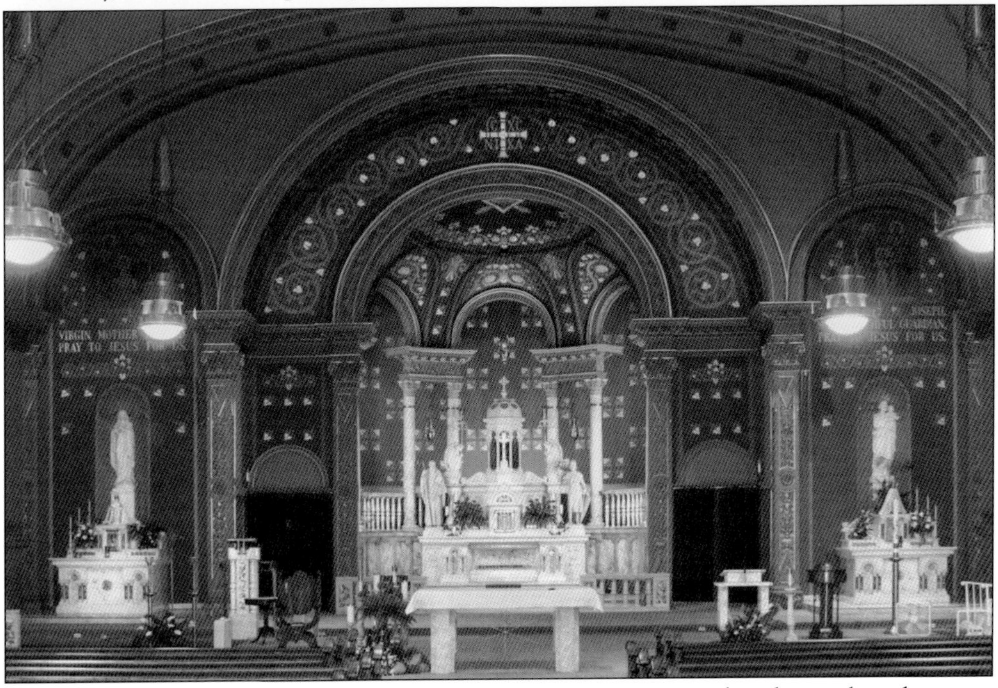

Inside the church, a view toward the east reveals the Romanesque arches that outline the entire front of the church. There are literally arches within arches, culminating in the apse that covers the main altar. Some have gone so far as to describe the church as "Byzantine Romanesque."

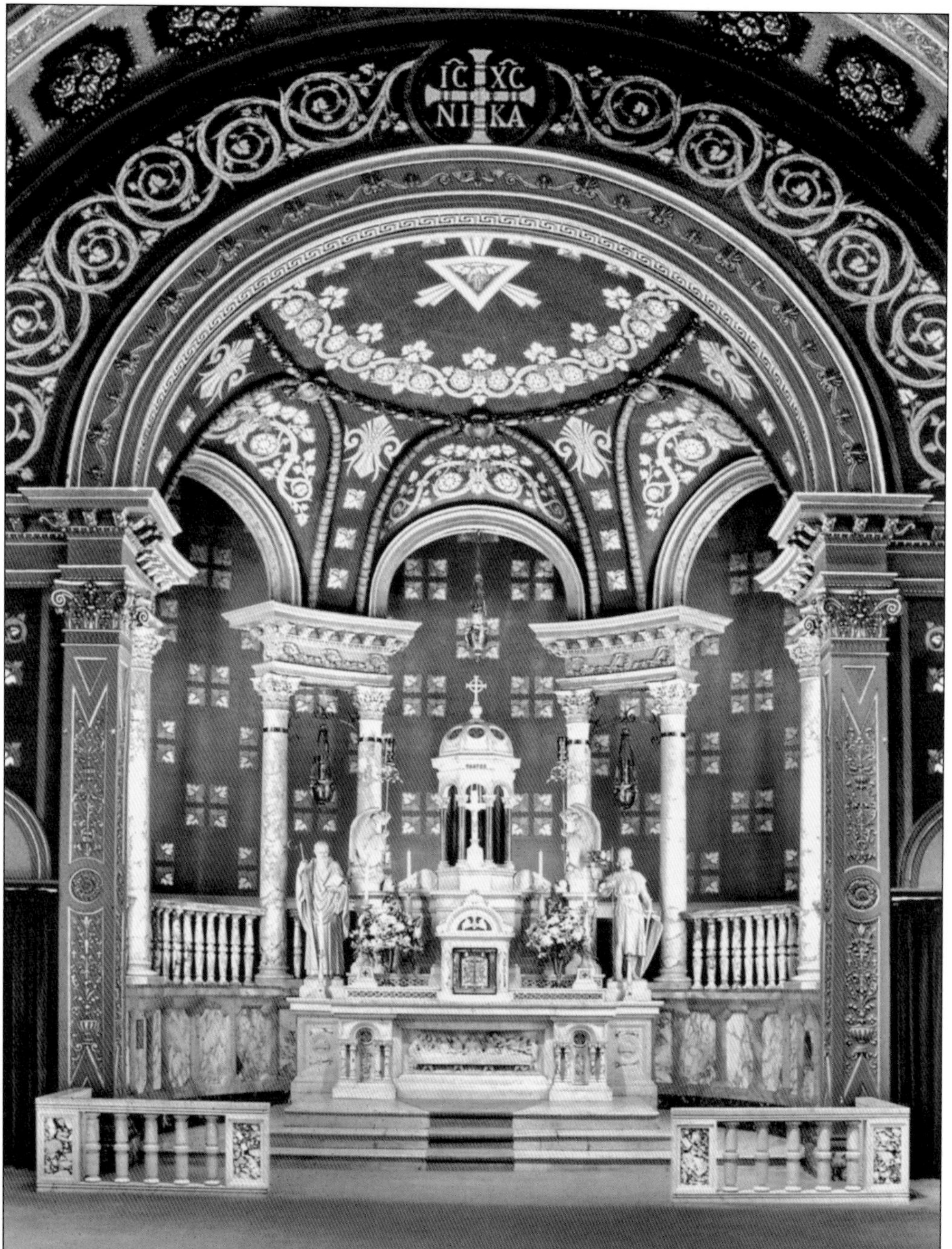

The magnificent sanctuary of St. Procop is delineated by a system of seemingly concentric, rounded arches. The combined genius of architect Uhlrich and engineer Fugman is exemplified in the design and execution of the three inner arches that form the base of the apse above the altar. In keeping with the Romanesque theme is the inclusion of a classical colonnade and six marble columns that support the apse via a double set of capitals.

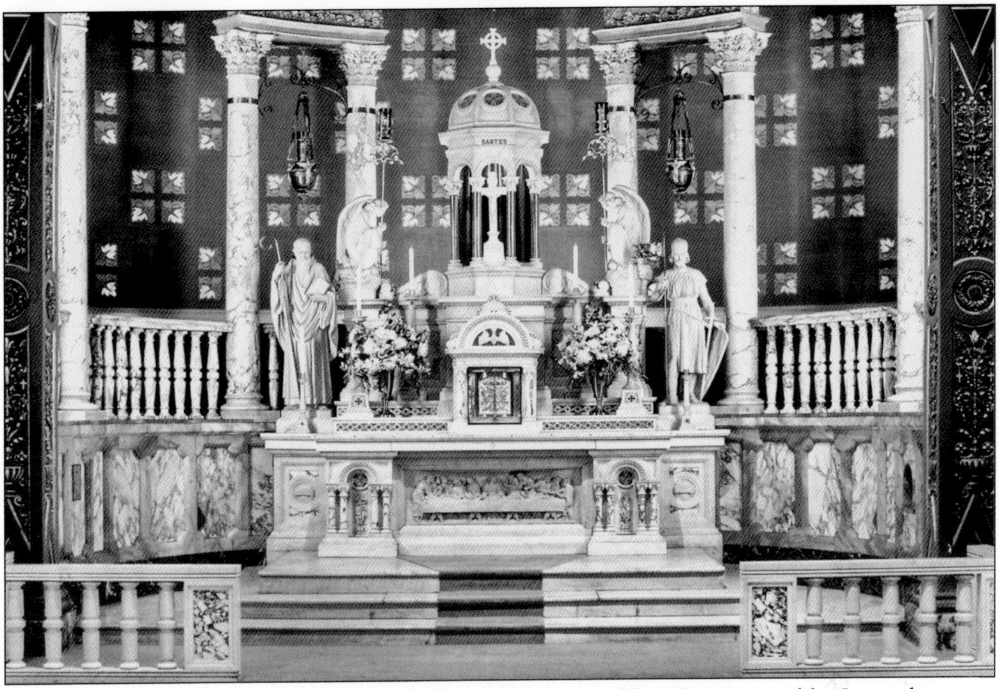

The high altar is white marble with small columns of a golden Sienna marble. Insets between these columns are white with purple breccia (a type of sedimentary rock). The steps are of a somewhat different white marble. The large pillars in the colonnade are a yellow breccia, and the spindles are white and gray breccia. The wall beneath the colonnade is of golden Sienna marble with insets of a white and purple breccia.

The statue on the left is St. Procop (around 970–1053), the namesake of the church. He lived in Bohemia in the late 10th and 11th centuries and became the Roman Catholic Church's first Czech saint in 1204. The statue on the right is an image of St. Wenceslaus (907–935), duke of Bohemia and ultimately the king of the Czechs. He has become the patron saint of the Czech people.

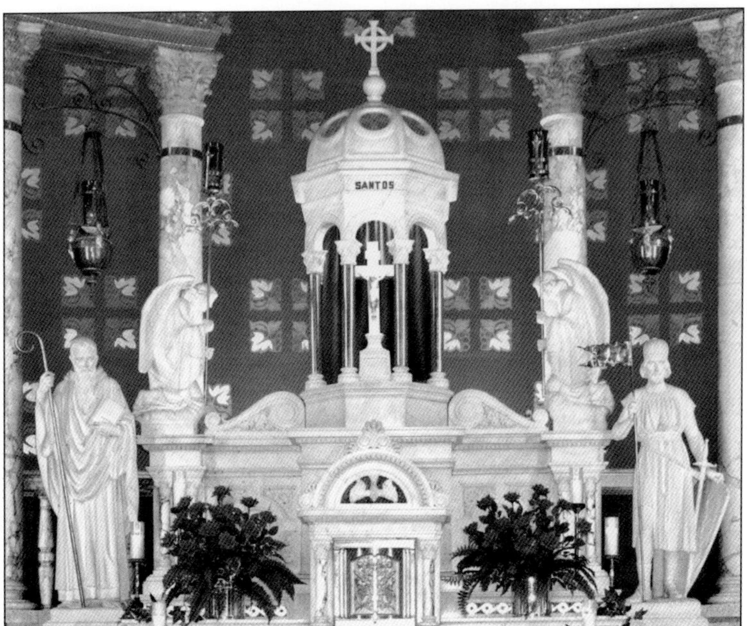

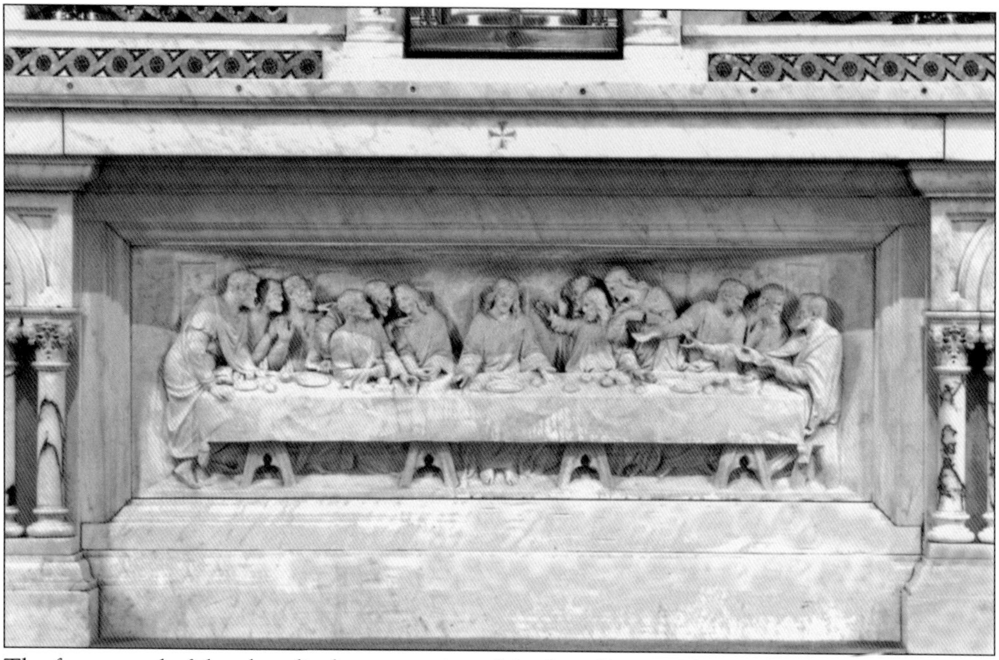

The front panel of the altar displays a carving of the Last Supper. Notice the detail, especially in the tablecloth's textures and wrinkles.

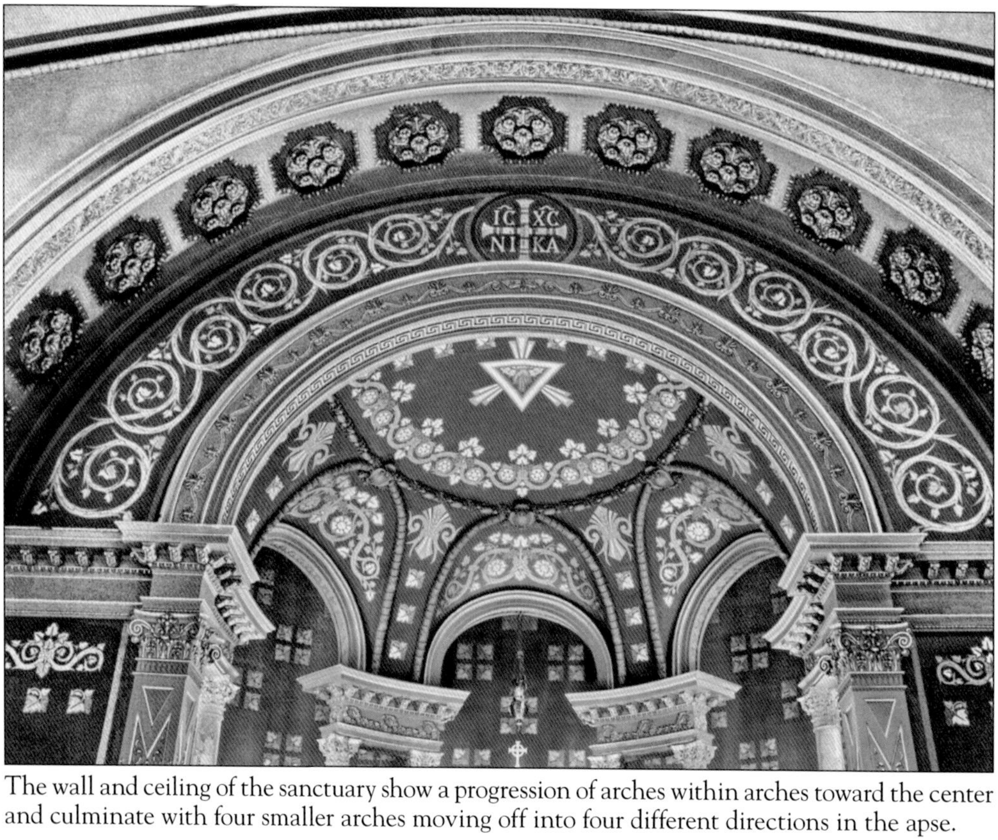

The wall and ceiling of the sanctuary show a progression of arches within arches toward the center and culminate with four smaller arches moving off into four different directions in the apse.

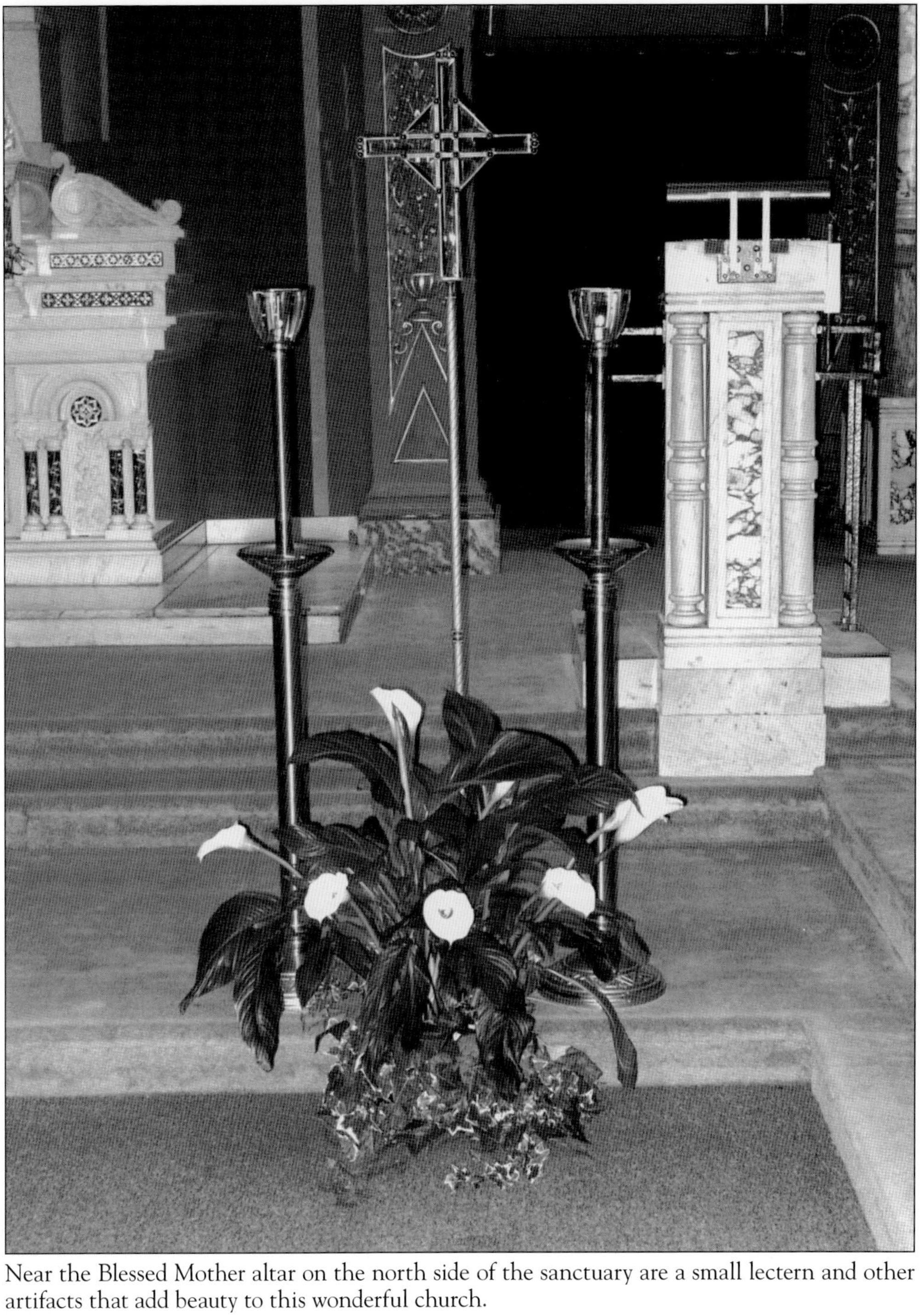

Near the Blessed Mother altar on the north side of the sanctuary are a small lectern and other artifacts that add beauty to this wonderful church.

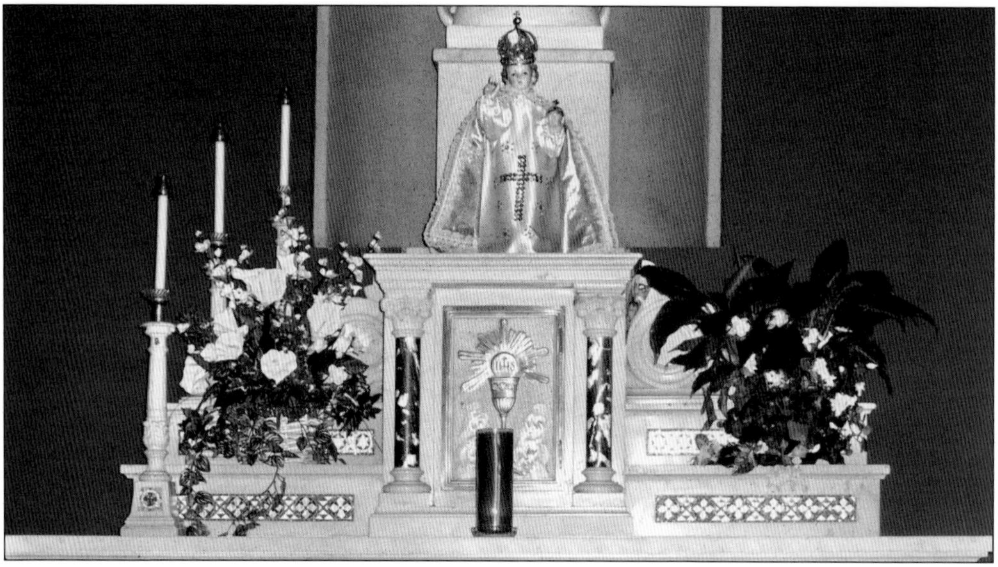

On the north side of the sanctuary is the Blessed Mother altar, and to the south is the altar of St. Joseph, each identified by lettering on the front panels. These altars are white marble with gray streaks and have eight small pillars of red marble with white texture. On this page are the upper and lower sections of the Blessed Mother alter.

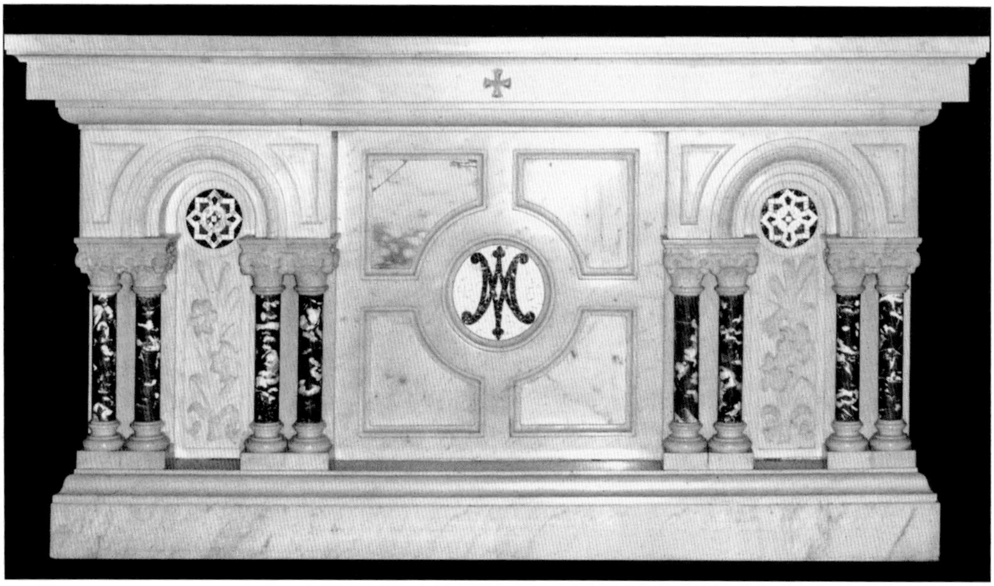

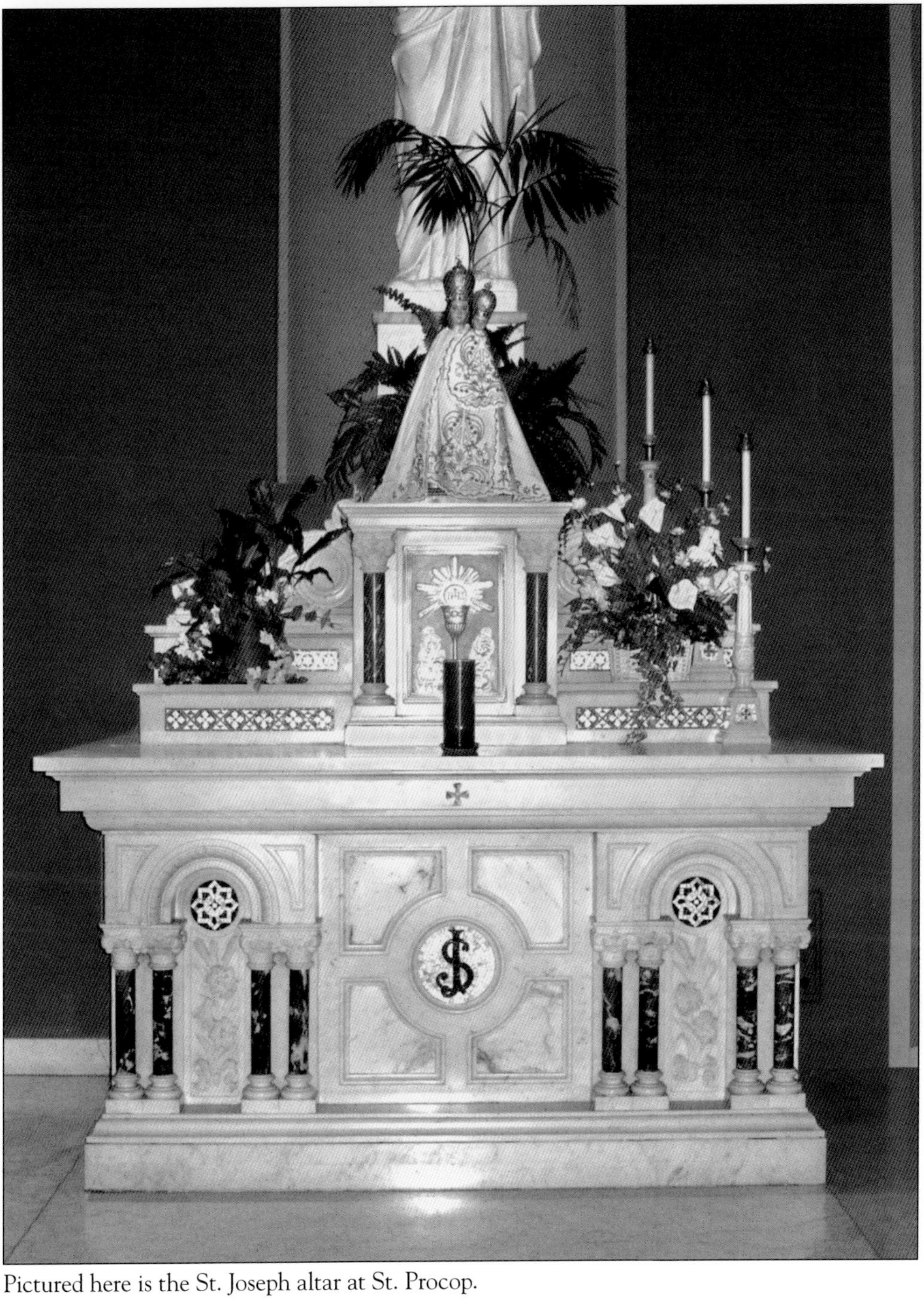

Pictured here is the St. Joseph altar at St. Procop.

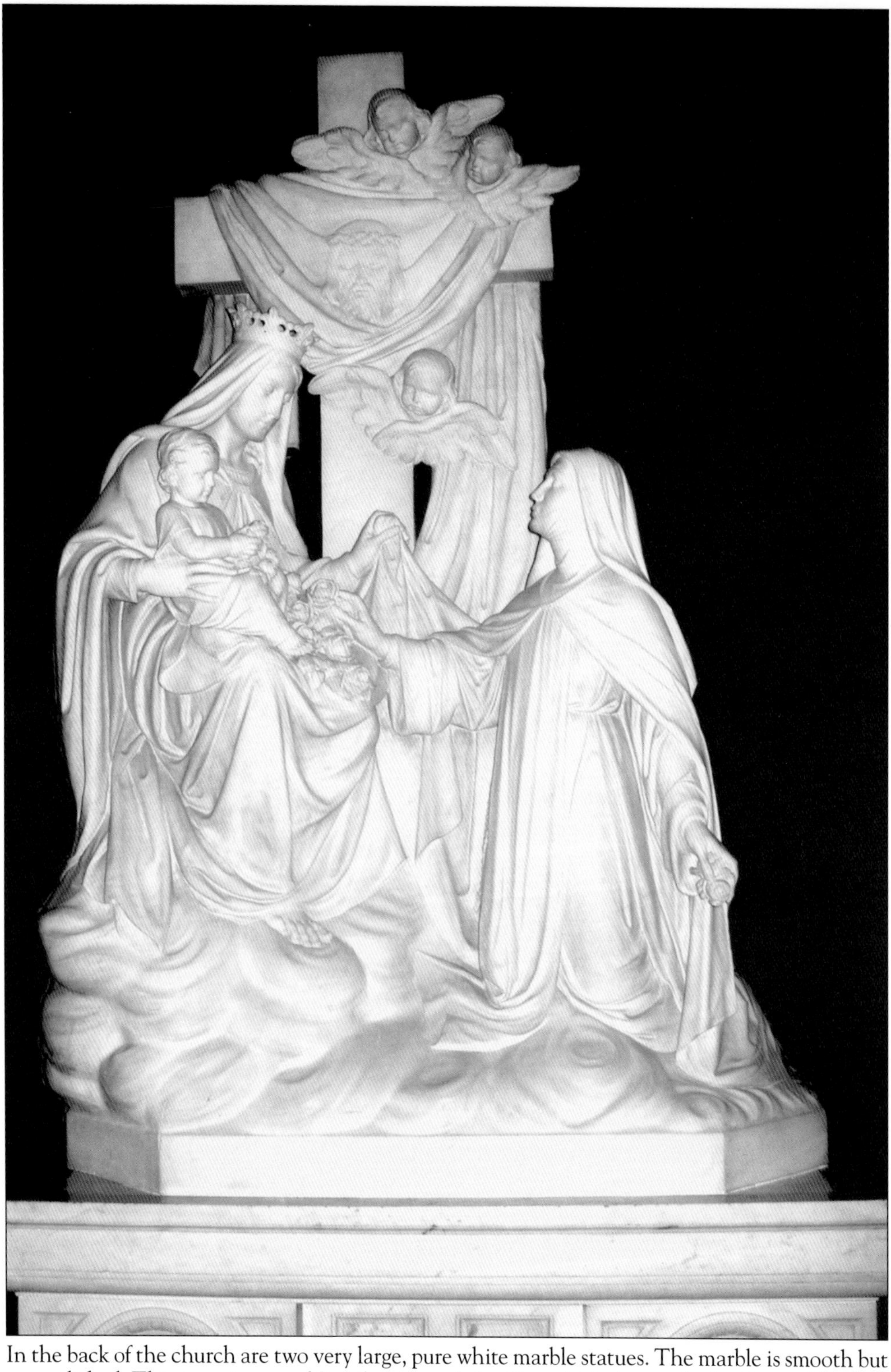

In the back of the church are two very large, pure white marble statues. The marble is smooth but not polished. This is an image of St. Therese and the Blessed Mother with the Christ Child.

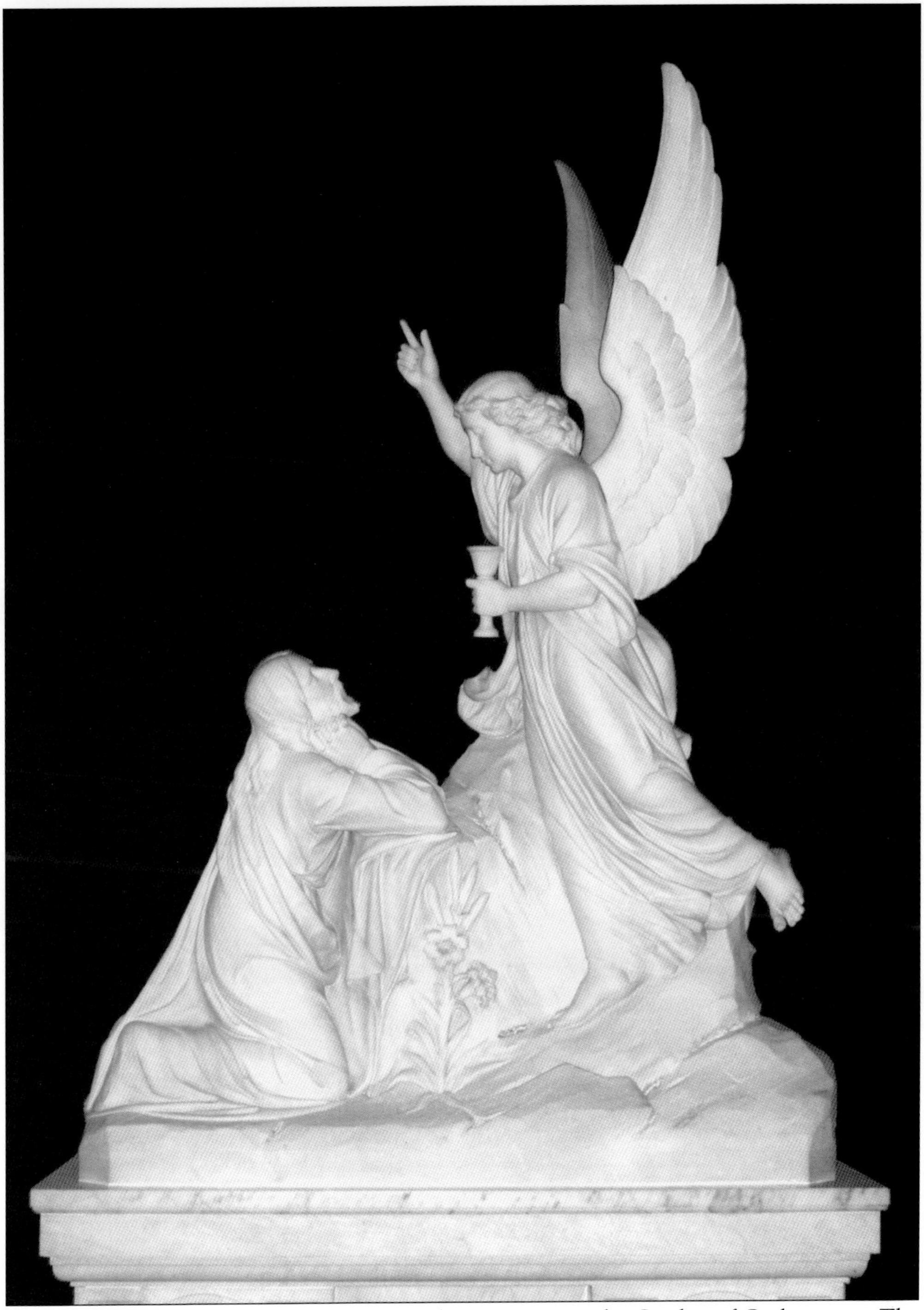

This image is a moving representation of Christ's agony in the Garden of Gethsemane. The degree of detail and texture of these sculptures is truly remarkable. The sculptor of these statues is unknown.

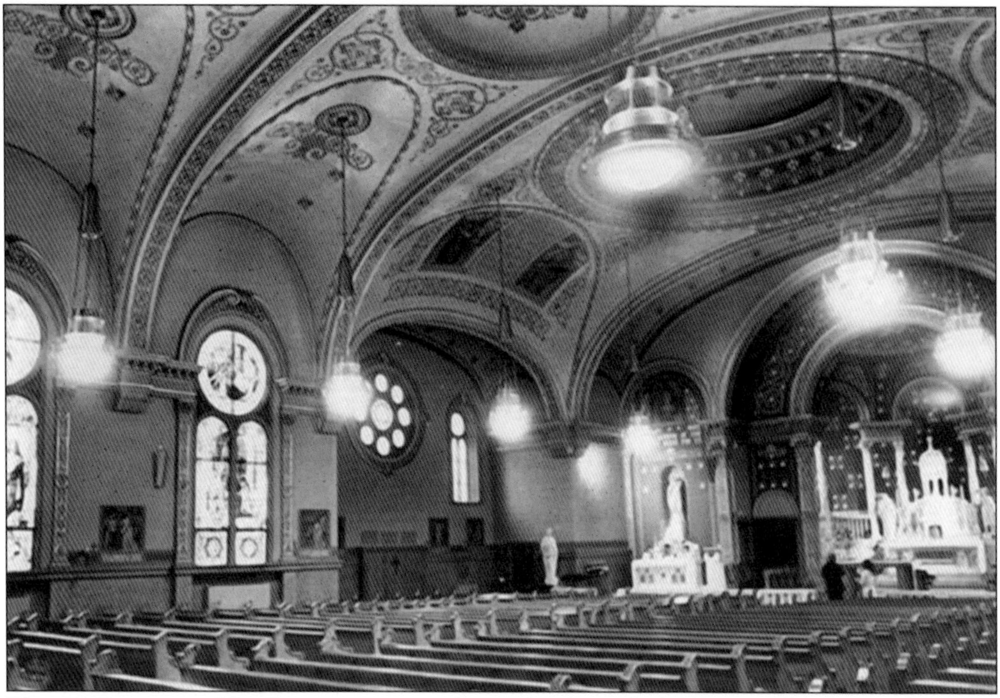

This 1947 picture of St. Procop's interior shows the decorated dome and frescoes. (Cleveland State University, *Cleveland Press* photograph.)

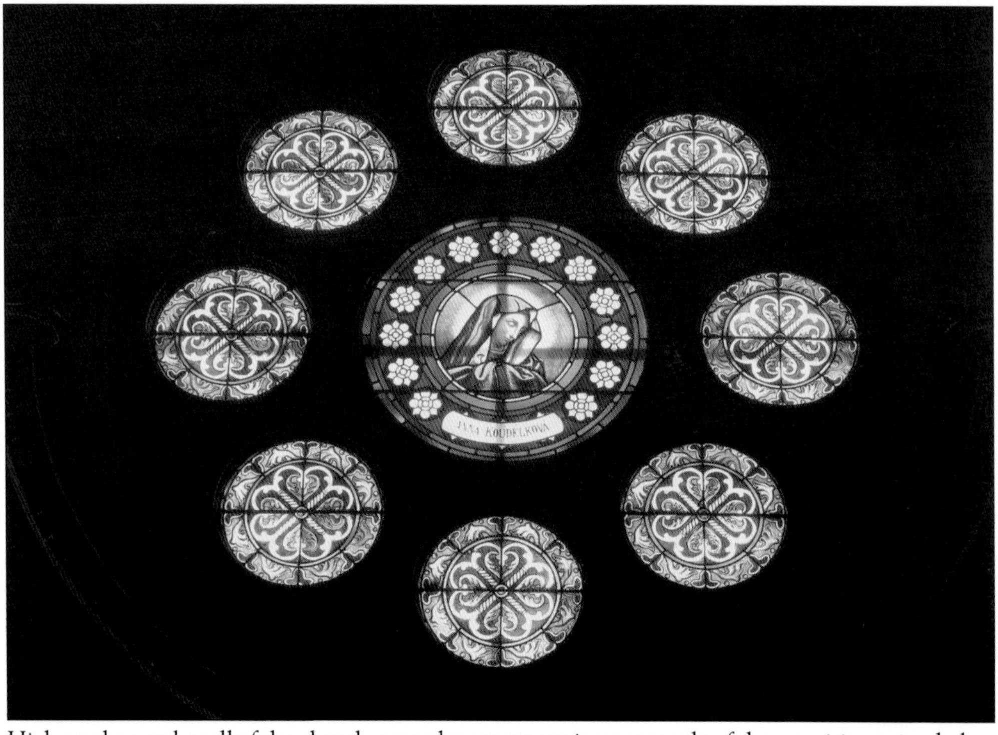

High on the north wall of the church, near the sanctuary, is an example of the exquisite stained-glass murals of St. Procop. This is one of a pair of circular arrays; one on each side of the church.

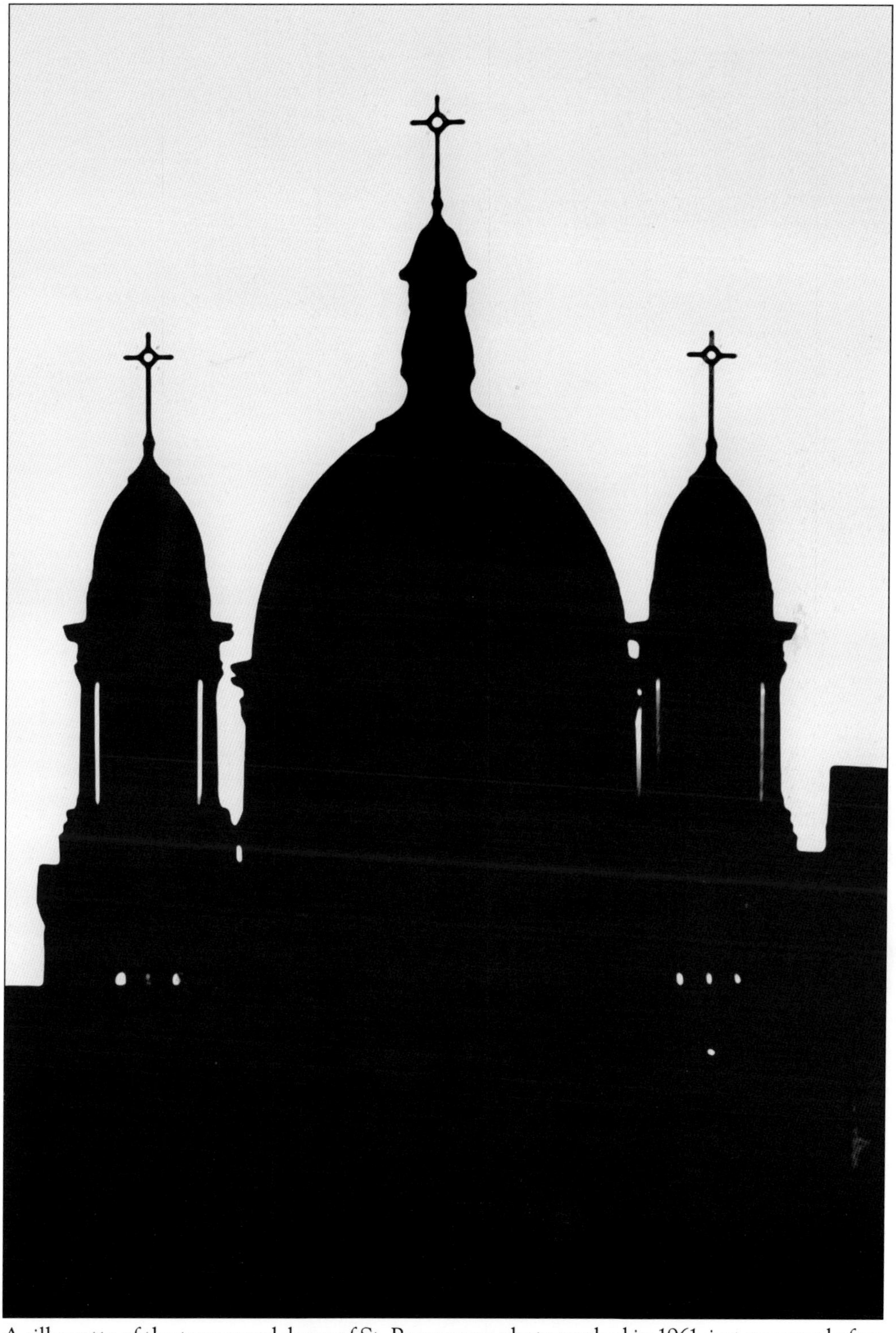

A silhouette of the towers and dome of St. Procop was photographed in 1961, just one year before they were taken down. (Cleveland State University, *Cleveland Press* photograph.)

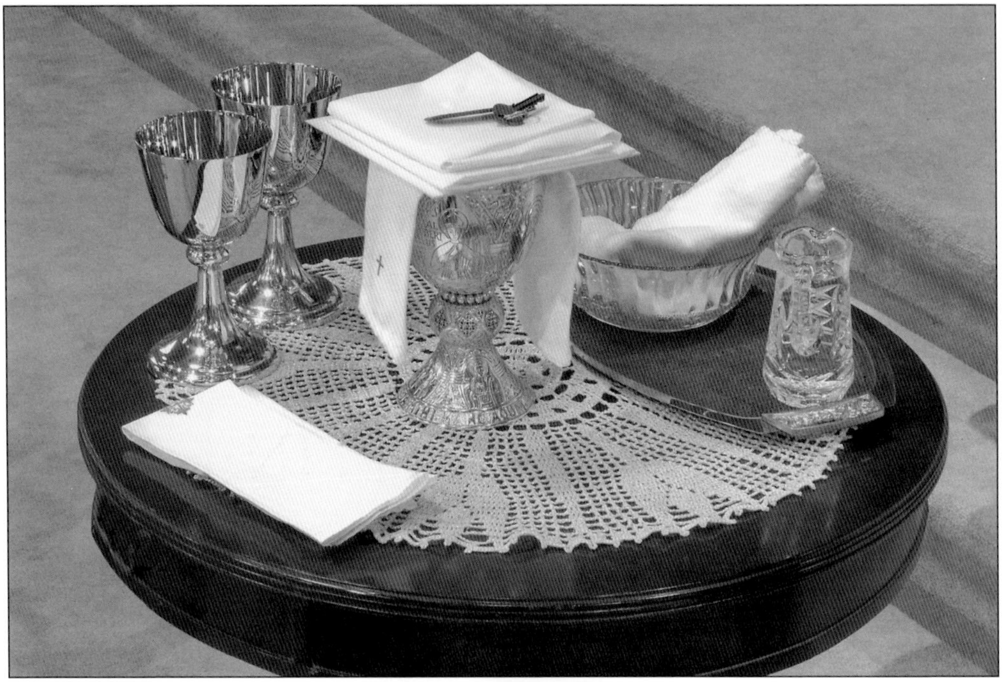

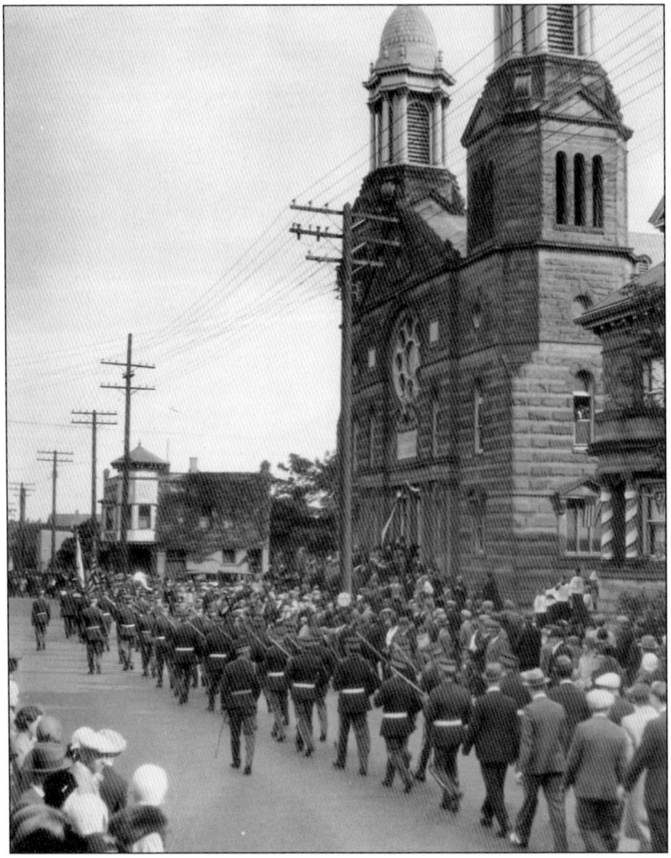

On a Sunday morning, Sr. Annette meticulously sets out the Mass vessels. She served as administrator of St. Procop for its last seven years.

The St. Wenceslas parade passes St. Procop Church on September 30, 1930. (Cleveland State University, *Cleveland Press* photograph.)

Seven

St. Wendelin

Rev. Joseph Koudelka, the pastor of St. Michael Church on Scranton Road, first approached Bishop Ignatius Horstmann about the possibility of establishing a parish to serve the needs of the Slovak community. Horstmann recognized the language difficulties this community faced and the parishioners' desire to continue their ethnic traditions. On May 3, 1903, a group of parishioners received the bishop's approval to found a new parish. This new parish was given the name St. Wendelin. The next step was to find a location for the new church. Property along Columbus Road near West Twenty-Fifth Street had become available; it consisted of two lots measuring 120 feet by 330 feet. On the property stood a brick building, which was purchased for $6,500. The front part of the building was remodeled into a parish house, and the rear of the building was transformed into a two-room school. On one side of the property was the Phoenix Brewery, and on the other stood a tavern.

The parish founders took bids and made decisions about the construction of the new church. During the summer and fall of 1903, a new wooden frame church and convent were constructed. The church was built and furnished for just over $14,000. The Pearl Street Bank loaned the parish $11,000 to help cover the costs of construction. On Sunday, December 6, 1903, the first Mass was held in the new St. Wendelin Church. Father Koudelka was the celebrant as the community gave thanks to God for this new place of worship. The collection at that first Mass totaled $90.17. The Christmas collection tallied $344.47, and the parish income for that first year totaled $7,560.

By 1924, however, due to rapid expansion of the congregation, a new school and church had to be built. Architect William Jenson designed the new church, and the project was completed in late 1925 at 2281 Columbus Road. In 1942, improvements were made, and the present stained-glass windows were installed.

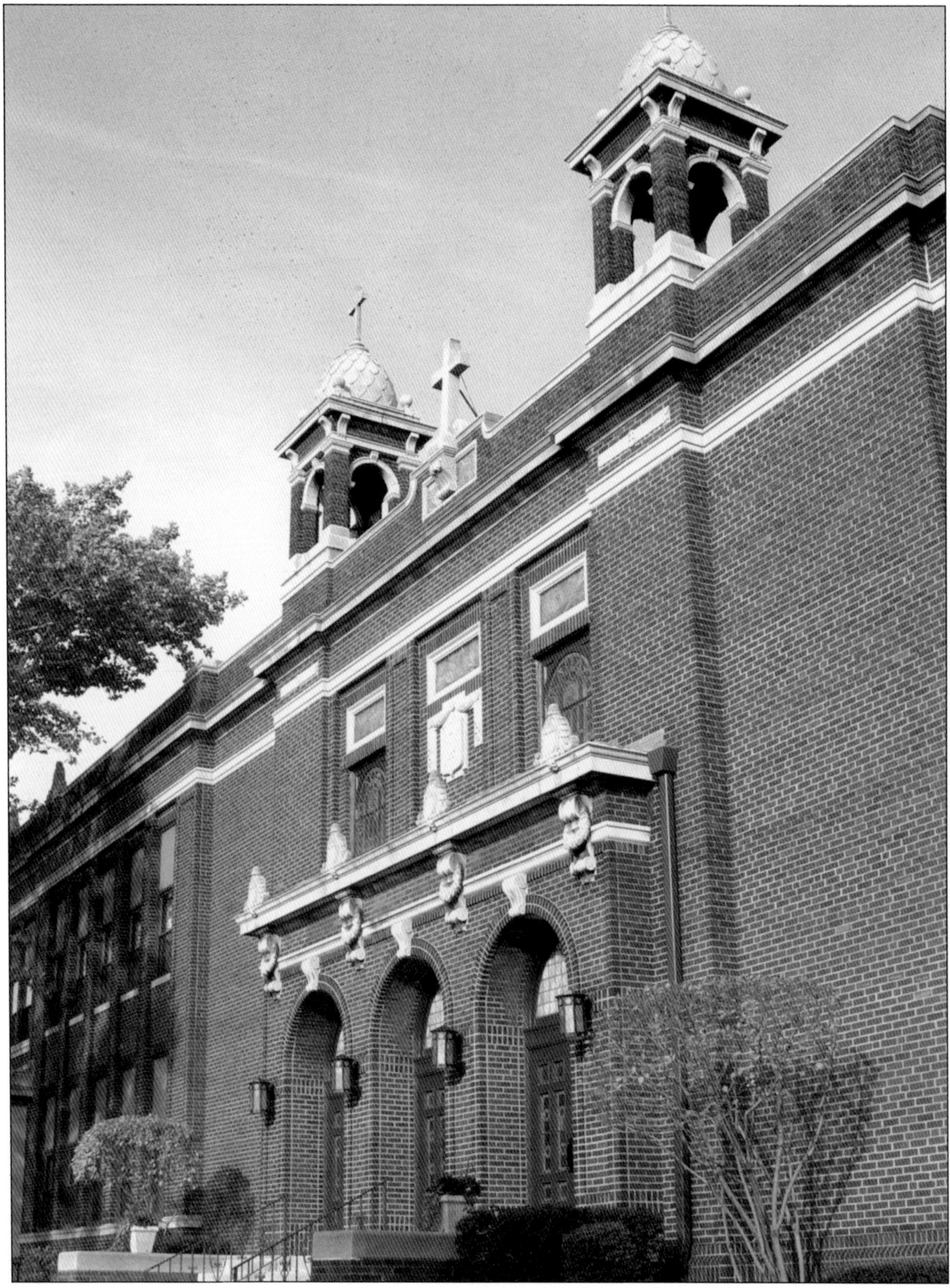

The facade of St. Wendelin presents a well-maintained and stately appearance. The church and school are both in one building. Over the years, it has become a neighborhood landmark.

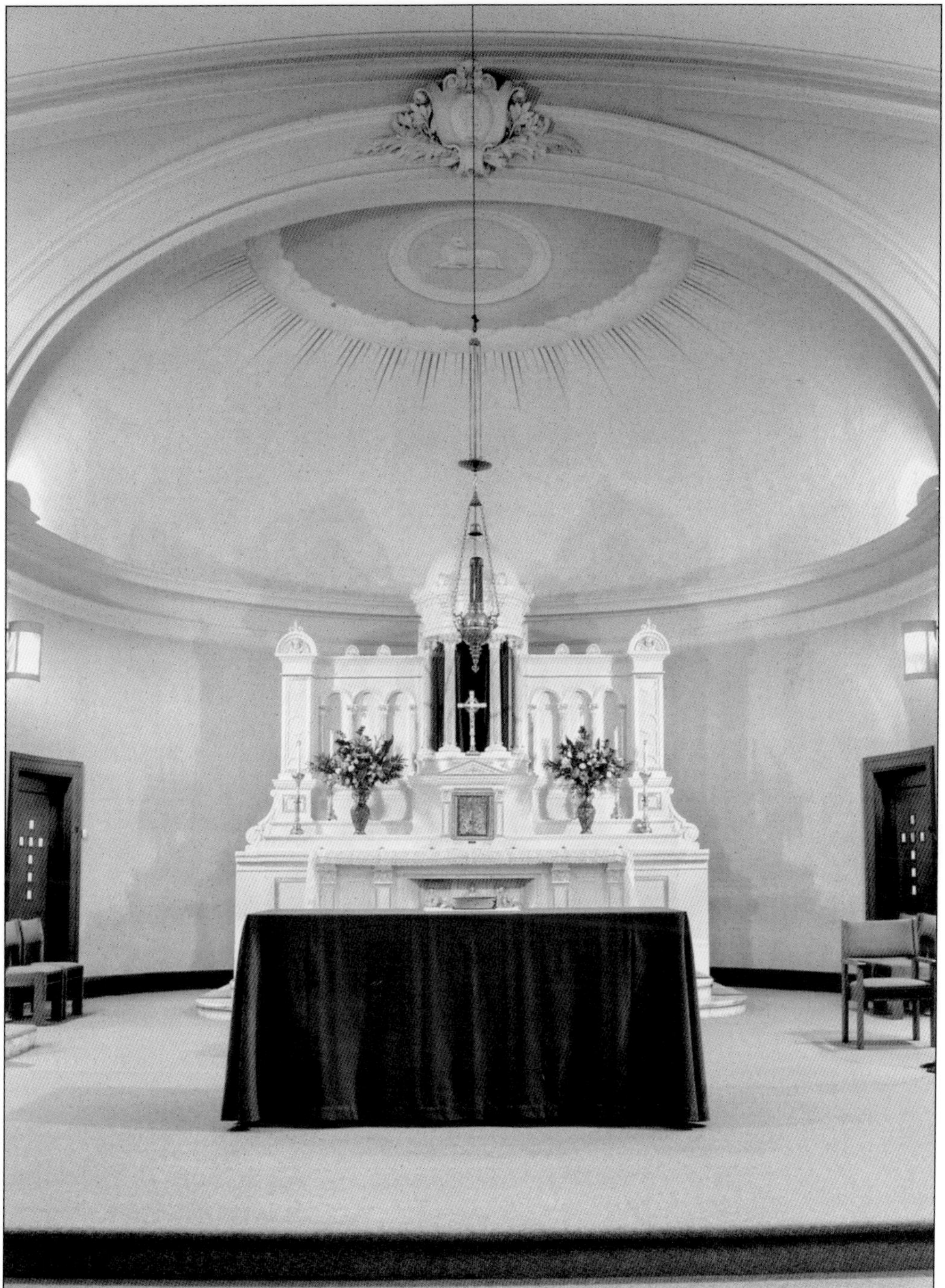

Inside the church, the low altar is situated fairly close to its predecessor, and the brilliant white high altar is below a shallow dome bearing the symbol of the Agnes Dei. The apse is delineated by both horizontal and vertical curves made up of a wide molding and a rounded arch, respectively.

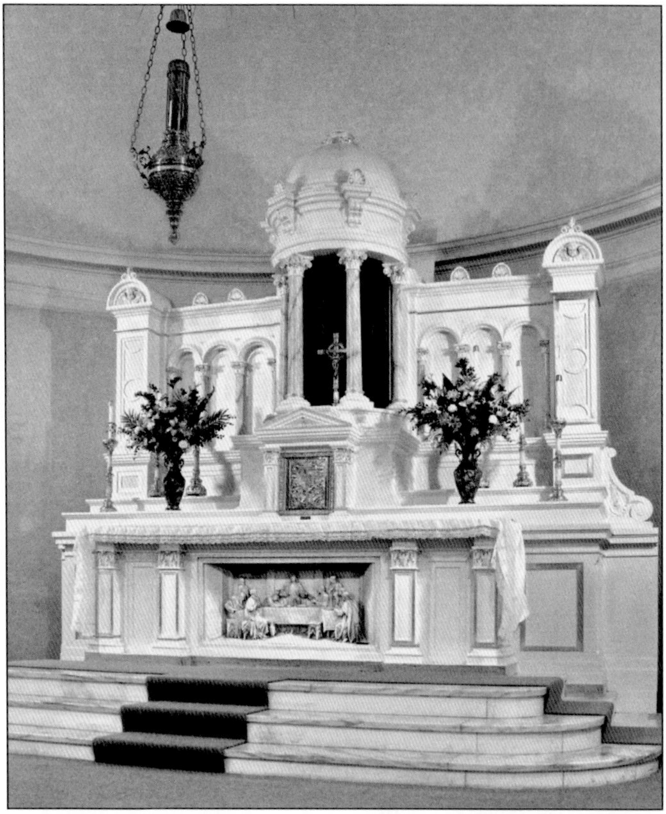

The delicately textured white altar has a somewhat classical theme with small pillars between the rounded arches and larger pillars beneath the rounded crown—in keeping with the Romanesque style.

At the center of the altar is the tabernacle, housed in a classical temple with implied pillars, caps, and pediment above.

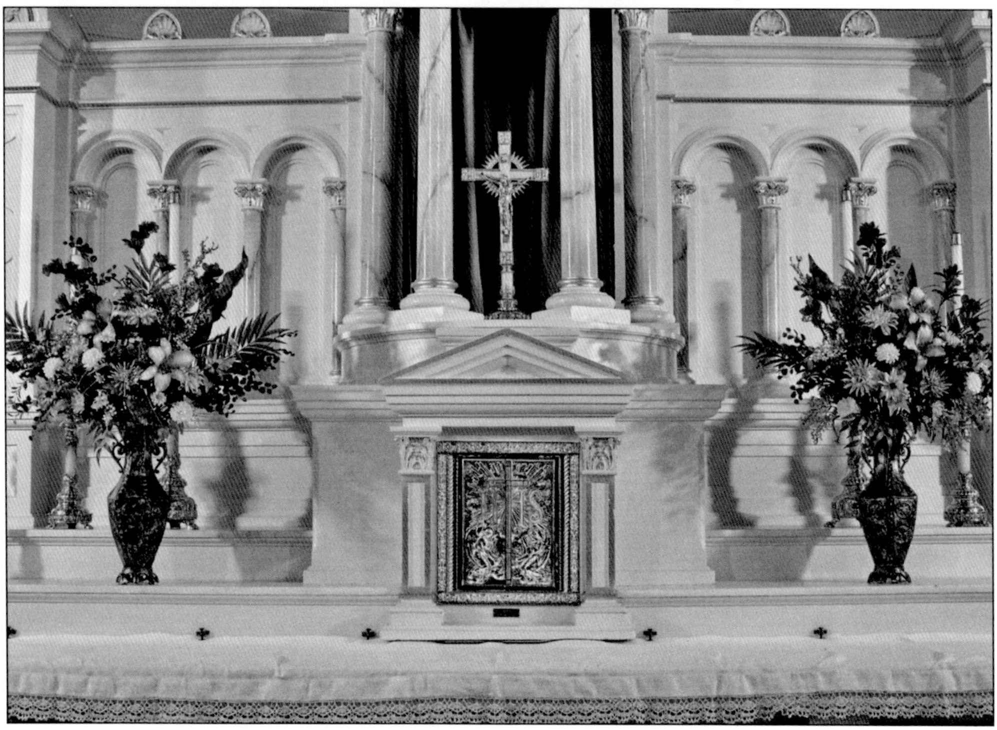

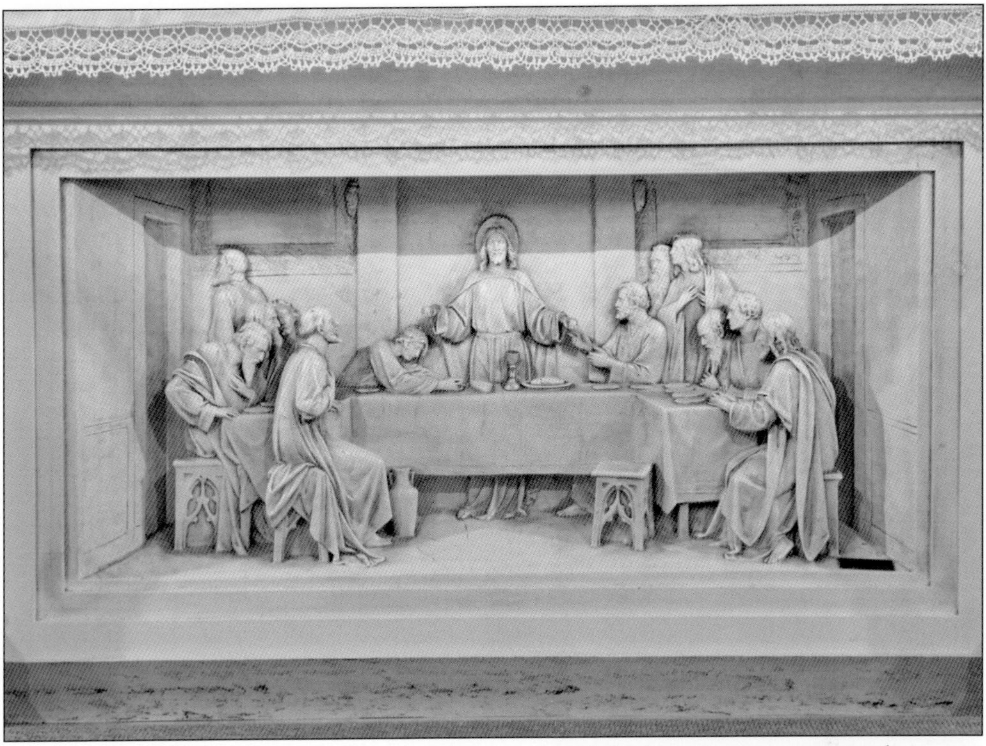

As with many altars of the period, a detailed carving of the Last Supper occupies the center panel of the altar.

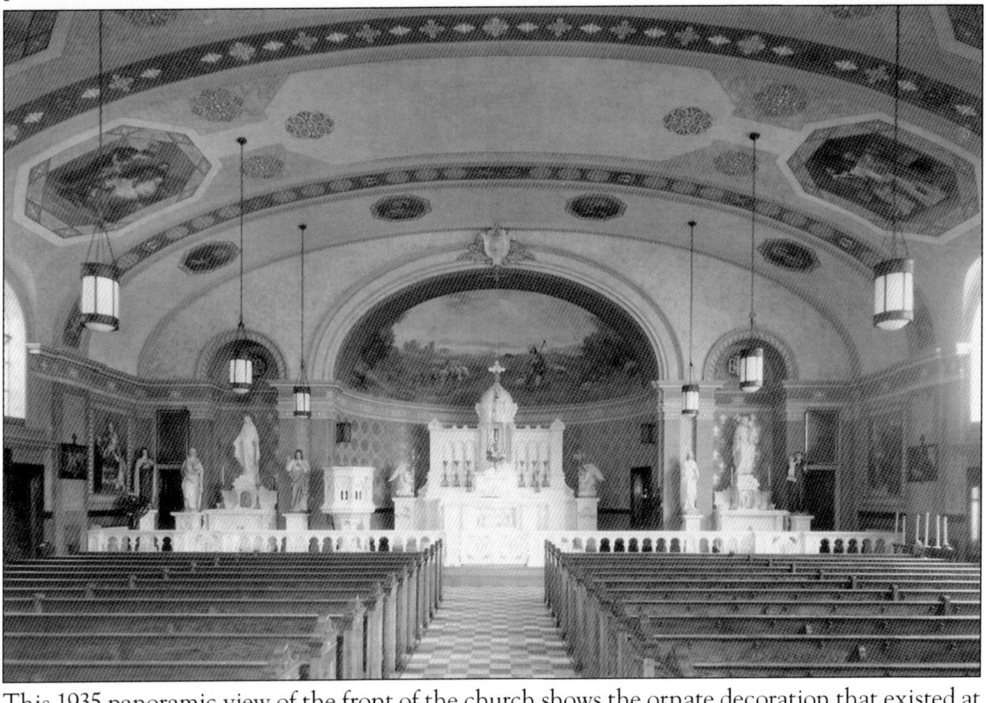

This 1935 panoramic view of the front of the church shows the ornate decoration that existed at the time. (Cleveland State University, *Cleveland Press* photograph.)

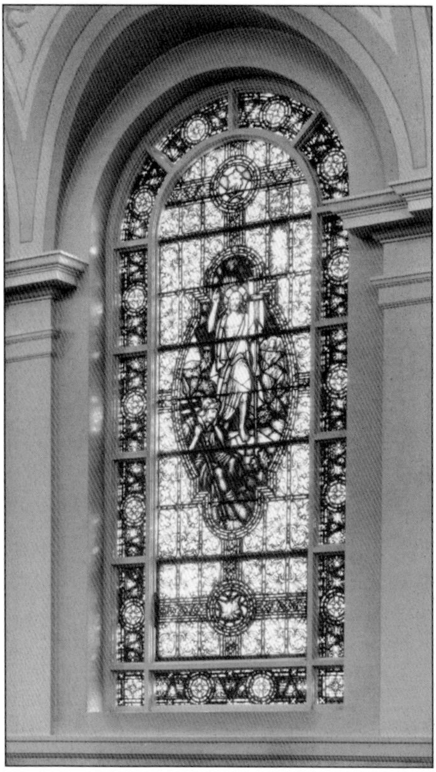

The exceptionally ornate stained glass at St. Wendelin was installed in 1942 and replaced the old factory-like windows. The cost of each of the new windows was $700.

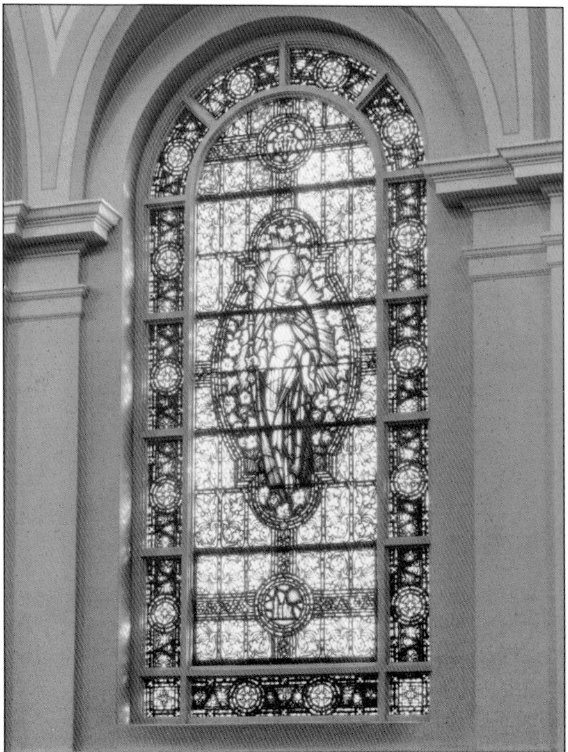

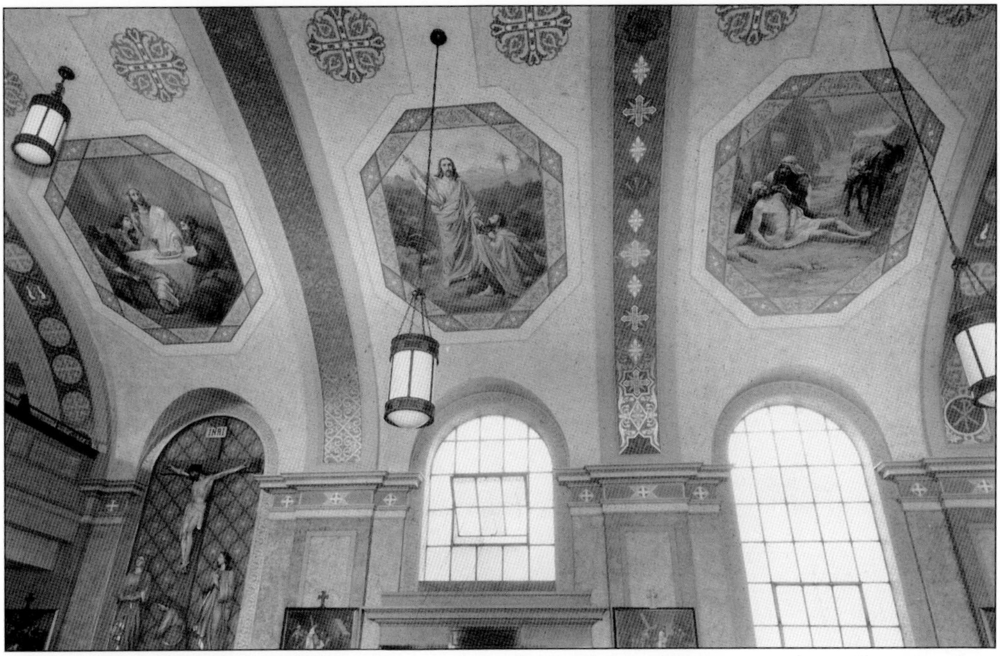

Prior to 1942, the church had plain-glass windows, but it also had frescoes on the walls and ceiling that are not there today. These two plates show some of the ceiling frescoes depicting events from the life of Christ. (Cleveland State University, *Cleveland Press* photograph.)

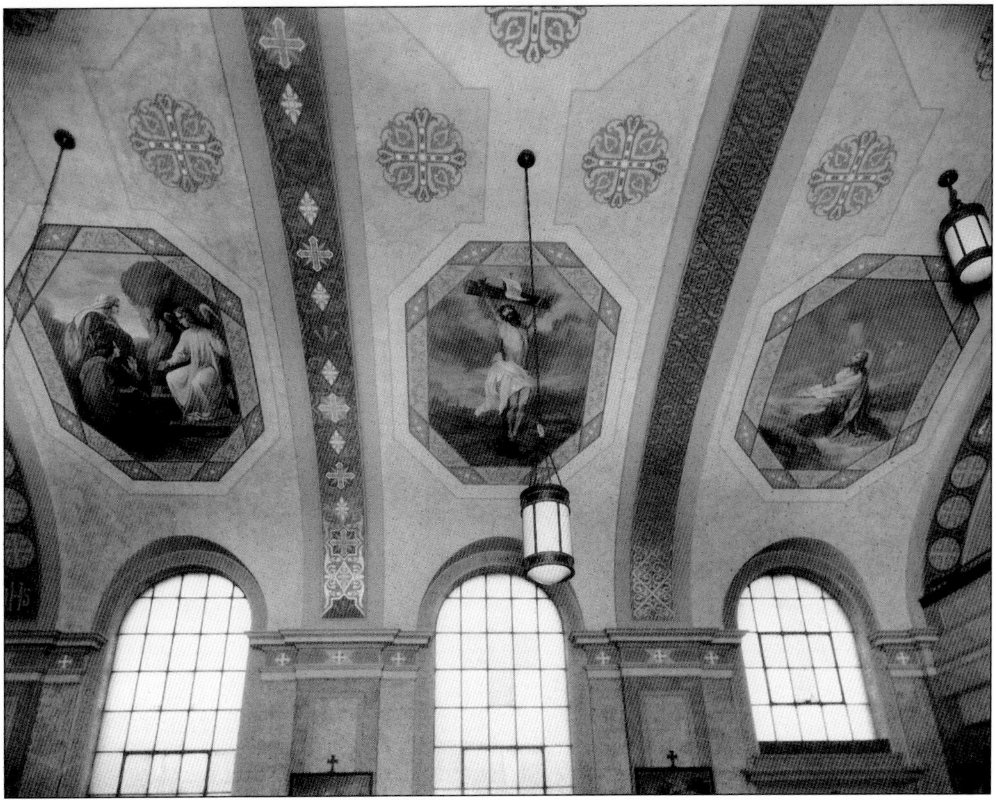

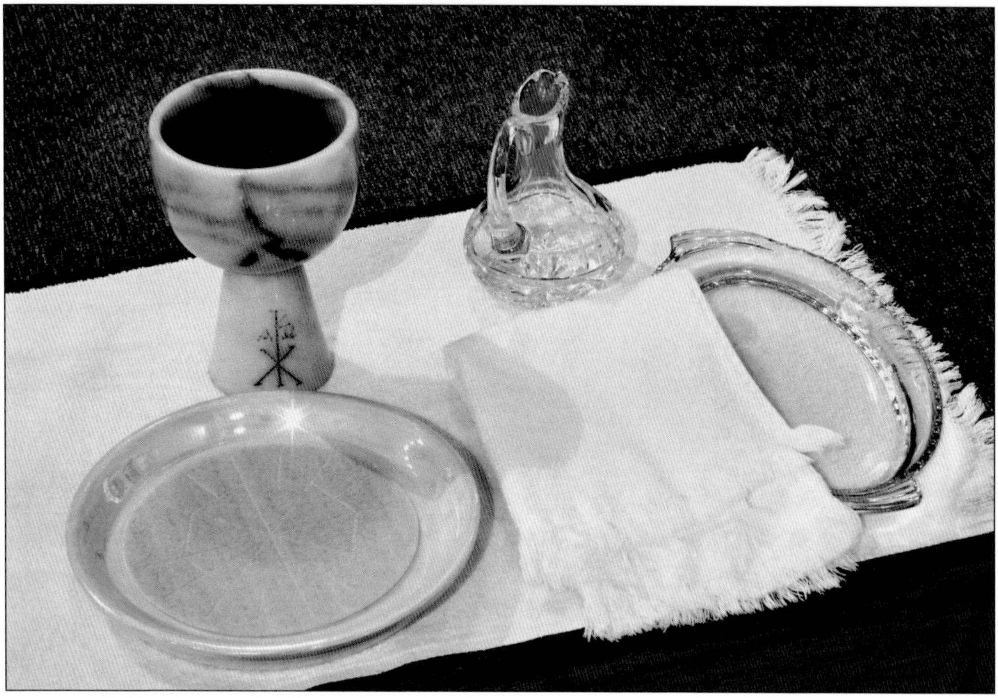

Next to the low altar is a table with the unconsecrated host, the chalice, and the vessels for the next day's Mass.

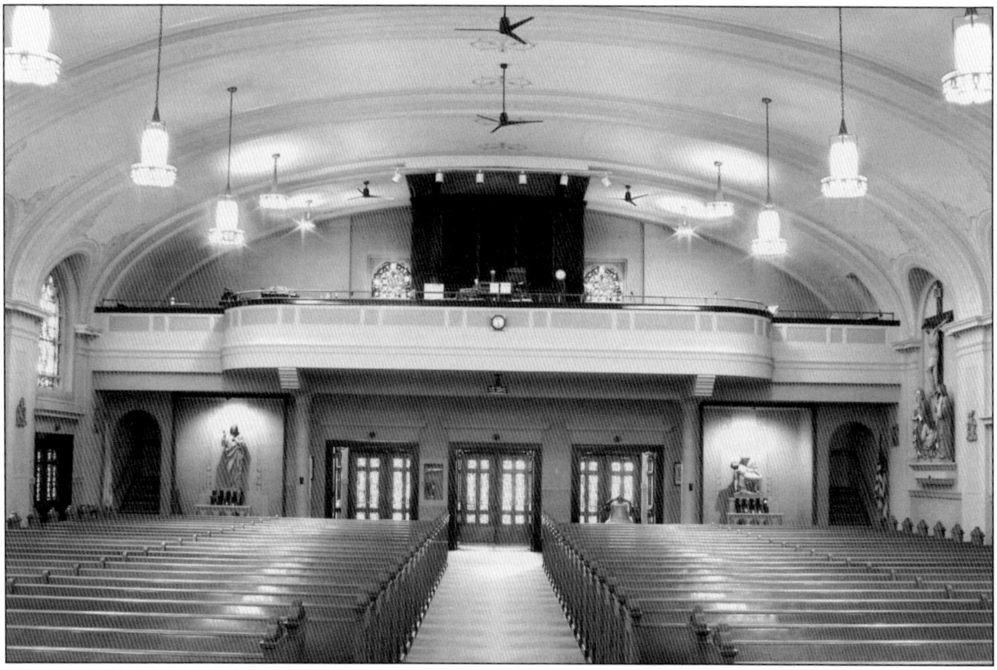

The nave of the church, as seen from the altar, has wide, elliptical arches with decorations above the windows. In the back of the church, beyond the doors to the right, is a bell that had been removed from the bell tower and repaired in 2002. It is still waiting to be placed in its permanent location.

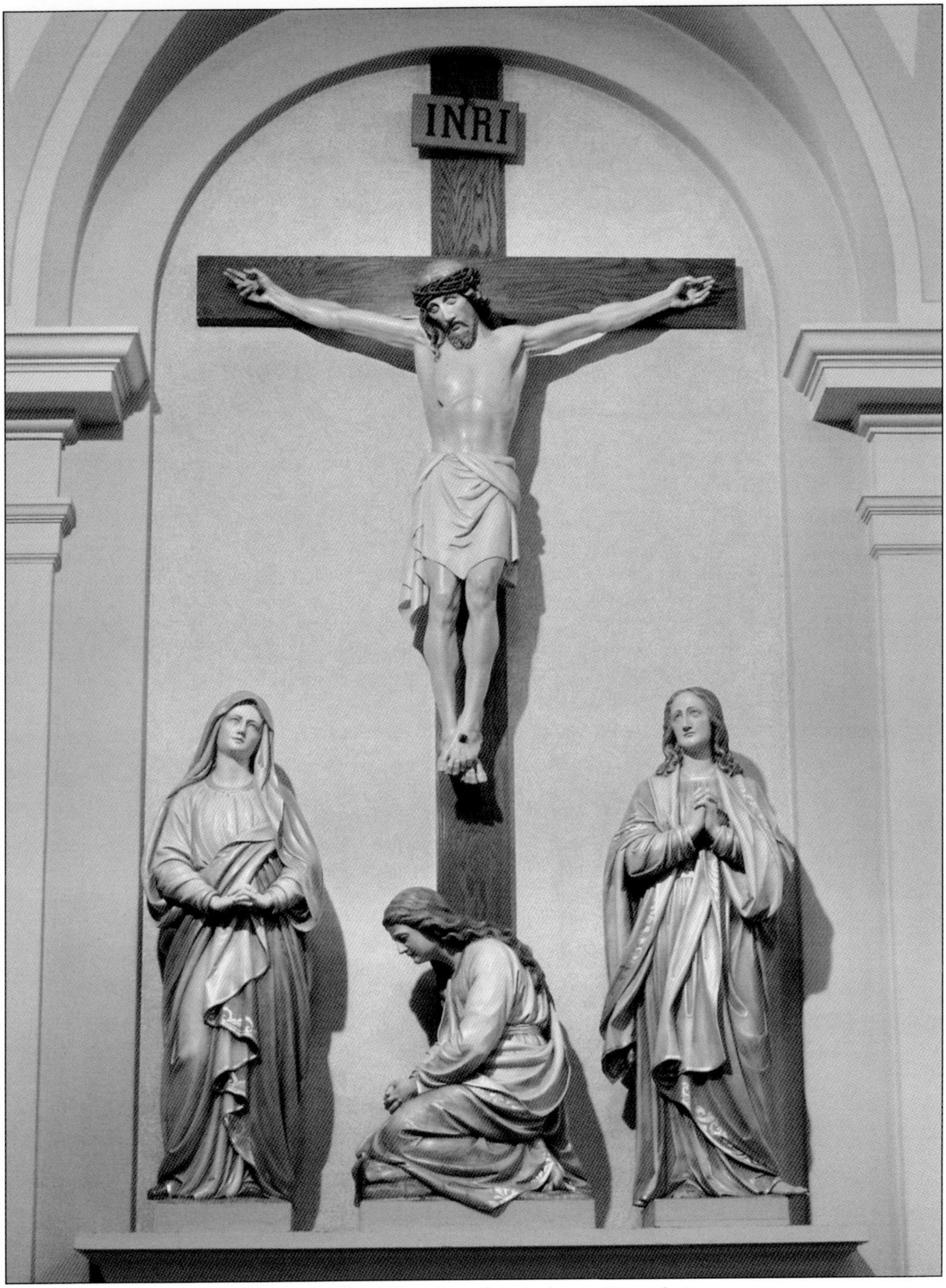

On the north wall, toward the back of the church, is a large Crucifixion scene.

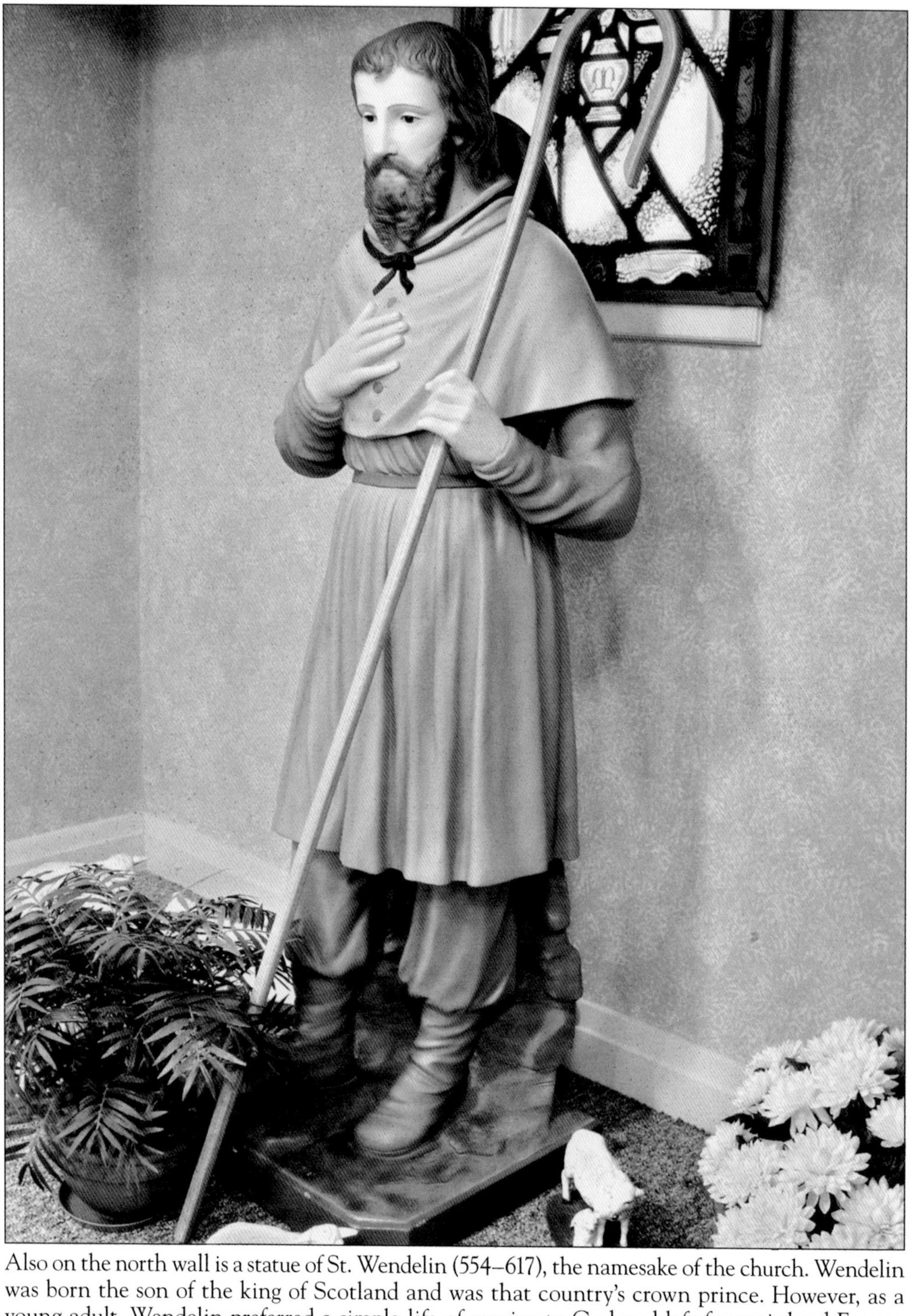

Also on the north wall is a statue of St. Wendelin (554–617), the namesake of the church. Wendelin was born the son of the king of Scotland and was that country's crown prince. However, as a young adult, Wendelin preferred a simple life of service to God and left for mainland Europe without his family's knowledge. He became a Benedictine monk and was ultimately appointed abbot of the monastery at Thopley in Germany. It was only after his death that his family was informed of his whereabouts.

Eight
St. Casimir

One of the most burning desires of the Polish immigrants that settled on the northeast side of Cleveland was to be able to worship God in a Polish American church led by a Polish American priest. Their prayers were answered in 1892 when Bishop Ignatius Horstmann gave his consent for the formation of a new church. Initiating the project was a Czech priest, Fr. Peter Cerveny, who was an assistant pastor at another parish. Under his leadership, a small group of devoted people overcame adversity and built the new church called St. Casimir.

By 1912, the young church/school had already become too small, and a new church was planned at 8223 Sowinski Avenue. In 1921, it was essentially finished. The architect on the project was William Jansen, whose building measured 155 feet by 64 feet and could seat 1,200 parishioners. Two stately square bell towers with octagonal crowns dominate the exterior of the brick church. The three rounded arches over the porticos belie the Romanesque style found within.

(Authors' note: St. Casimir is a church of unusual aesthetic and artistic value and is deserving of an extensive photographic study. Unfortunately, even though the pastor of St. Casimir gave his permission and blessing to do this study, circumstances prevented its completion. Consequently, the limited number of pictures that follow do not do this fine church the justice it deserves.)

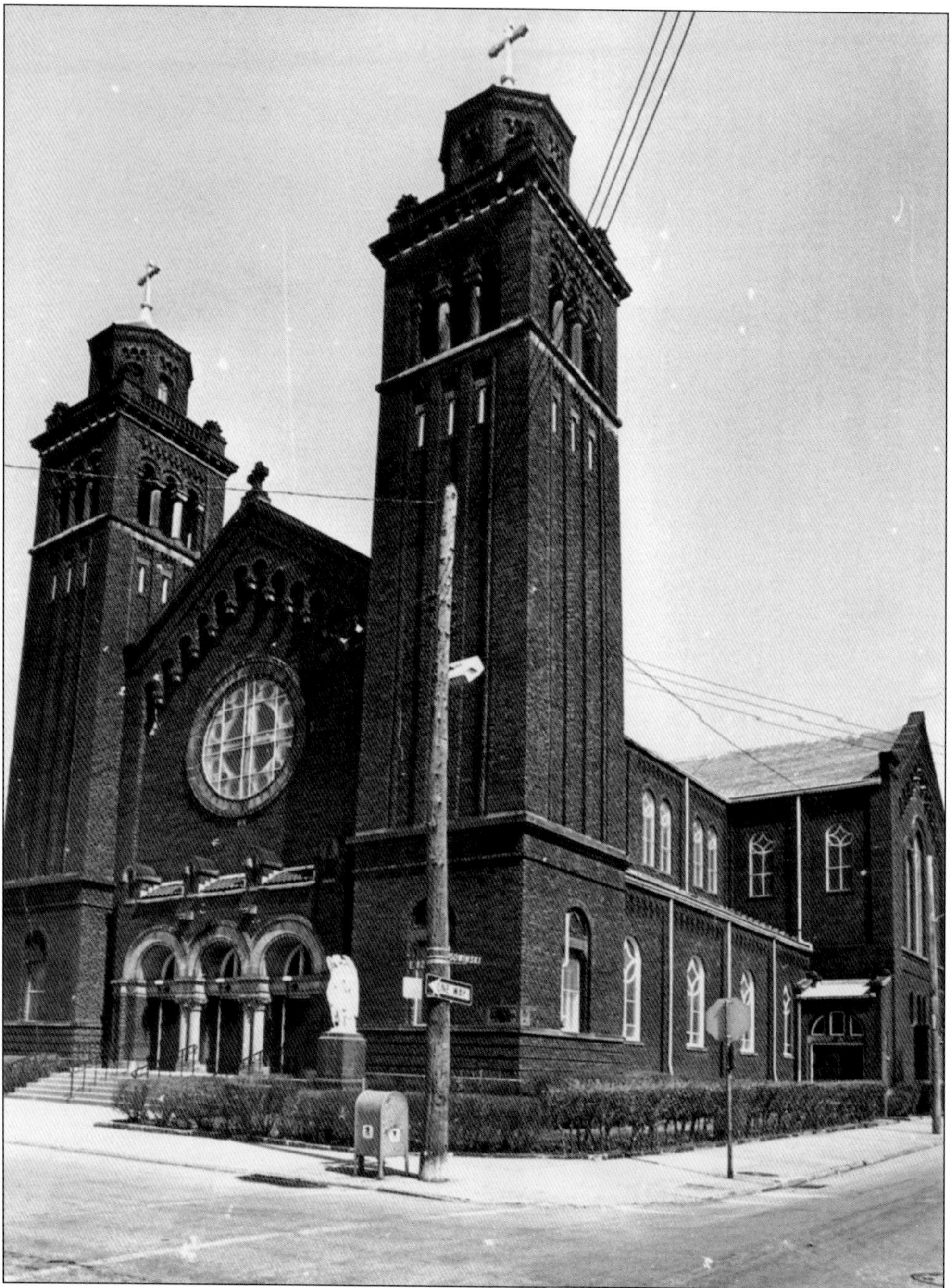

The stately St. Casimir Church towers over the corner of East Eighty-Second Street and Sowinski Avenue. (Cleveland State University, *Cleveland Press* photograph.)

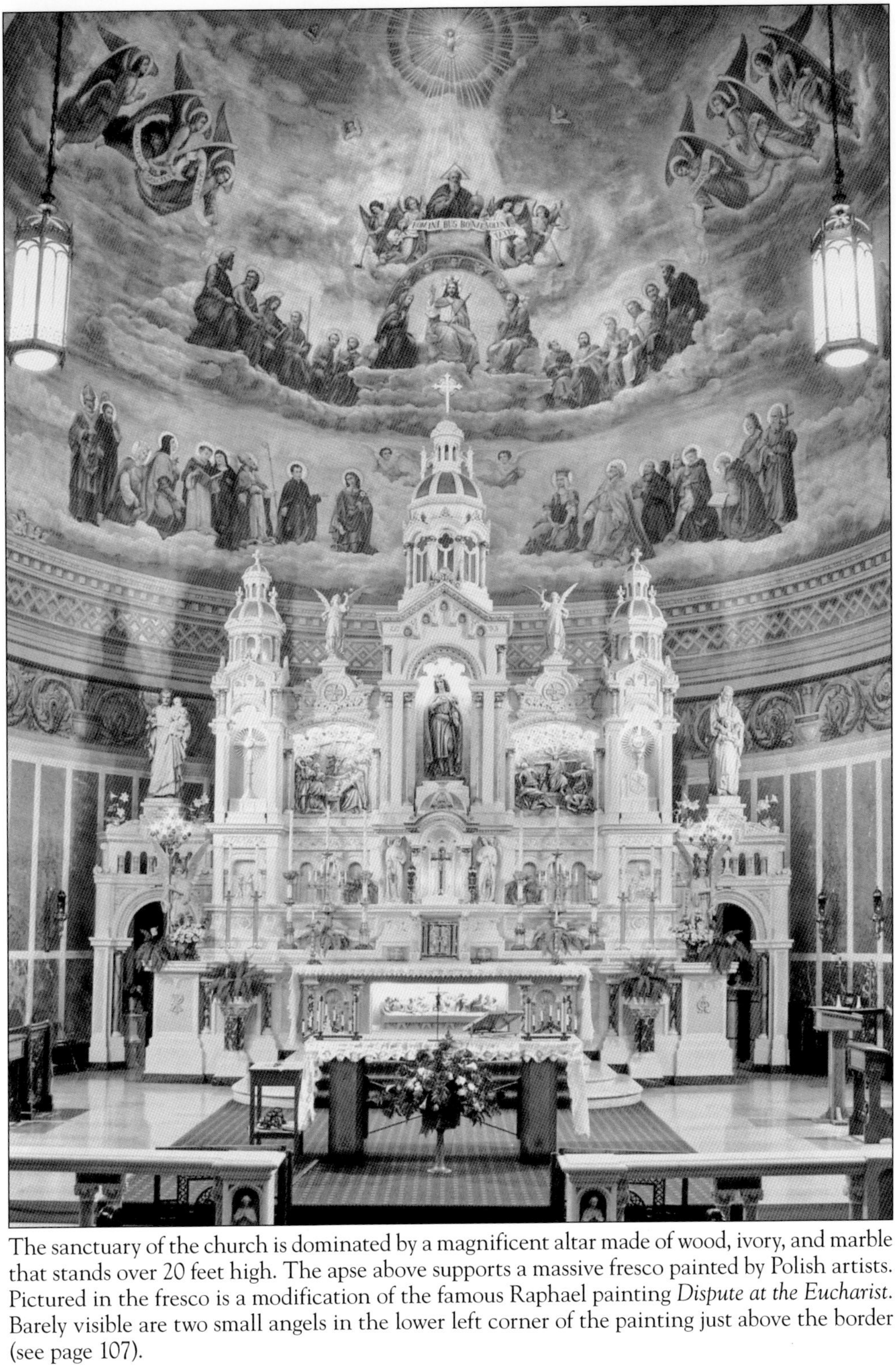

The sanctuary of the church is dominated by a magnificent altar made of wood, ivory, and marble that stands over 20 feet high. The apse above supports a massive fresco painted by Polish artists. Pictured in the fresco is a modification of the famous Raphael painting *Dispute at the Eucharist*. Barely visible are two small angels in the lower left corner of the painting just above the border (see page 107).

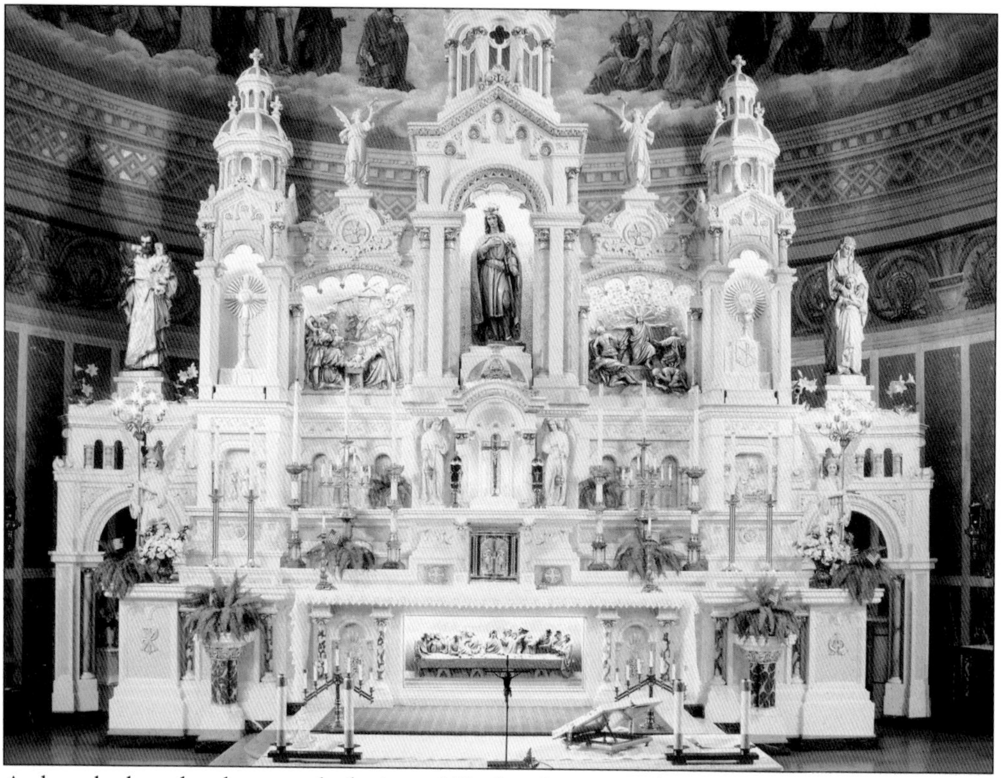

A closer look at the altar reveals the incredible detail contained in it. Featured in the center is a statue of St. Casimir (1458–1484), whose father was both king of Poland and the grand duke of Lithuania. His mother was Queen Elizabeth of Austria. When his father went to Lithuania for an extended period, Casimir became the king of Poland. St. Casimir is the patron saint of both Poland and Lithuania.

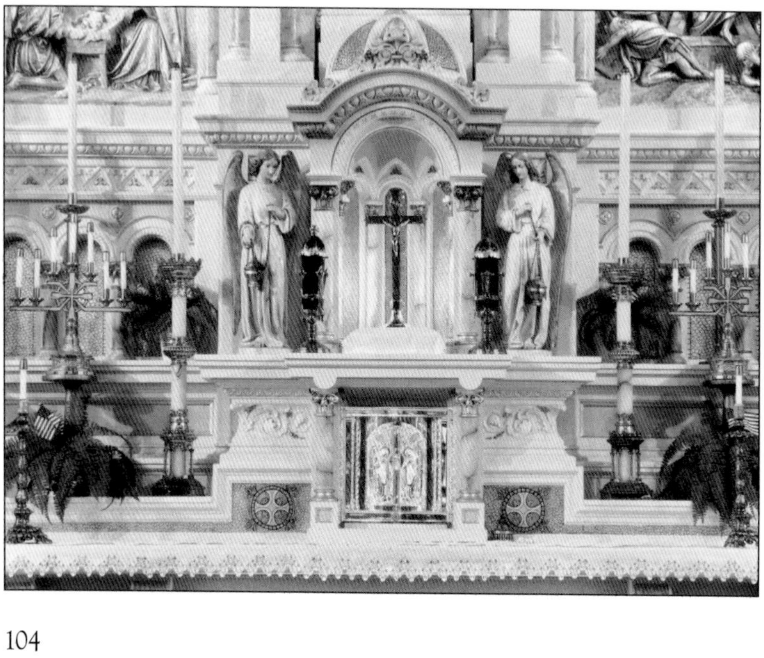

Look closely at the altar and more detail is revealed. Note the intricate mosaic above the crucifix, inside the arches, and next to the tabernacle.

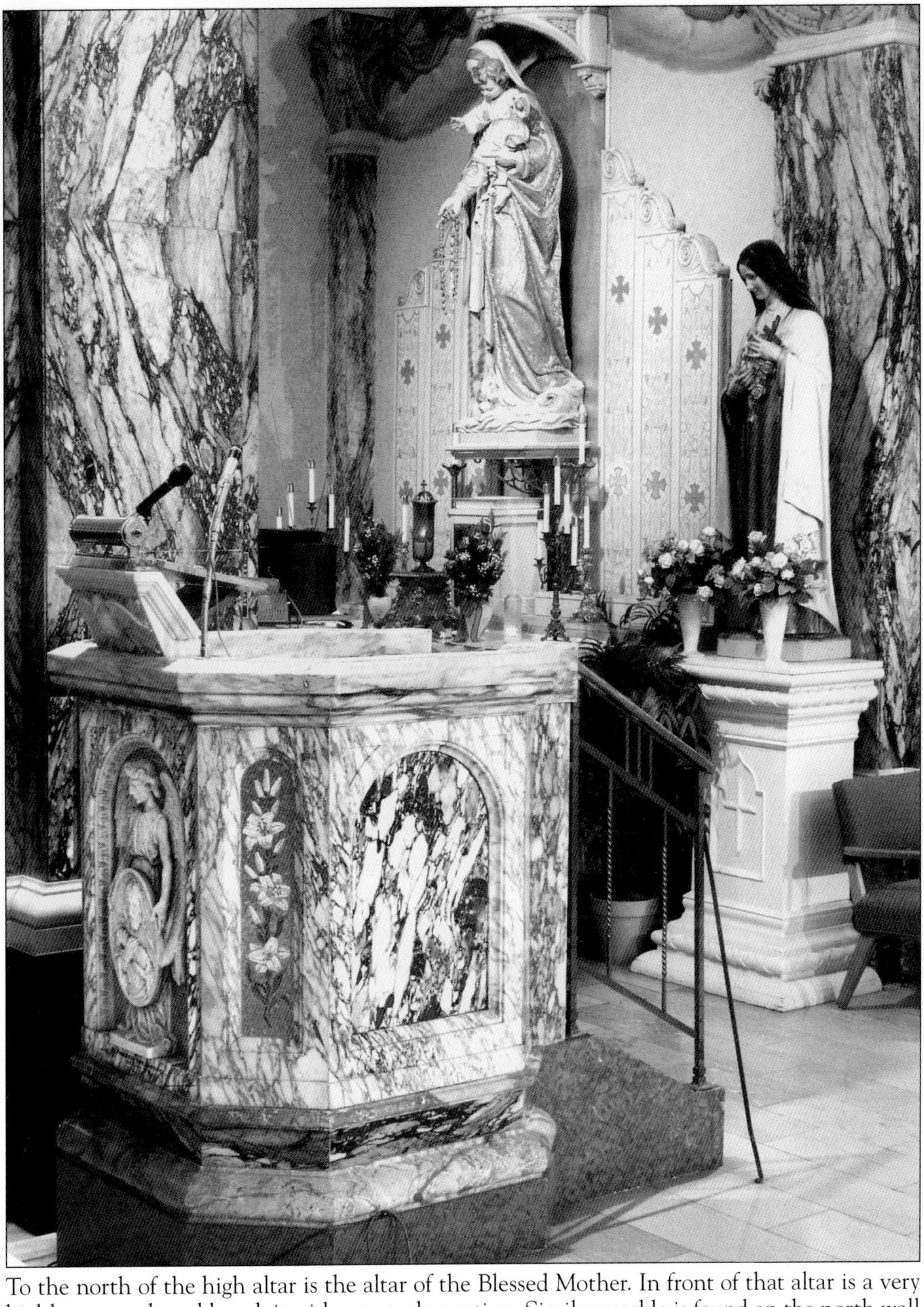

To the north of the high altar is the altar of the Blessed Mother. In front of that altar is a very highly textured marble pulpit with ornate decoration. Similar marble is found on the north wall itself, behind the statue of St. Therese, and in a square column in the corner next to the altar.

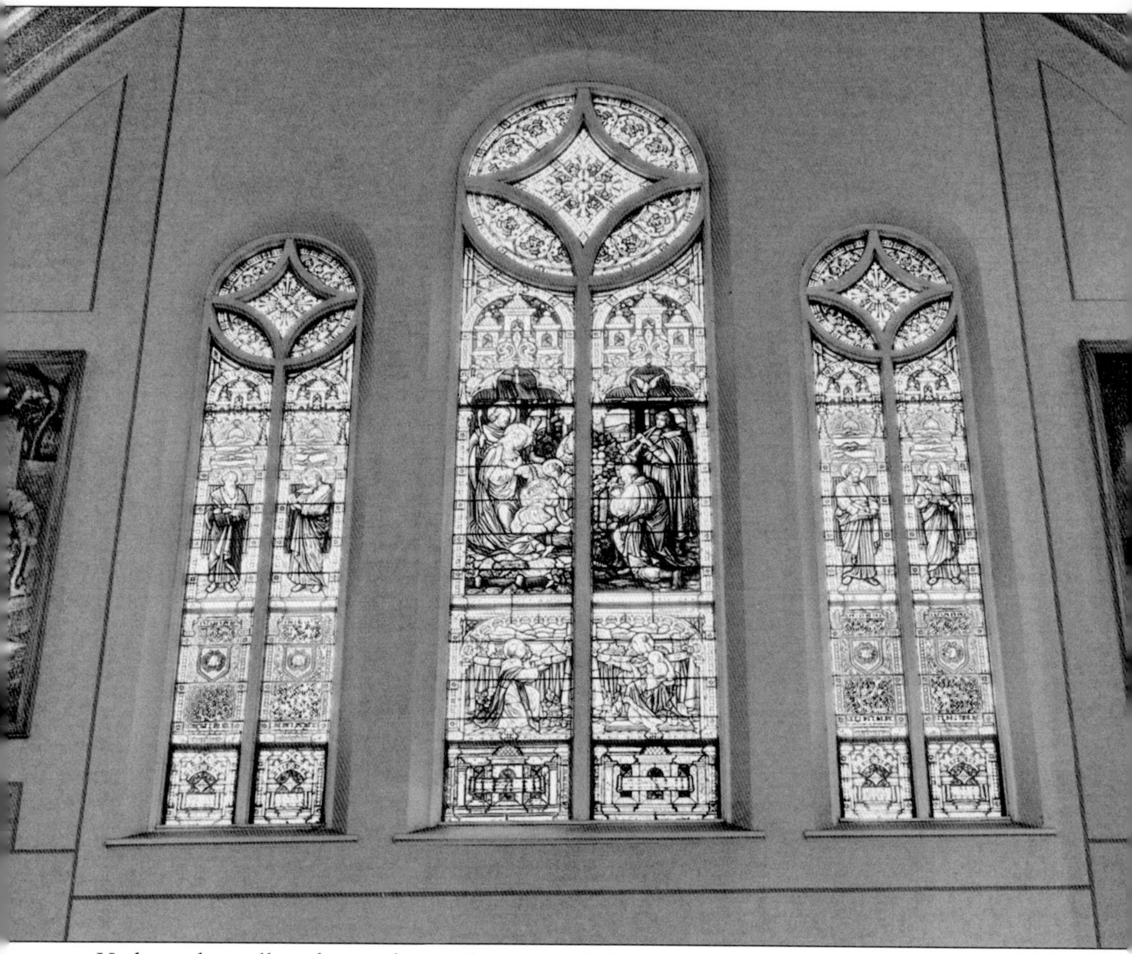

High on the wall in the north cruciform area of the church is one of the arrays of stained glass; this one depicting the Nativity.

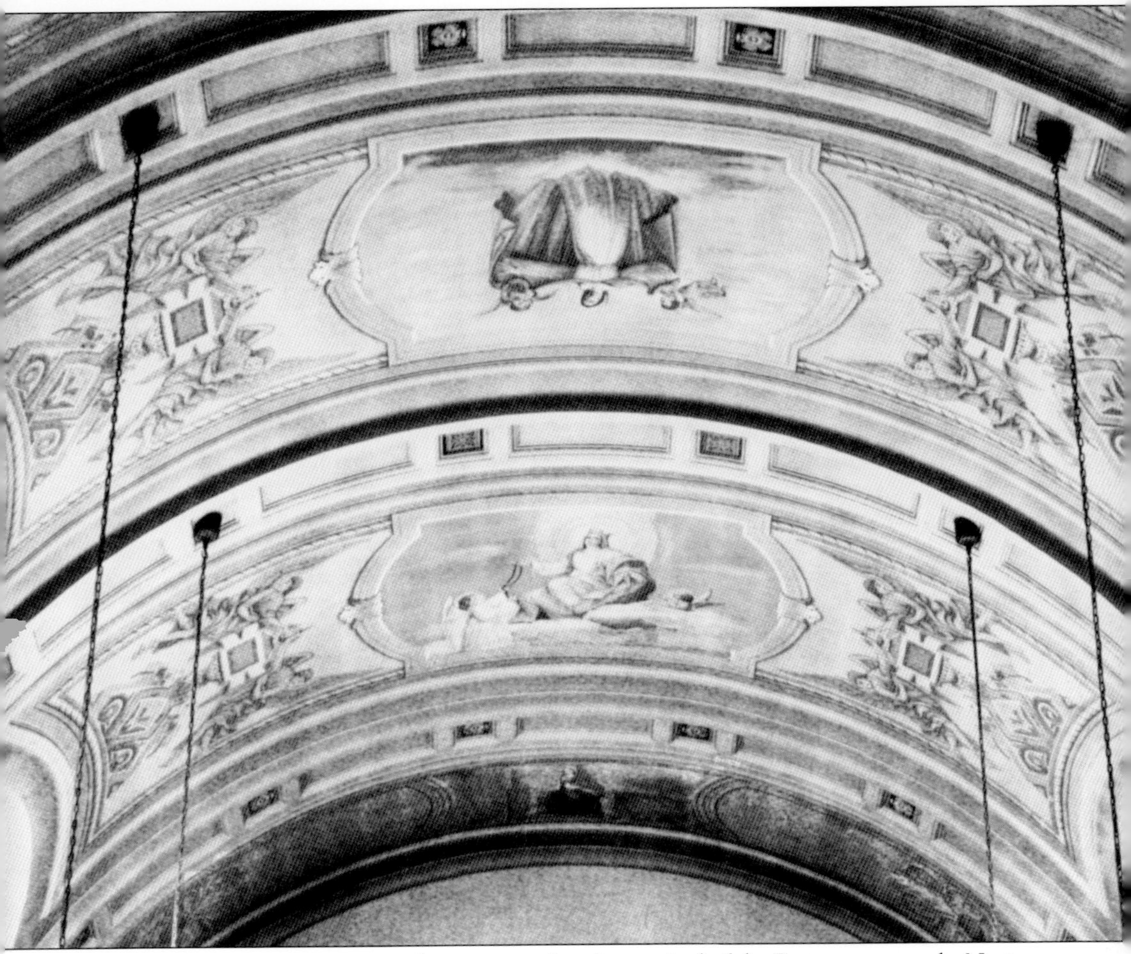

The ceiling of St. Casimir possesses the curves and arches typical of the Romanesque style. Notice how the frescoes were painted in alternating directions.

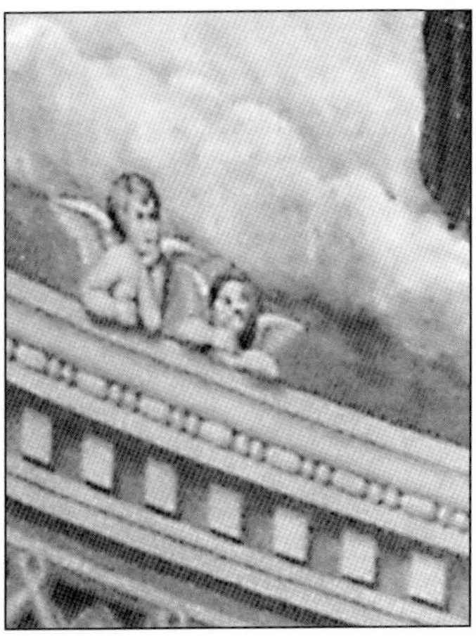

As the story goes, while the fresco on the apse was being made, two young children watched the entire process. Impressed by the children's continued interest, the painter included them in the fresco as two young angels watching from the far left side of the scene.

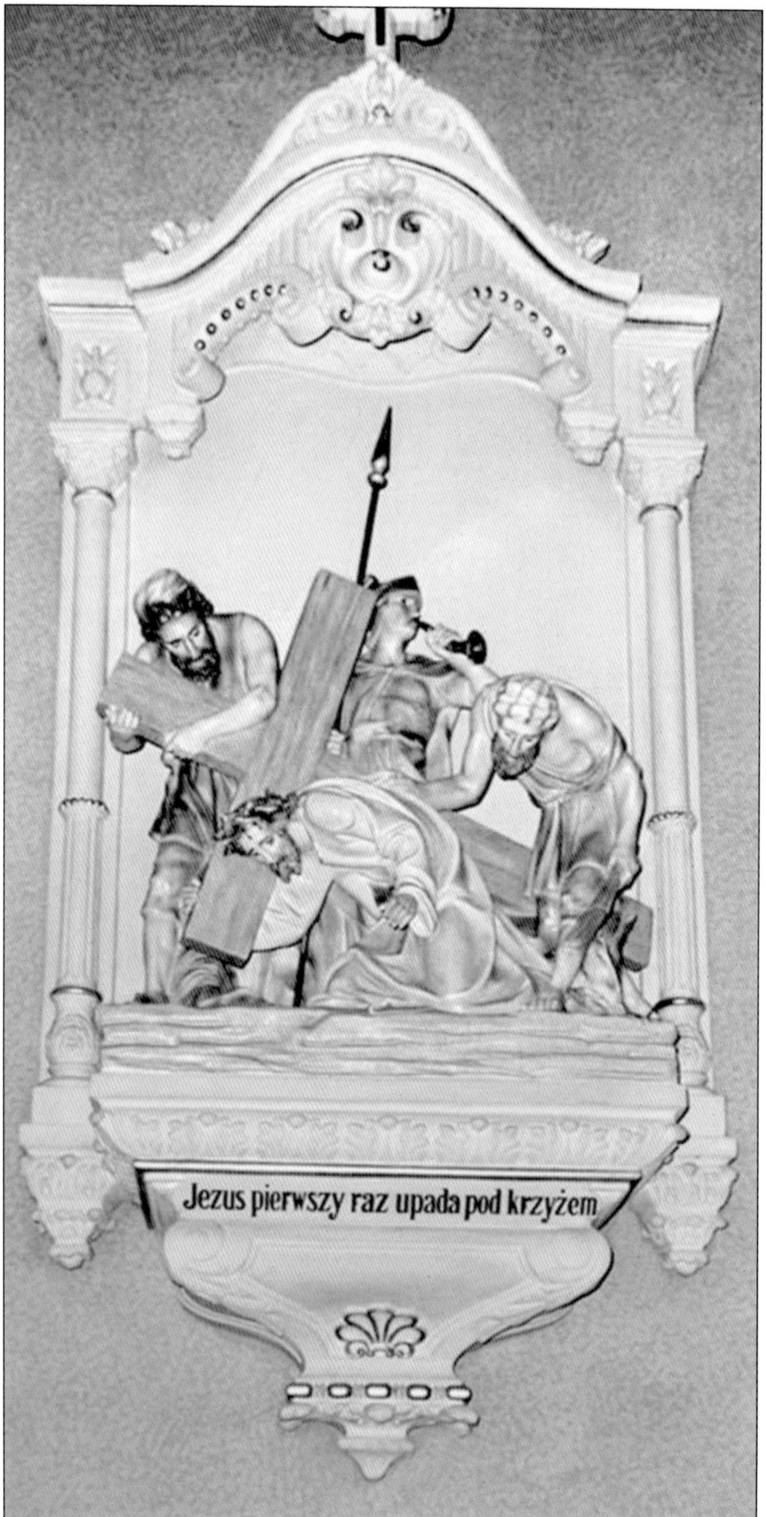

One of the Stations of the Cross is pictured here. Its Polish inscription translates as "Jesus falls for the first time."

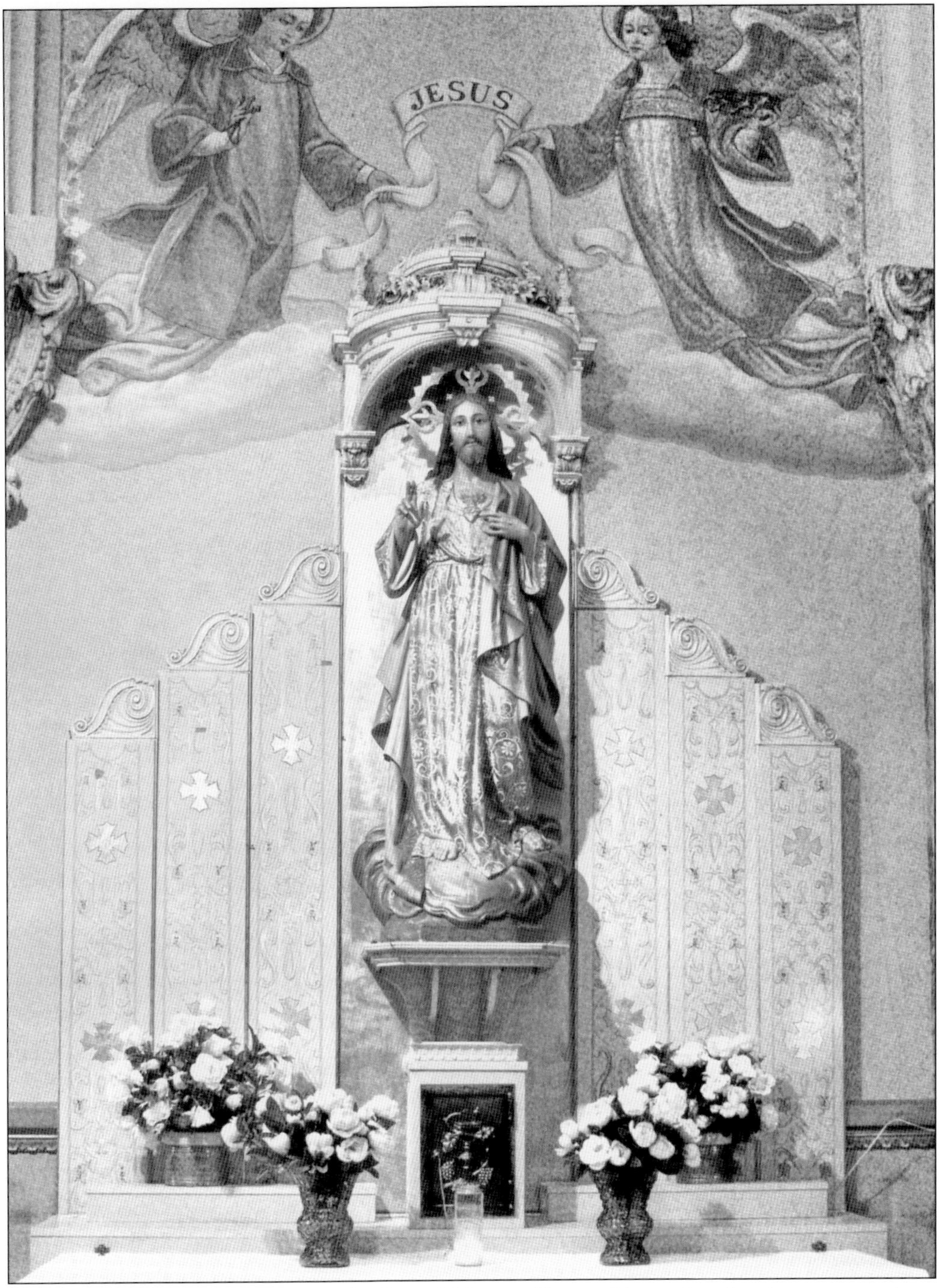

To the south of the main altar is the Sacred Heart of Jesus. Above the altar is an ornate icon screen; a fresco is above that.

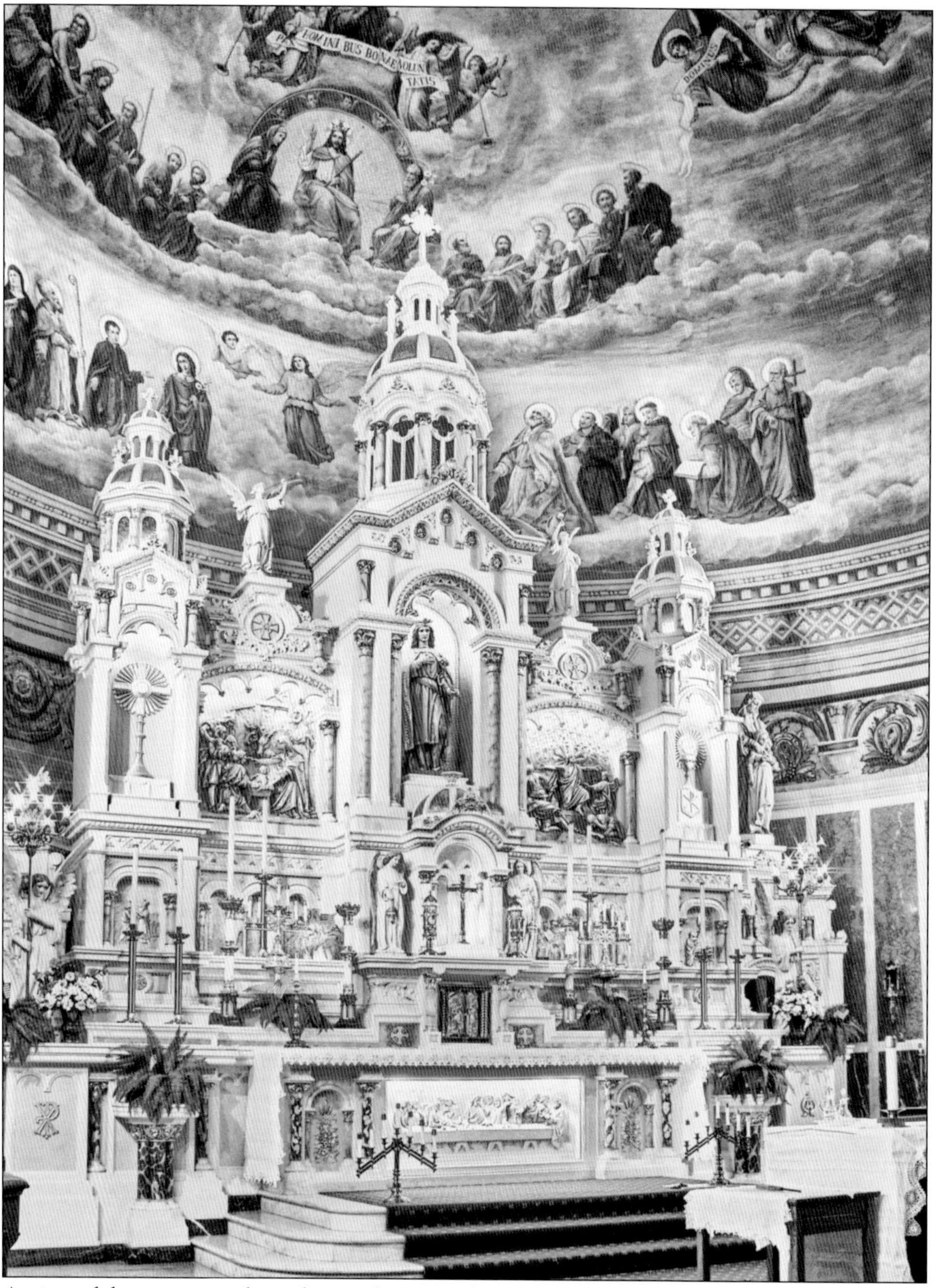

A view of the sanctuary from the north corner shows the magnificent altar below the fresco of the celestial scene conceived by Raphael.

Nine

St. Mary of the Immaculate Conception

In 1905, Bishop Ignatius Horstmann sent Fr. John Carroll, pastor of Holy Name Parish, to administer to the residents of the farmlands in the far southeast corner of the city. The Bedford area was designated as a mission to Holy Name. Soon Sunday Mass was celebrated at the old town hall on Bedford Square, which was rented by the diocese for $1. By 1910, a church and school were built on Paul Street for a developing, predominantly Hungarian congregation, but this facility still remained a mission under the authority of Holy Name. Finally, in 1921, Fr. John R. Hagan became the first pastor of the new parish of St. Mary. A new school was initiated immediately.

By 1928, a brand-new brick church was built on property at 300 Union Street. Then, in 1951, the church and school were expanded due to overwhelming need. In 1957, the school had to be expanded again. By the late 1960s, even more expansion was again unavoidable. In December of 1968, a new church was planned, and on December 8, 1969, on the Feast of the Immaculate Conception, the first Mass was celebrated at the new church. In its 75-year history, St. Mary became the mother parish to St. Jude (1945), St. Monica (1952), St. Pius X (1952), St. Barnabas (1956), St. Martin of Tours (1960), SS. Cosmas and Damian (1963), Holy Trinity (1965), and Our Lady of Guadalupe (1967).

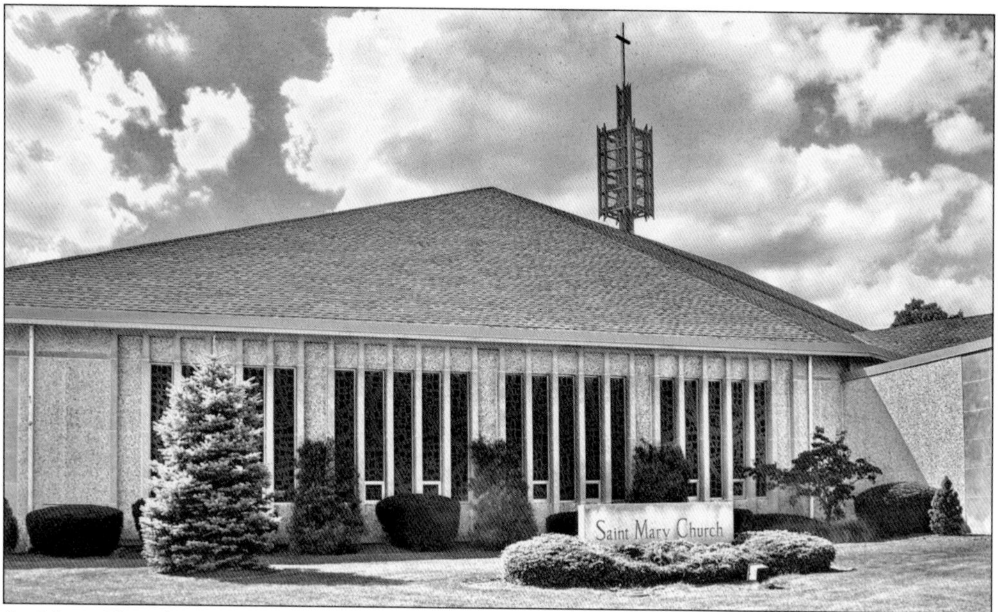

St. Mary Church, unlike traditional designs, presents a low profile that emphasizes width rather than height or length. This view shows only the east facade up to the center entry portal on the right. The actual building extends equally to the west.

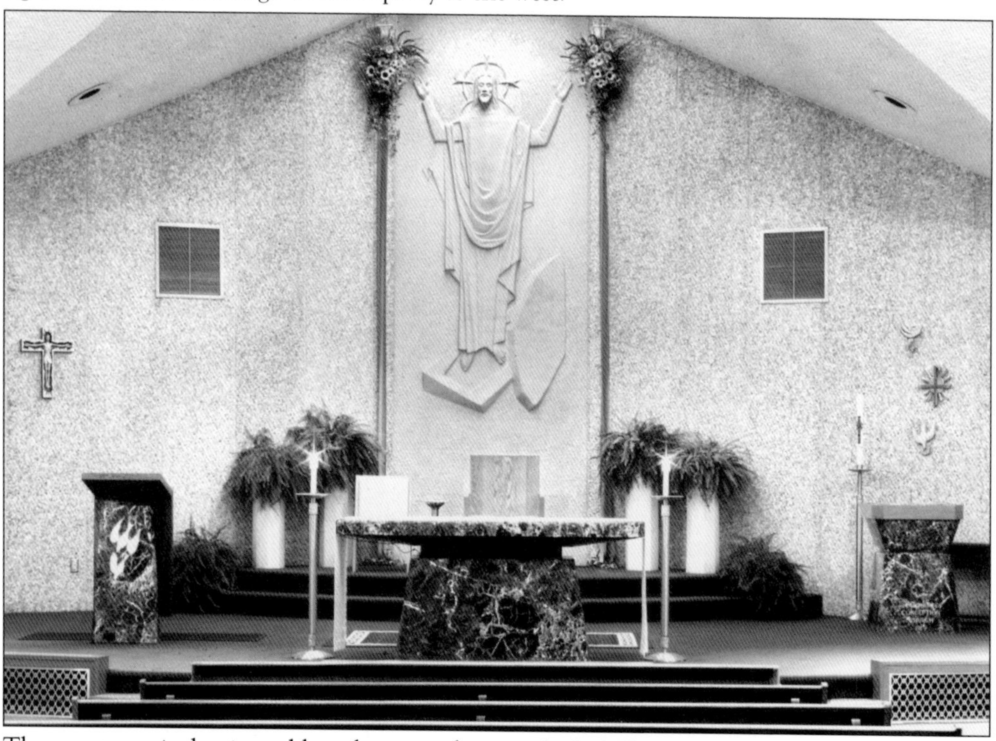
The sanctuary is dominated by a large sandstone relief of Christ extending to the crest of the ceiling just below a skylight. The church was designed to conform to Vatican II; consequently there is no high altar. The rich textures of the black marble altar, lectern, and baptismal enhance the simplicity of the sanctuary.

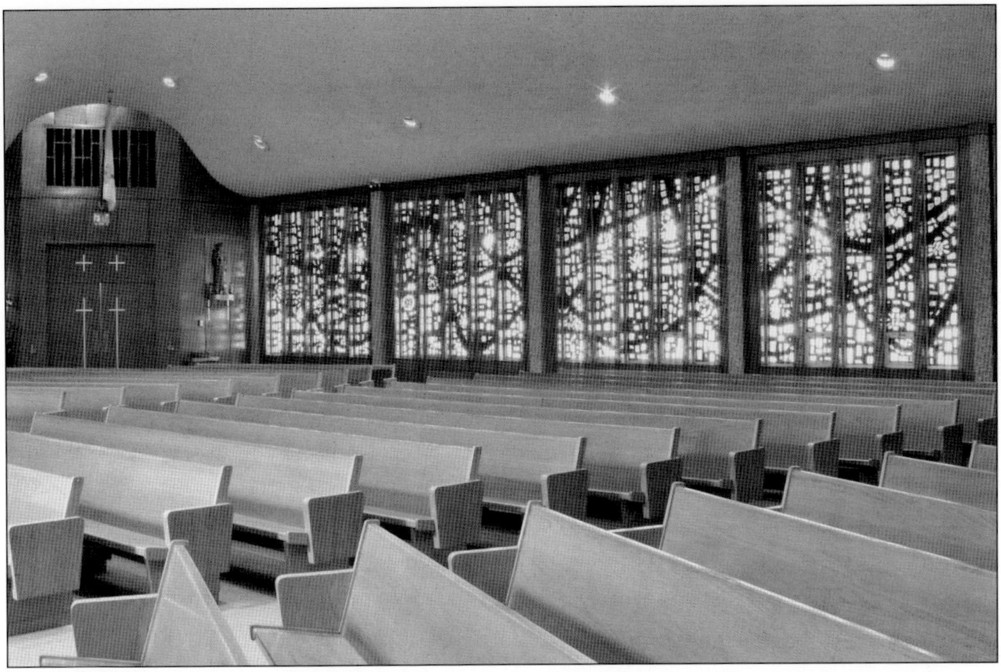

A solid wall of multicolored glass backs the west side of the nave. The right center aisle is in the foreground. There are seven sections of pews forming a semicircular configuration around the altar.

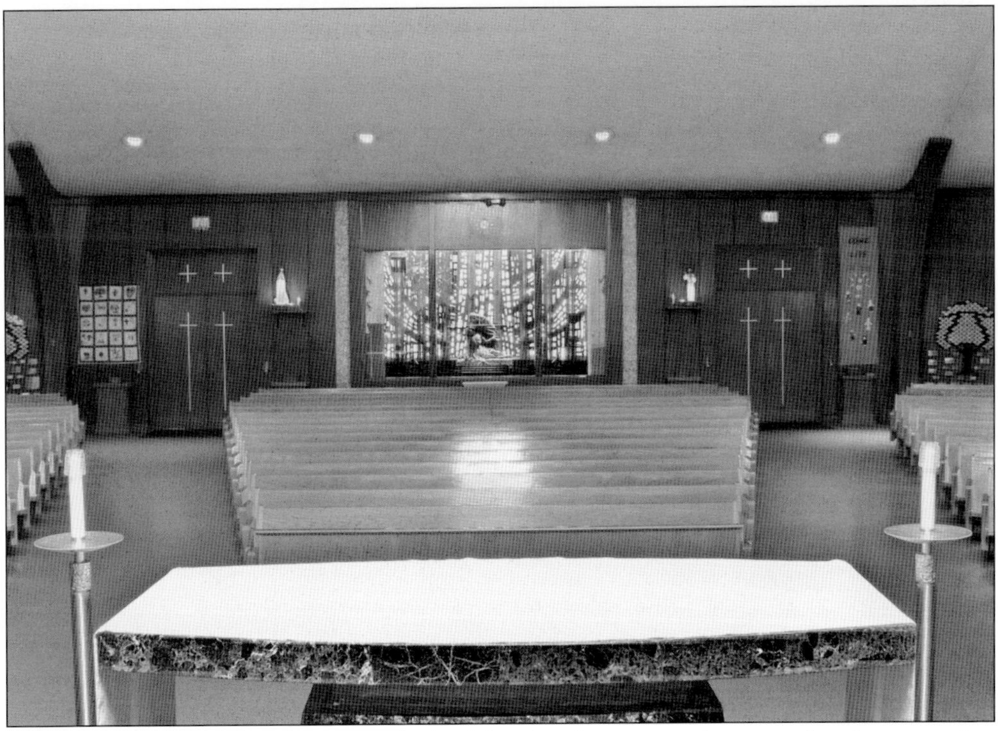

Looking from behind the altar to the back of the church, one sees the unusual crying room that features a magnificent statue before an impressive wall of colored glass.

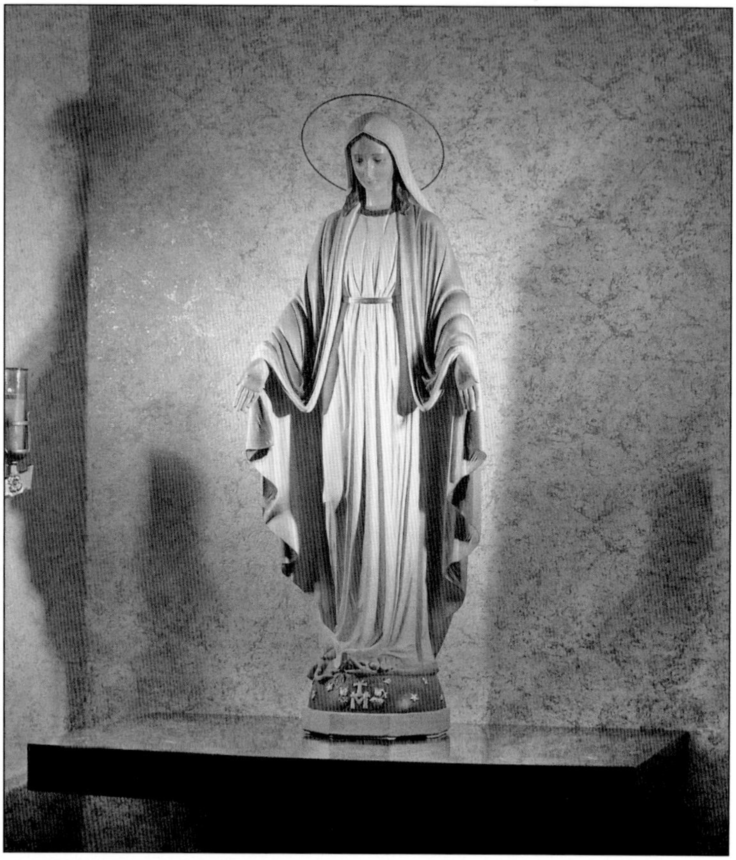

To the east of the sanctuary is a shrine of the Blessed Mother. St. Mary has no altar of St. Joseph.

To the west of the alter is a marble pedestal supporting the tabernacle rather than a St. Joseph shrine. The shape of the tabernacle and pedestal arc in keeping with the geometric design of the objects in the sanctuary.

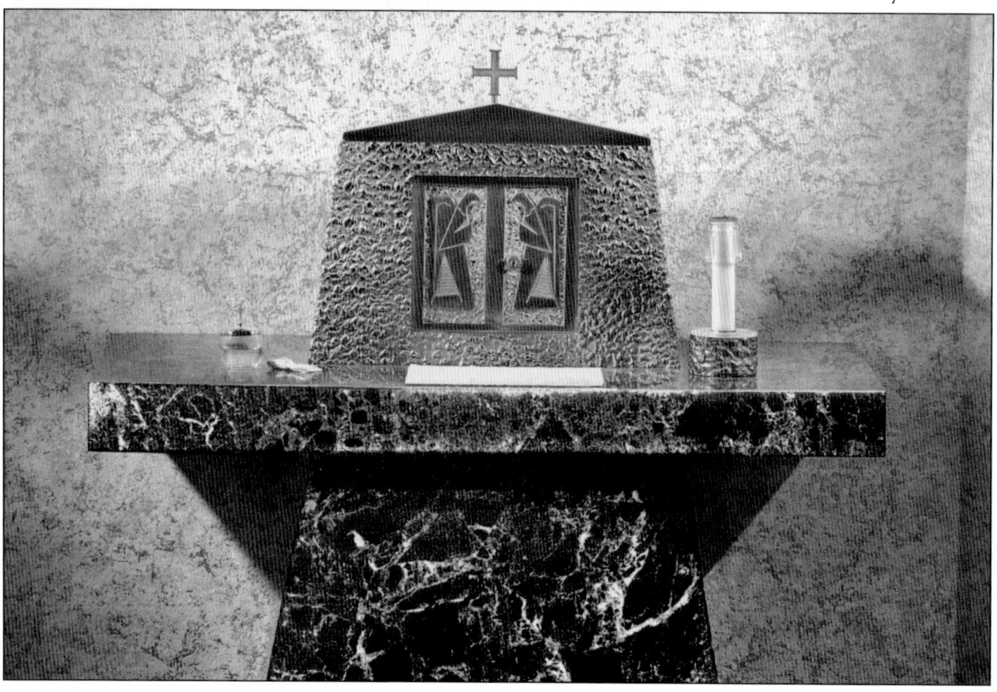

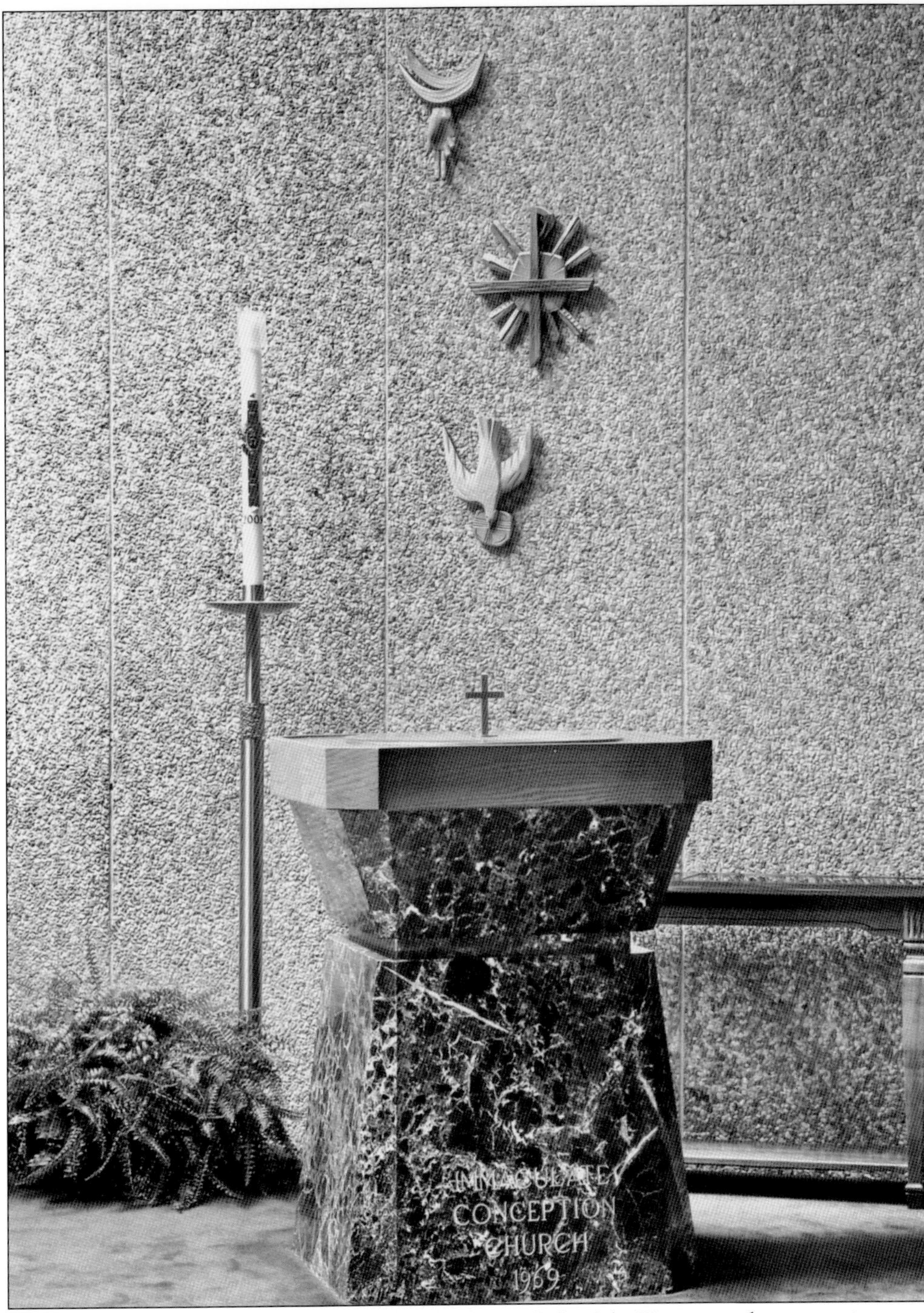

The impressive marble baptismal stands before the symbols of the Trinity on the composite stone wall behind it.

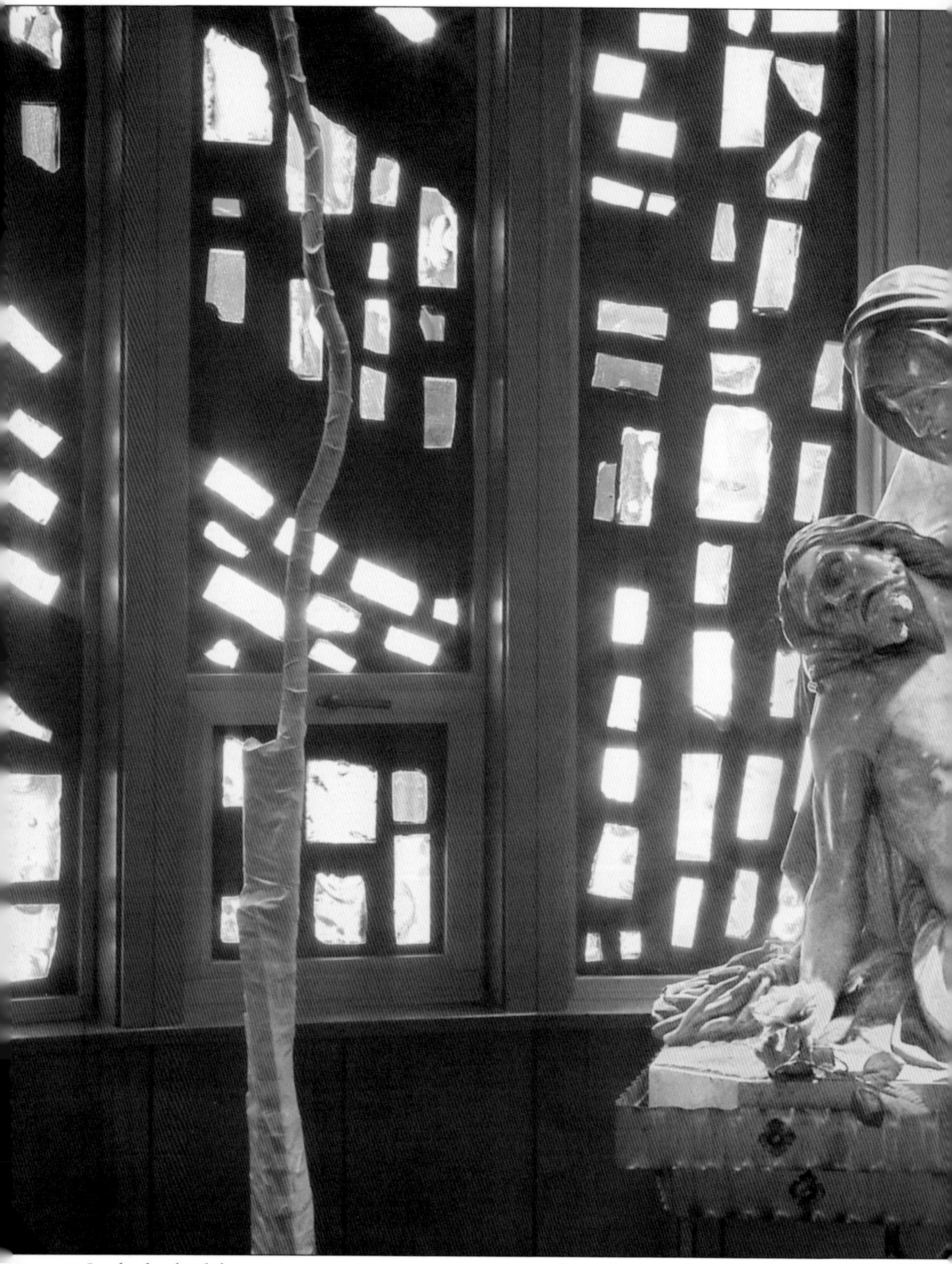

In the back of the crying room is an evocative statue of the Blessed Mother embracing the body of Christ reminiscent of the *Pietà of Michelangelo.* The colored glass provides a dramatic backdrop

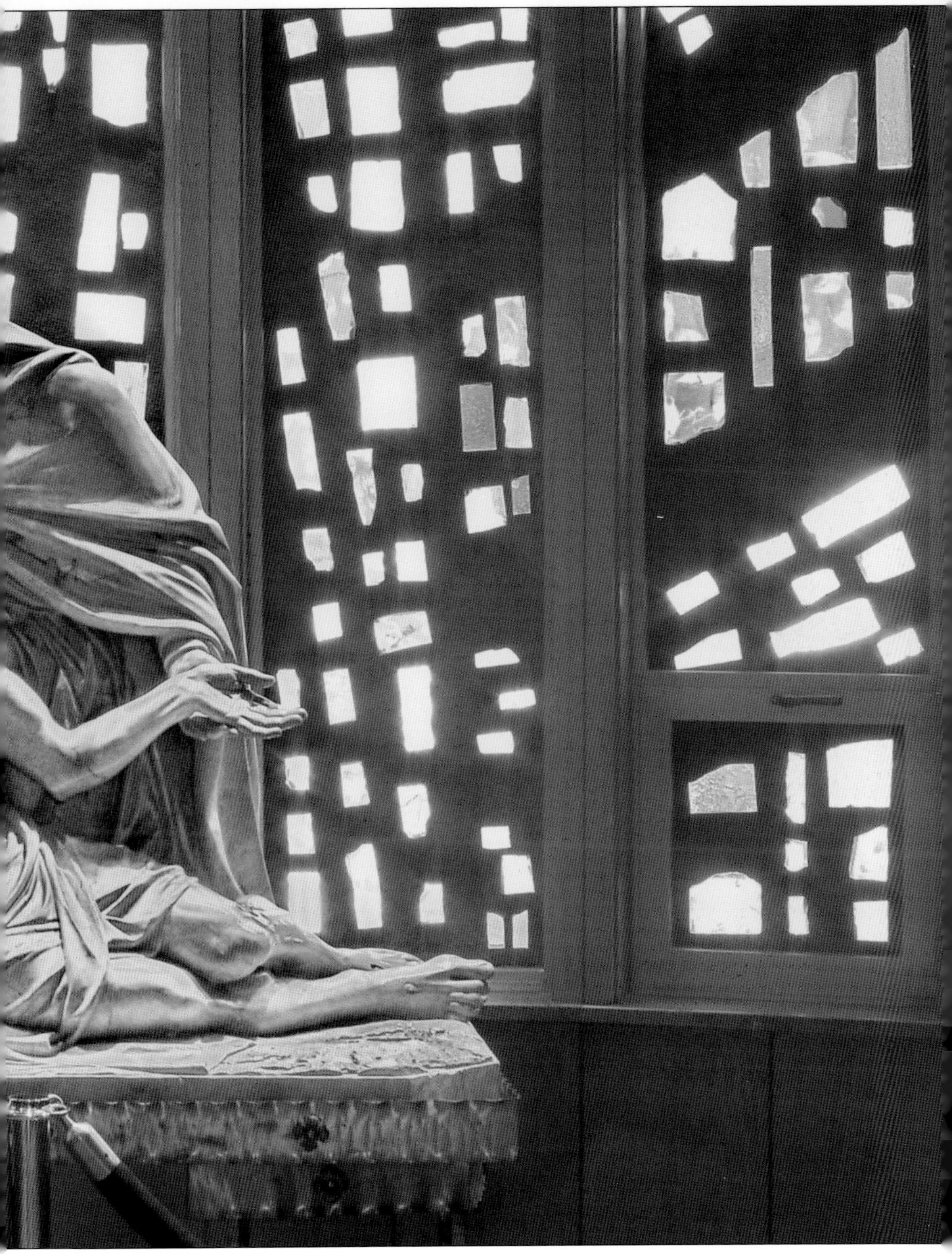

for this unusual image.

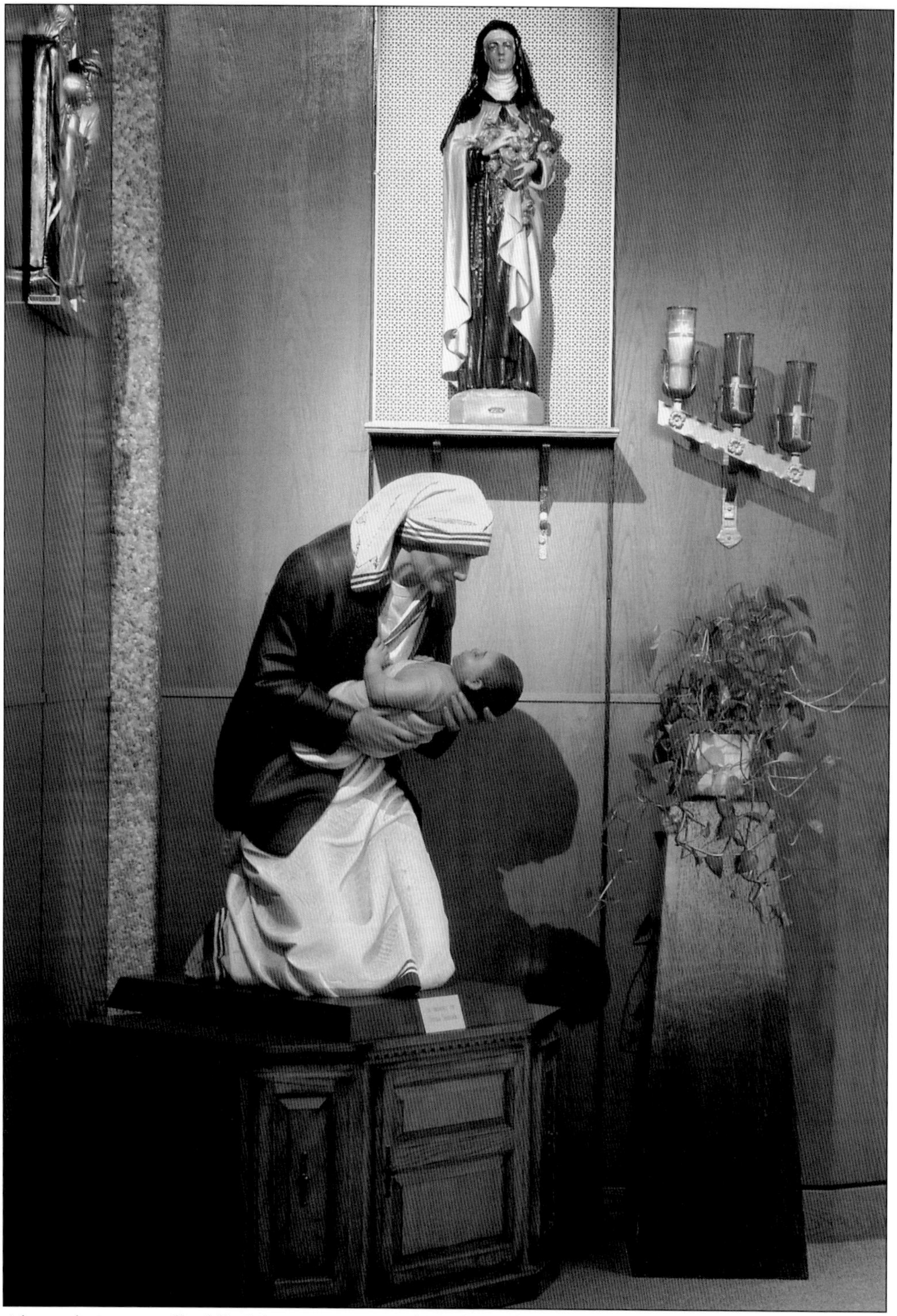

Along the west wall of St. Mary is a statue of Mother Theresa attending to a baby. Above her is an image of St. Therese. The former image was given to the church by a parishioner in memory of her mother.

Ten

Our Lady of Mercy

In 1915, parishioners petitioned Bishop John Farley to start a Slovak parish in the area of Cleveland called the Heights (today's Tremont), arguing that St. Wendelin Parish, the nearest Slovak church, was too far away for children to safely walk to school. Before a decision was made, the petitioners purchased property with a store and three houses on it. Unfortunately the bishop denied their petition. Prior to the bishop's denial, however, the store was converted into a small church called St. John the Baptist, one of the houses was converted into a school, and another house became the rectory.

By 1917, the would-be founders of the new church were desperate and stuck with a large ($13,000) mortgage. They approached the bishop of the Polish National Church in Scranton, Pennsylvania, of the Byzantine Rite. A priest was sent, and the parish began. However, it was not a Roman Catholic church. When Bishop Farley died, his successor, Bishop Schrembs, looked favorably on the new church and took it into the fold of the Catholic diocese. In 1922, the name was changed to Our Lady of Mercy, and the deed was turned over to the diocese. The first pastor was Fr. Francis J. Dubosh. Within a few years, the church's debt was paid off, and a new school was built.

Little by little, the church prospered. In 1948, Bishop Edward F. Hoban authorized the building of a new church at 2425 West Eleventh Street. The architects were Stickle, Kelly, and Stickle, and the cost was estimated at $157,000. In October 1949, the new church was dedicated. In attendance was Bishop Hoban (celebrant), the governor of Ohio, the councilmen, judges, and other dignitaries.

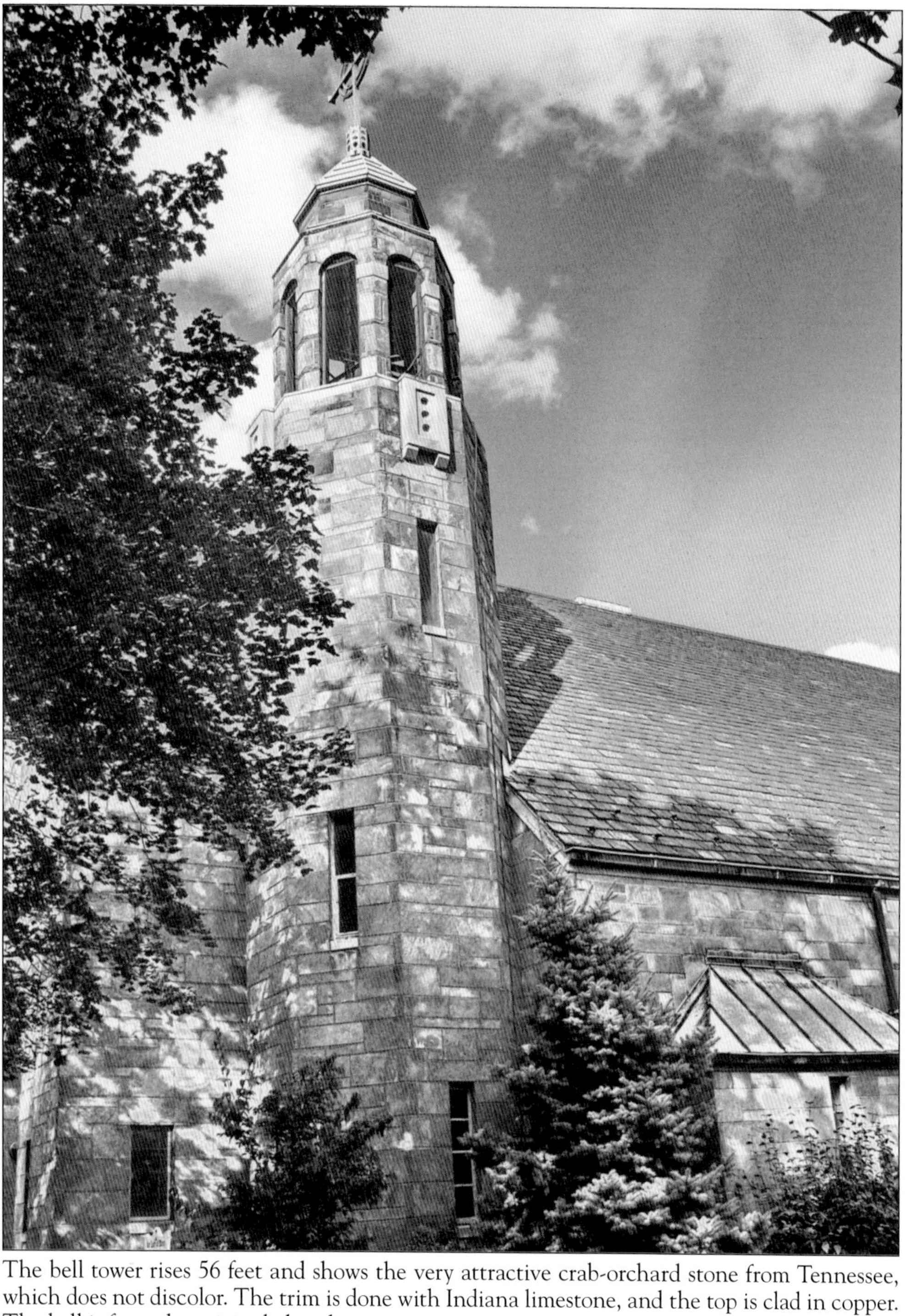

The bell tower rises 56 feet and shows the very attractive crab-orchard stone from Tennessee, which does not discolor. The trim is done with Indiana limestone, and the top is clad in copper. The bell is from the original church.

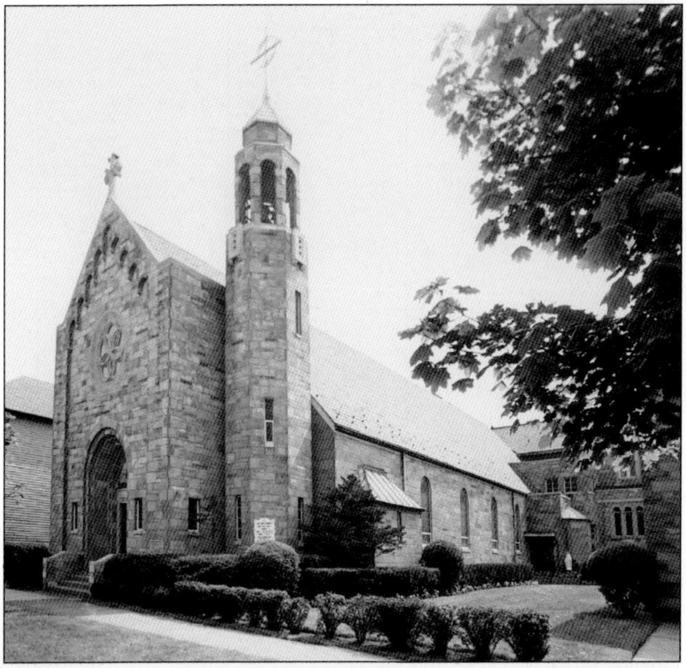

The rounded entrance seen here is consistent with the Romanesque style; however, the octagonal bell tower is more typical of the later Renaissance style. It is also referred to as Modern Romanesque, which is common among Slovakian churches. The church provides seating for 500. (Cleveland State University, *Cleveland Press* photograph.)

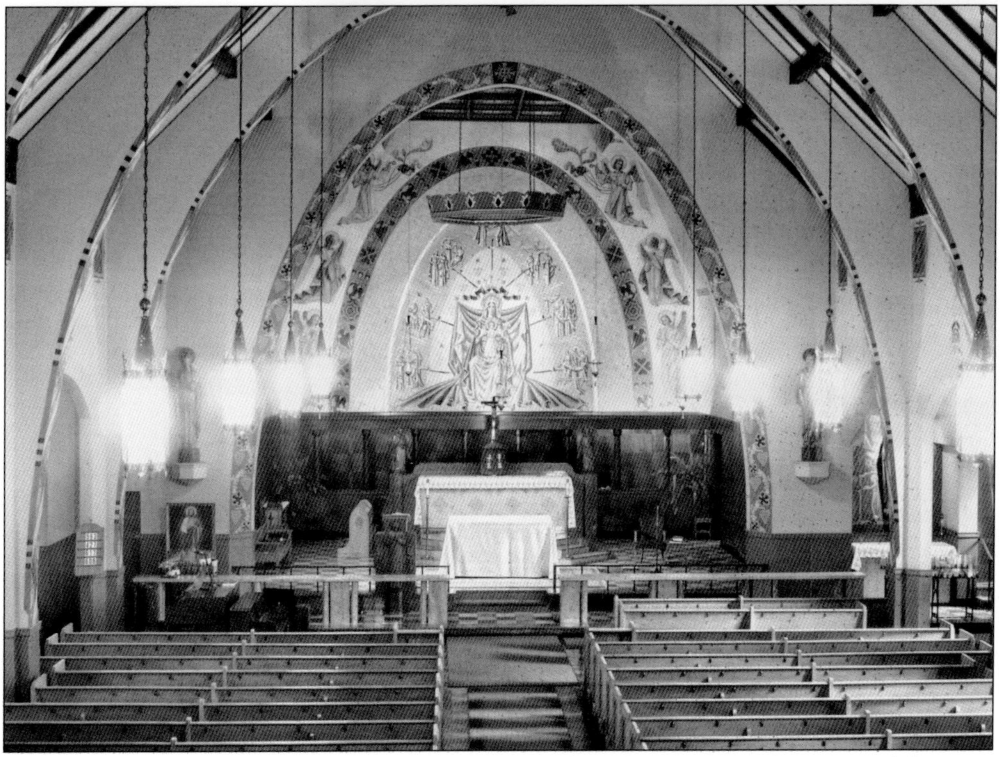

The interior architecture is decidedly Romanesque, but there is one apparent modification. In most Romanesque churches, the arches are flattened to produce a broader, more horizontal effect, but here the arches are narrowed and elliptical to create a vertical motif, which is consistent throughout.

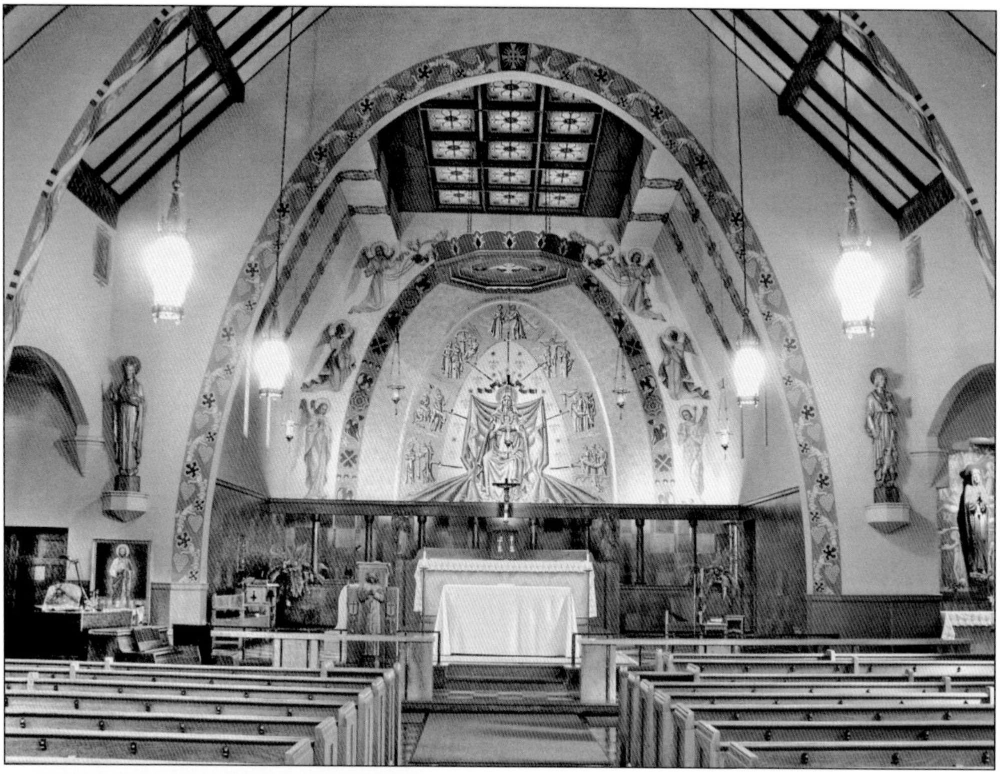

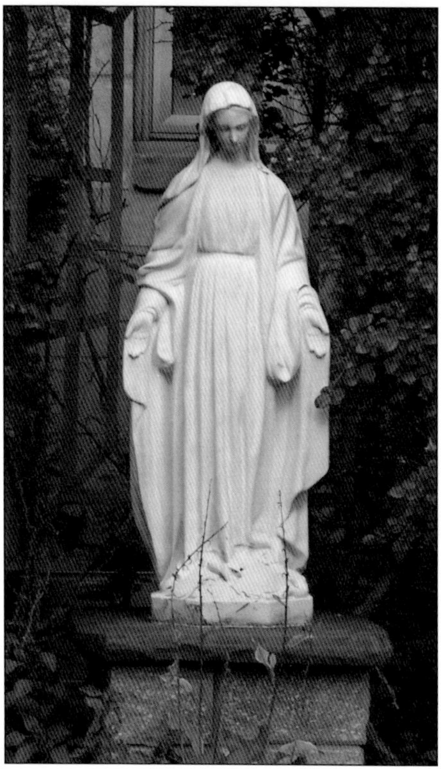

Our Lady of Mercy's interior decoration is decidedly Slovak. The ribbon-like geometric design seen throughout the church building resembles the free-flowing design found on traditional Slovak costumes. The two large wooden statues on either side of the center sanctuary were carved from Italian linden wood; the left is an image of Christ the King and the right is John the Evangelist. There are many artifacts from the Eastern Rites of the Church, as well as the Eastern Orthodox along with the traditional Roman Catholic features.

In the garden to the south of the church is a statue of the Blessed Mother, the namesake of the parish.

The high altar is made from white and brown marble from Italy and is backed by a decorative wall of highly textured light and dark brown marble. Two carved oak cherubim, symbolizing the Ark of the Covenant from the Old Testament, flank the altar.

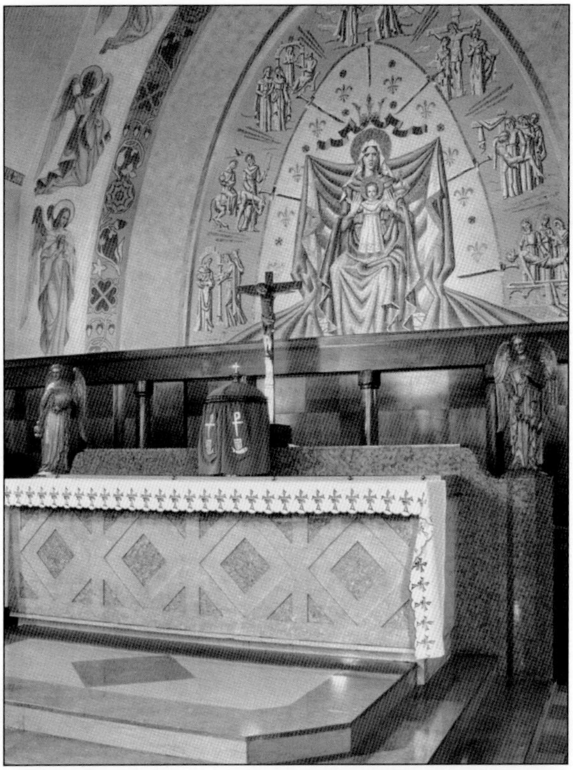

The most prominent aspect of the church is the large mosaic behind the altar that is made from Venetian glass. It depicts Our Lady of Mercy holding the Christ Child, and scenes surround her from her life, referred to as the Seven Sorrows or Seven Swords of Mary. In the mosaic, each scene has a sword pointing toward the Blessed Mother. The Sorrowful Mother is the Patroness of Slovakia.

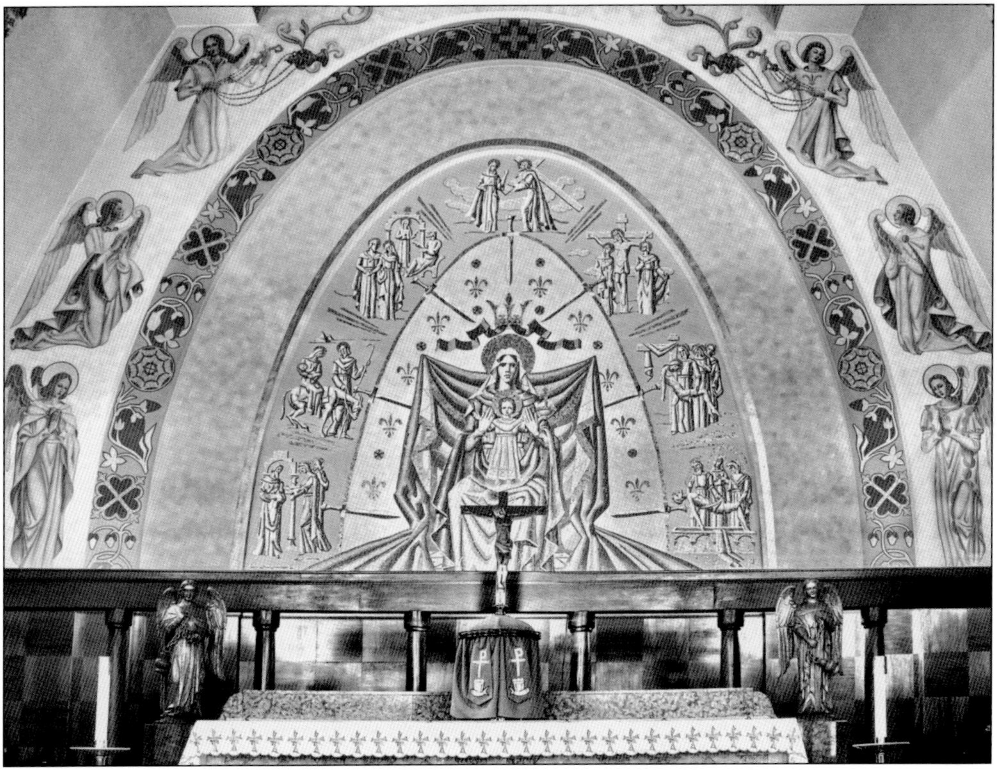

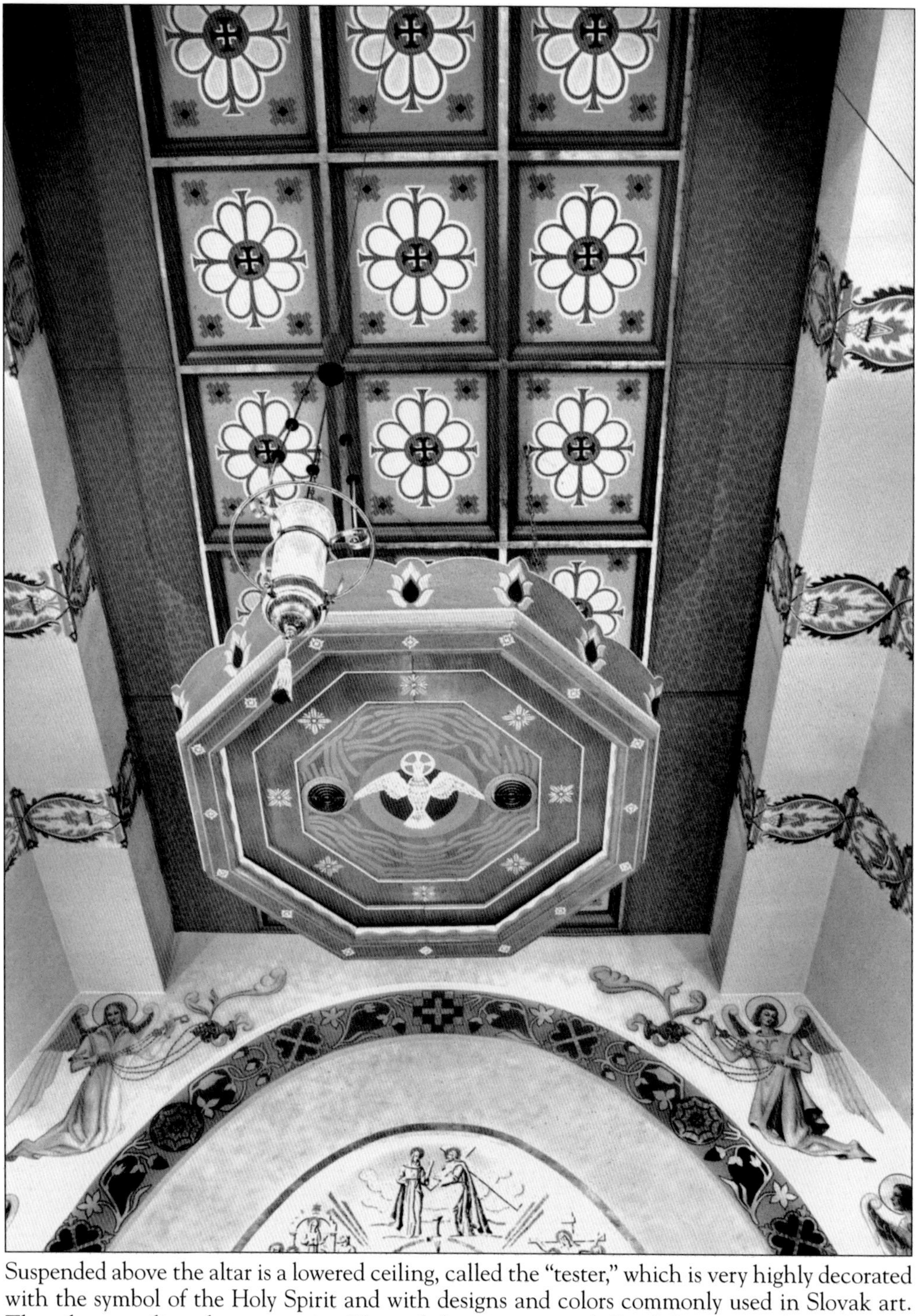

Suspended above the altar is a lowered ceiling, called the "tester," which is very highly decorated with the symbol of the Holy Spirit and with designs and colors commonly used in Slovak art. The vibrant ceiling above contains 15 panels bearing pastoral, floral decoration that enhances both the large and small crosses contained within.

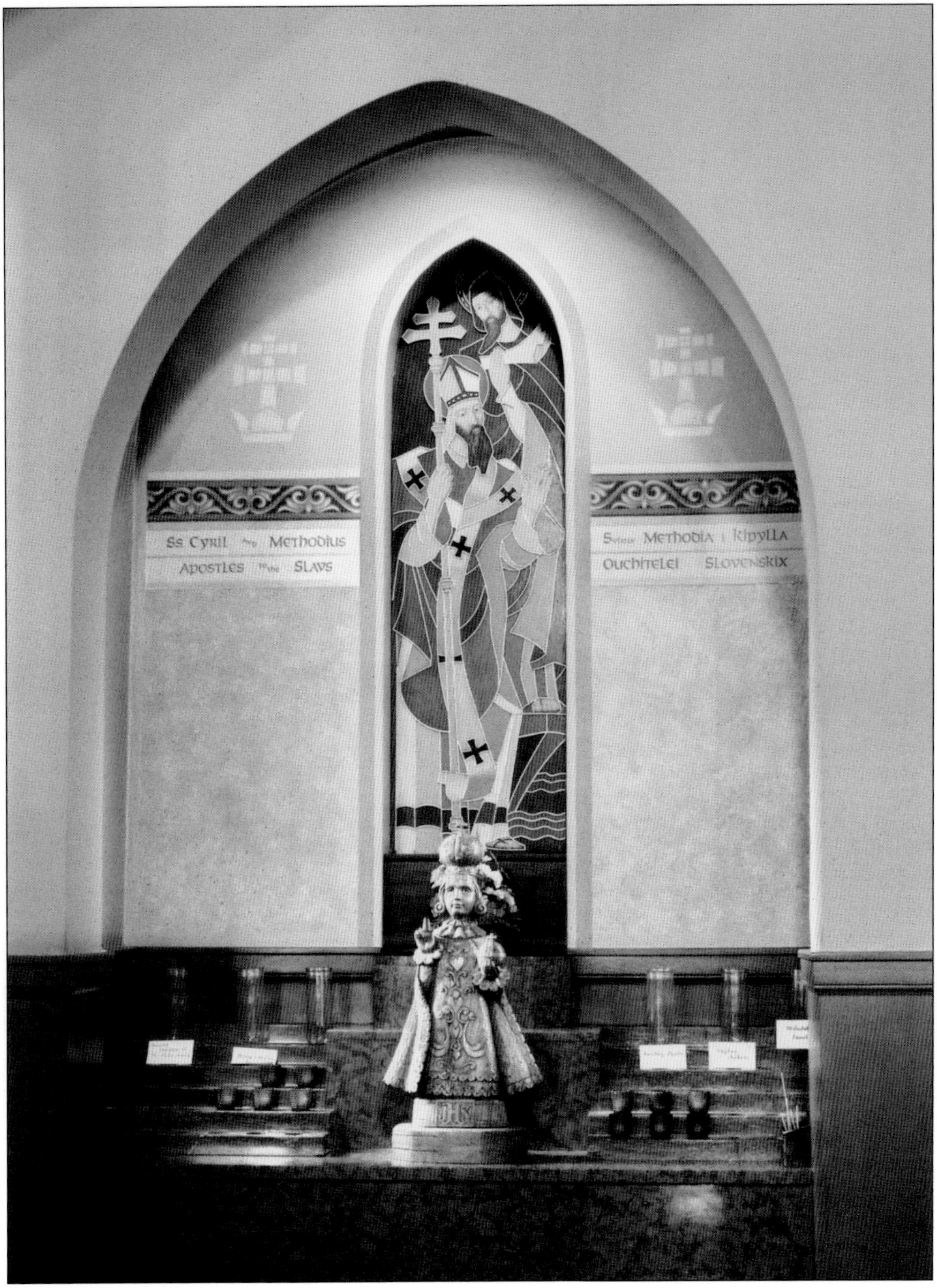

On the north wall of the church is a shrine to the patron saints of the Slavic people, St. Cyril and St. Methodius. These two Greek saints were sent by the Pope to convert the "barbaric Slavs" to Christianity in 988. The figures are made of enamel, and a carved oak statue of the Infant Jesus of Prague completes the shrine. (This shrine is another feature of Our Lady of Mercy that blends the Eastern and Western Rites of the Church.)

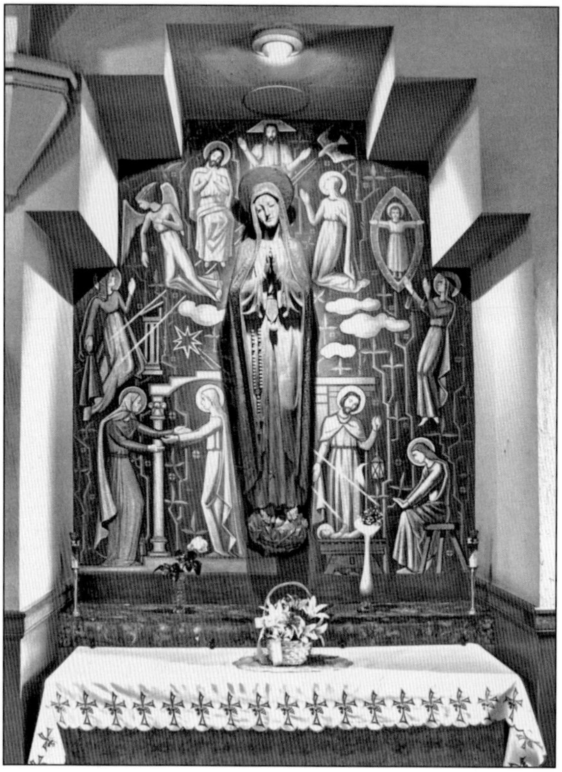

On the south side of the main altar is the altar or shrine of the Blessed Mother. Above the altar is a hand-carved, Italian linden wood statue of Mary with a rosary. Behind her is a mural depicting the Hail Mary prayer.

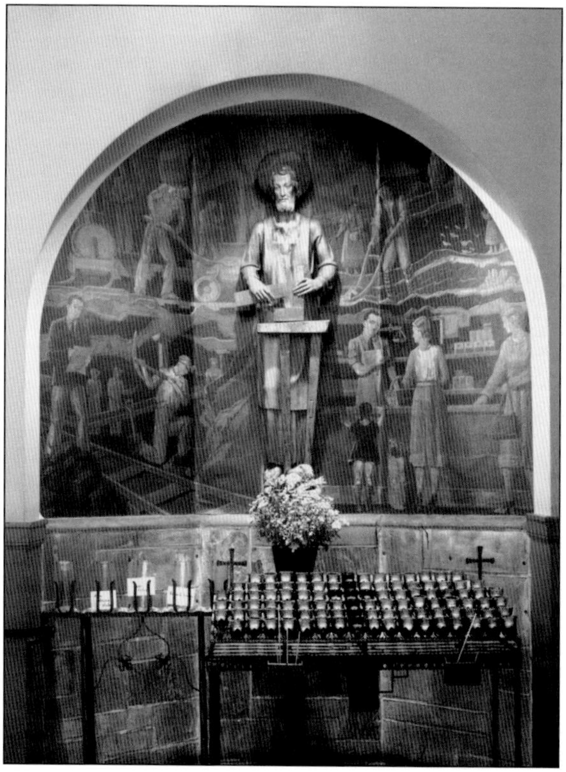

On the south wall of the church near the Blessed Mother altar is a shrine of St. Joseph the Worker. It contains an Italian linden wood statue of St. Joseph with a mural behind him depicting the humble life of the people of the parish who toiled in the fields of Slovakia before working in this country's steel mills, coal mines, and commercial establishments.

The windows of the church depict the life of Mary and are unusual insofar as they are "transparent murals" made by a European artist working in New York. The window on the right is a rendering of the Dormition of Mary, a teaching of the Eastern Churches that the Blessed Mother "fell asleep" on Earth before her body and spirit were reunited and assumed into heaven.

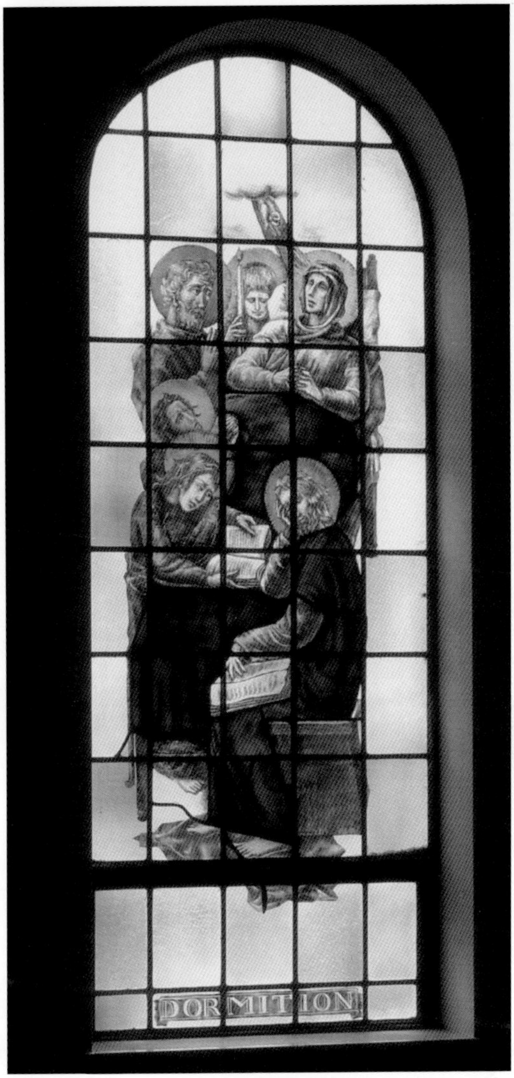

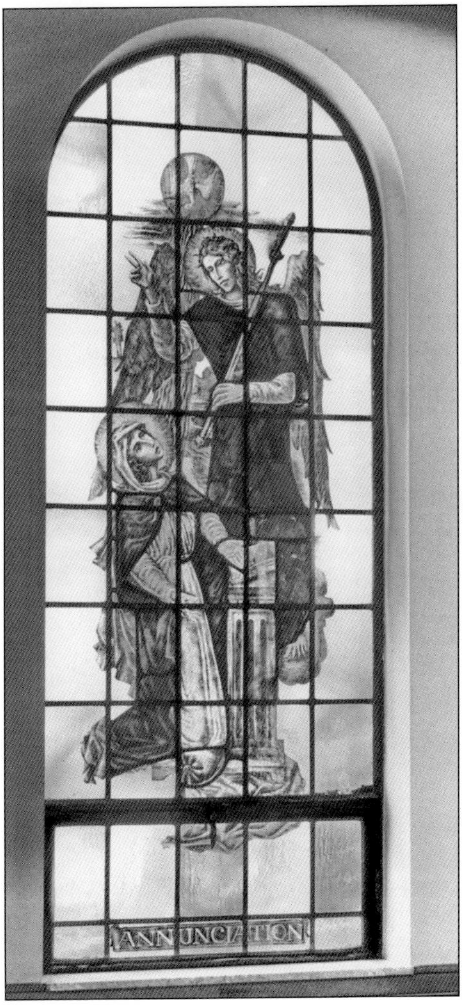